A History of Public Administration

A History of
Public Administration

E. N. Gladden
M.Sc.(Econ.), Ph.D.(Public Admin.)

Volume I
From Earliest Times to the Eleventh Century

FRANK CASS: LONDON

First published 1972 in Great Britain by
FRANK CASS AND COMPANY LIMITED
67 Great Russell Street, London WC1B 3BT, England

and in United States of America by
FRANK CASS AND COMPANY LIMITED
c/o International Scholarly Book Services, Inc.
P.O. Box 4347, Portland, Oregon 97208

ISBN 0 7146 1310 X

Printed in Great Britain by Stephen Austin and Sons Ltd., Hertford

Contents

Introduction

Historians have always paid considerable attention to the problems of power and the wielders of power, whose importance cannot be gainsaid. On the other hand much less has been said about administration and those who carried it out on behalf of the leaders. This too is understandable, for the activities of the leaders are often spectacular, providing the very essence of a good story, while those of the administrators are inherently pedestrian. Yet today, when more and more attention is being given to the history of particular activities, to specialist as opposed to general history, there is surely a case for attempting to redress the balance between government and administration. At a time when the scope of public administration is continuingly expanding — to many persons with a frightening impetus — and more and more thought is necessarily being given to research into its nature and problems, much profit could well be derived from a better understanding of the administrative lessons of the past, so far as they can be deduced. Furthermore, even a cursory investigation of the administrative context of earlier ages raises the suspicion that administration, like human nature, may not have varied very much since human society began. If this should prove to be the case there could be much to be said for regarding administration as a common factor in all historical situations, a sort of general essence in time and place by which the entire human story can be co-ordinated. This present book is an attempt to provide a highly selective introductory history of this vast subject, with special emphasis on its public aspects.

Public administration serves so many fields of activity and in such a diversity of forms that it can be approached from a number of viewpoints. Selecting universal history as the context, public administration, despite its ubiquity, suffers from not being regarded as a major activity within that context, and from, in fact, being essentially a subordinate or supporting factor in government, which is itself a subject that has not been too well served by the general historian. While accepting the signposts of universal history we have to relate such specific administrative incidents to the system of government with which they were associated.

In any case there are many gaps in the record, some of which will eventually be filled. It has to be admitted that administration is not an exciting activity at best, and administrators themselves, who are in the most favourable position to interpret their own activities, are not prone to dwell upon them, much less to set them down in writing and thus to place on record the problems they have had to face and the methods they have had to employ to solve them. Consequently, many of the existing gaps are not there because the record has been erased by tragic destruction or sad neglect. Although there have been plenty of such instances, once the individual administrator died the record itself was beyond creation. Yet, despite these gaps in the historical record, the surviving material is abundant and in some instances not easily manageable. Many fine studies of administrative events, periods and incidents have been made by scholars: many first-rate accounts, sometimes on comparative lines, exist of the administration of specific realms — states, kingdoms, principalities, institutions — but not by any means enough to build up an integrated explanation of public administration as an essential ingredient in human experience and endeavour, such as scholars have been able to attempt on an universal basis with commendable success in other specialist fields. The author has therefore chosen to select from the human record — as far as it has come within his inevitably limited knowledge — certain periods and phases when public administration can be clearly seen in contemporary perspective, to arrange these instances in a suitable historical pattern, but to leave it largely to the reader to discern the ebb and flow of administrative development and to sense, somewhat vaguely perhaps at this stage, their underlying contribution.

The specific incidents in, or pieces of administrative history thus sketched in are inevitably slanted from different standpoints, and neither selected nor directed to sustaining a particular thesis, other than to reinforce the points already made of the subject's inherent continuity, universality and essential subordination. There are in fact a large number of possible approaches to public administration similar to those applied to other fields, but there are six that might have been adopted as the basis of such a history, all of which have contributed ingredients to the resulting picture. These can be classified as (1) Direction and Top Management, (2) Functions and Organization, (3) Personnel, (4) Techniques, (5) Biography, and (6) Theory.

(1) *Direction and Top Management.* This represents the normal

approach to the subject by administrators and historians without distinction. Viewed from the governors' level the subject is concerned with the exercise of power, the deployment of resources, the determination of policies and the control of the administrative machine. The sphere of government extends to religious observance and the deployment of armed power. At this level, rulers and governors themselves participate in administration, in varying degrees, although they are not necessarily aware of it as a specific activity, or they appoint deputies, i.e. ministers, with power both to govern in their name and to manage the affairs of the realm on their behalf. Division of labour is quickly manifesting itself with the increasing complication of affairs, and the extending responsibilities of government. Normally the historian is here concerned with the form and powers of government and not in separating its administrative aspects, although the specialist in public administration must do so.

(2) *Functions and Organization.* The extending functionalization of society and government, arising out of the process of specialization, calls for changes in the structure of government. Consequently, rulers and their ministers become increasingly involved in organizing. The actual extent of such functions varies from system to system, with time and place, and with the level of operations: e.g. imperial, national, regional, local. To be effective, and indeed often to facilitate such developments, public administration has to be broadly and suitably based. Its organization, or structure, must be suited to the purposes it is devised to meet. Senior administrators are concerned in securing the services of human agents who are sufficiently skilled in deploying the essential resources and in running the machinery of government. At this vital level the public services in the various functional spheres can be usefully analysed and compared.

(3) *Personnel.* As we have seen, from the very beginning the supreme administrator has found it necessary to delegate some or most of his administrative responsibilities and functions. He has normally employed in this office a member, or members, of his own family or household, but a time comes when the public officials form an occupational group with its own place in society. A new art of personnel management develops, imperceptibly at first, formulating precedents and rules for dealing with the public business, and of such matters relating to the regulation of their occupational practices, touching upon such matters as precedence and authority, discipline, grading and selection, training, advancement and so forth. As history unfolds, realms extend, governments develop, officialdom becomes professionalized. The public

services can be compared and their effectiveness assessed. Bureaucracy becomes one of society's problems.

(4) *Techniques*. Public officials soon develop their own techniques, an internal sphere closely related to the functional, (2). Where they are called upon by the ruler to undertake tasks, or to provide services, that are not solely administrative in form, in addition to being administrators, they need to be masters of such crafts and operations as, in other circumstances, would be left as a matter of course to the governed. There are, however, basic developments and techniques of society that play an important part in determining the scope and nature of administration; especially those activities concerned with communicating and record-keeping, in which the public administrator has a special interest. These cover the use and development of language, the invention of writing and of media suitable for its perpetuation — such as papyrus and paper — of printing, telecommunications, office machinery and latterly computers. Such developments which have been basic to the development of civilizations have a closely related and vital influence in the shaping of administration as an instrument of government.

(5) *Biography*. Since administering is essentially a human activity it is important to understand what the individual official actually does. Only the involved official can know precisely how the machine works and it is to his experience the student must turn, if he can discover it. The lives of administrators, where they have been recorded, are therefore of prime importance, but in this sphere there is much that has not been recorded. Existing accounts tend naturally to concentrate upon the actions of the leaders, at the decision-reaching or policy-making levels; their relationships with the rulers, with their subordinates, if they have any, and with the administered; their effectiveness as the agents of the governors; their attitudes to their profession; the techniques they have to acquire and the routines and methods of their daily work. On such matters there is much to be gleaned, not only from the general histories and the specialized studies, but from the autobiographies and biographies of statesmen and other public figures, and of course from the official papers themselves. Nor should fictional reconstructions be overlooked which interpret the ways and manners of a particular age, among which, for example, may be cited Lady Murasaki's splendid *The Tale of Genji,* which, in probing the ways of Japanese society in the tenth century, contains a good deal of incidental information about the conduct of public business of the time.

(6) *Theory*. Finally there are the philosophies which have influ-

enced the development of public administration and the theories that have been, or are being advanced to explain its place in the general scheme of things. Those of the past have survived in an extremely piecemeal way, while those that are currently being adumbrated are numerous and inevitably lack authority. A good deal can be gleaned from the theories of government offered by political writers as far back as Aristotle, and more so with the appearance of the so-called Administrative State. Latterly the development of general administration, both as an art and science, has been assiduously examined, particularly in the fields of industry and business enterprise, with special emphasis on the theories of organization, decision-making, management and so forth. There is growing support among scholars for the idea that public administration, well accepted as an art, is in fact also a science which can be learned and applied. We need not go all the way with these contentions to appreciate what an interesting field of human endeavour and inquiry is emerging here.

These six approaches are by no means exclusive: many others are possible, depending to some extent upon the specific interests and objectives of the inquirer. The separate pieces of public administrative experience out of which the present work has been built have not been chosen to illustrate specifically any of the six approaches. Some of the sections of the work contribute to more than one of the viewpoints. A key to the appearance of the six themes in the present volume is provided by references under the six headings in the index.

In conclusion, may it be suggested that, apart from its appeal to the general reader who is interested in the world around him and in its roots in the past, this *History of Public Administration* should be of particular interest to the student, practitioner and teacher of government, and especially of public administration. Somewhere within the vast area of the survey, in which there are inevitably many gaps both in period and level of activity, it should be practicable for the interested reader to fit his own special interest or experience of administering, and to relate it to mankind's administrative experience as a whole. In this way it should be possible for almost any interested reader to make his own contribution to the overall picture; while the teacher of public administration, unavoidably concerned with a particular period or specialist activity, should be helped to perceive the broad flow of administrative development and to place his own teachings in their appropriate context. History in this way, regarded from many viewpoints, can add both interest and meaning to Public Administration, a subject in which even the expert often finds it difficult to provide his students with a co-ordinated picture of the several sectors he is being called upon to study.

This History of Public Administration is presented in two separate parts: Volume I — *Early Public Administration,* covering the period from the beginnings to the eleventh century A.D., and Volume II — *Modern Public Administration,* covering the period from the eleventh century A.D. to the present day.

BIBLIOGRAPHICAL NOTE

The works quoted in the footnotes may be divided broadly into (1) specialist historical studies in specific fields and periods of public administration, and (2) works on other topics, especially government, which contribute incidentally to the history of public administration. Works in both categories are legion. In fact, there are few histories which could not be assigned to one category or the other. There would therefore be little point in adding to these lists.

Little attention has been given to the history of public administration in a general or universal sense and it is therefore difficult to afford useful guidance in this field. One could of course quote multi-volume works on the history of public administration like T. F. Tout's *Chapters in Mediaeval Administrative History,* or L. D. White's studies in the administrative history of the United States, which began with *The Federalists* (1948), but these fall squarely into category (1) above; or to Arnold Townbee's *Study of History* or K. A. Wittfogel's *Oriental Despotism,* which fall into category (2).

However, there are signs of changes in the air. In 1964 the Fondazione Italiana per la Storia Amministrativa, of Milan, inaugurated their series of *Annuali* which bring together scholarly monographs on the history of public administration. In 1969 the Institute of Governmental Studies, University of California, Berkeley, included in its 'Vistas of History' series a stimulating brochure on *Perspectives on Administration,* by G. D. Nash. In 1971 Scott Foresman and Co. of Illinois have included in their 'Topics in Comparative History', series a group of articles on *Bureaucracy in Historical Perspective.*

CHAPTER 1

IN THE BEGINNING : 20,000 to 600 B.C.

Since we are committed to begin at the beginning it is important to look at some of the milestones in the development of humanity, which are of course well enough known today. On the evidence of skeletal remains and primitive tools the anthropologist and the archaeologist have been pressing back the beginnings of man and his subsequent development along a number of experimental lines, with such labels at Neanderthal, Sinanthropus, Pithecanthropus, Rhodesian and *Homo Sapiens,* to as early as seven hundred thousand to a million years B.C., although it was not until about 35,000 B.C. that the infancy of mankind seems to have given way to the hunter stage, which lasted till the emergence of agriculture and settled communities about 6000 B.C. Only then does substantial evidence begin to accumulate of organized government and the existence of public officials. The first representative civilizations are already upon the scene somewhere between 4000 and 3000 B.C. (although recent discoveries at Jericho and elsewhere suggest that there was already a settled town on this site at least two thousand years earlier!). Written records are vital both to the recording of history and the expansion of administration. But writing was not invented before the fourth millennium B.C. and obviously evidence of administration before this is hard to come by.

THE NATURE OF ADMINISTRATION

First comes the initiator or leader to render society possible, then the organizer or administrator to give it permanence. Administration, or the management of affairs, is the middle factor in all social activity, unspectacular but essential to its continuance. In simple communities the headman, or ruler, is the wielder of power, able to perform, or at least personally to direct, all the activities involved in running the show, or government, as we call it. Very soon, however, the wielding of power, whether personally by a despot or on behalf of the community by less-autocratic authorities, becomes more than one man can cope with, however able he may be. Functions have to be shared, or delegated, and the first administrators or managers emerge to operate under the leader's direction. Such administration long remains the prerogative of the leader and his family relations, but sooner or later others have to be brought in to participate, and the class of administrator emerges in which can be discerned the first public officials. Broadly such a community can now be divided into three class bands: at the top the governors or manipulators of power, in the middle the managers or administrators who see to the carrying out of the behests of the governors, and the large lower class of workers and slaves who undertake the productive work of the community. A hard and fast line cannot be drawn between the governor and the leading officials nor can the more menial official be excluded from the worker group, but in the main the public administrator figures in the middle band.

PRIMITIVE PUBLIC ADMINISTRATION: TWO MODERN EXAMPLES

Although history, as the story of human development, and our knowledge of public administration are largely a consequence of writing, whose invention made the permanent recording of human activity possible, it must be obvious that societies were developing and administration was being carried on before the making of permanent records. Government, an early theme of history, obviously predated it to the very beginnings of civilization and, although administration as its subsidiary activity may not have called forth a deal of comment it can be rightly assumed that it existed long before the written record.

An analogy of this early unwritten stage of public administration can be discovered in the organization and government of tribal societies which have continued to exist side by side with our modern highly organized states. Numerous studies exist of such systems, a comparative examination of which would bring to light some interesting facts. It is proposed to select two for brief consideration here.

The first, by Schapera, is an interesting study of certain South African tribes.[1] The chiefs' duties cover much more than decision-making and leadership. The chief represents the people in his dealings with outsiders and attends to the organizing of important communal activities such as collective labour, ritual and war. In some instances he may act both as legislator and judge, organize agricultural activities and even care for the needy. In practice it soon becomes impossible for him to undertake all these functions personally and he may delegate powers on a geographical basis to sub-chiefs, members of his own family or others closely related who represent him in the areas. Apart from such local subordinates the chief will require personal assistants whose duties may be either advisory, i.e. to participate in the making of policy, or executive, to help him to carry out his routine tasks. Sometimes the two functions will be performed by the same person but it is upon the latter activity that the status of the official depends. Thus, although the evidence may be scanty the history of the public official can be traced back before the invention of writing.

The second study takes us much further. In his examination of tribal government in the area of Zaria in Northern Nigeria, during a century and a half from A.D. 1800 onwards, M. G. Smith provides a most interesting, in many ways, sensational, account of the extent to which administrative machinery can develop in the absence of efficient office facilities.[2] The period covers three successive regimes in the area: the Habe Abuja government, subject to the overlordship of the rulers of Bornu from 1800; the Fulani Zazzau government, vassals to the Emir of Sokoto, from 1865; and the modern Fulani phase under the British from 1900, during which the tribal system was retained and developed.

In all these systems the political and administrative sectors can be differentiated, specific administrative rules and procedures having been worked out. Government was 'conducted through a system of ranked and titled offices known as *sarautu,* each of which can be regarded as an exclusive permanent unit, a sort of corporation sole. Relations between offices of subordinate and superordinate rank-orders are highly formalized, while those between offices of co-ordinate status are not clearly laid down'[3]. Only a few of these offices were hereditary and the appointive offices could be held by freedmen, members of the royal family, eunuchs or slaves, all categories that we shall meet in our examination of the outstanding historical administrative systems. The kingship was not hereditary, for the Fulani rulers were consecutively selected from different dynasties. The ruler's power was thus restricted by custom and the specific division of responsibilities. As a counterbalance, it was necessary for him to keep as close a hold as possible on the administrative sectors, through which his instructions were implemented. He maintained close consultation with his senior officials, who had to see that his instructions were passed down the line. Informal councils of state were assembled, but their powers were limited. The local communities were controlled by chiefs, who were responsible to the king. He retained direct control of certain royal domains and his personal property, consisting mainly of slave-settlements. In addition to the large income from these sources the ruler received a large share of the state tax, a half-share of military-booty, tribute from vassal states and certain pagan tribes, death duties of office-holders and a portion of his predecessor's estate. Outgoings were also multifarious, although there was usually a surplus for the founding of further slave-settlements.

Such a brief statement as the foregoing fails inevitably to do justice to our author's remarkable study, but the subject cannot be left without a brief reference to the complex system of official positions that had already been worked out by the Habe and had left an impress upon their successors.[4]

At the top of the official hierarchy were *Rukuni,* or First Order Chiefs, who were known respectively as *Madawaki, Galadima, Wambai* and *Dallatu.* The *Madawaki* was greeted as Head of the Chiefs. He was military leader and had certain territorial controls. The king obtained his consent to all appointments and he acted as a sort of Master of Ceremonies. The *Galadima's* main task was the administration of the capital in the king's absence on campaign. He officiated at the marriage and naming ceremonies of the king's children. The *Wambai* also officiated at naming ceremonies and was responsible for the cess-pits and urinals of the king and the women of the palace; he was virtually the royal sanitary engineer! The *Dallatu* supervised arrangements for the war camps and deputized for the *Galadima.*

Below the *Rukuni* was a second order, known as the *Rawuna,* or turbanned officials. They were more numerous and included the principal assistants of the top officials. Among these may be mentioned the *Iyan Bakin Kasuwa* whose job was to supervise the markets of the capital and the villages.

Then there were the numerous *Fadawa,* or officers of the King's Household, under their chief, the *Sarkin Fada.* Of special interest among them was the *Cincina* whose duty was to spy out the news of the country so that he would be aware of any plots against the king. A number of these *Fadawa* had military functions.

The king's Eunuchs acted as officials of the inner chamber, under the *Makami Karami.* They looked after the royal house-hold and acted as messengers for the king. Among the latter was *Sarkin Ruwa,* or Chief of the Waters, who was the king's messenger to the fishermen and responsible for all matters pertaining to water.

Three other groups of officials included the principal servants of the king, certain royal office-holders, and the chief Koranic scholars who carried out important priestly duties.

Here surely was a remarkable quasi-bureaucratic structure developed by customary law and operating through a personal communications system. Its members were classified severally by function, rank-order and status and may be divided alternatively into public officials, household officials and slave officials, any of whom might hold either military or civil posts.[5] It is instructive to observe how many of the universal characteristics of officialdom are to be found in this system, which seems to lack only the advantages of the modern recording techniques, office machinery and accountancy methods which have rendered large-scale administrative services possible.

This interesting system of tribal administration embodies the process of division of labour which characterizes the rise of the official as a specialist administrative agent of the governing power. At first there is little distinction between the directive, law-making, adjudicative, religious, military, and productive, or economic, activities of the leader. As chief he is responsible for many, perhaps all, of the vital activities of the tribe. With the growth of larger governmental areas — probably as a result of conquest — and the increasing complexity of governmental functions, the division of labour is manifested, at first by the departmentalization of administration on a geographical basis, subsequently by the separation of powers and duties through the process of specialization.

As the tribe grows bigger and the chief gradually acquires the prestige of kingship the tendency is for government itself to become a specialist activity and for the social and economic sectors of the community to be centred elsewhere. But the ruler may continue to be responsible for his own household on the old lines and also for certain social and economic matters in which he is personally involved. He is still religious and military leader, and his personal duties are of a mixed executive, legislatory and judicial nature. He may soon relinquish religious matters to the priests and military matters to the generals — while still retaining final responsibility for both as the wielder of ultimate power — and gradually the civil duties of government will be distributed to separate institutions dealing respectively with executive, legislative and judicial matters. In all these spheres the assistance of officials will be needed, but particularly in the executive sphere within which the main day-to-day activities of government are carried out. This specialization of function, seen at work in tribal societies, is characteristic of government at all times and the several functions mentioned figure under all types of government, although their actual allocation varies infinitely.

At every stage and in every form of organization the official is the subordinate of the reigning power whether it be chief, king or corporate body — high priest, magistrate, military leader, legislator or chief executive. He is not the manipulator of power — the Ruling Bureaucrat of press and legend — but the specialist in management and administration. Sometimes the line is not easy to draw, for the power-holder may continue to administer, while situations constantly arise where the ruler delegates political as well as administrative functions to his chief assistants, who in this case also act in a dual capacity. If in such a situation the ruler is weak and his chief executive overpoweringly strong the immemorial division between power and administration is upset, but this is usually a fluid and unstable situation. Even in tribal societies there may be assistants of this kind to whom the chief delegates wide powers. In the Bantu, for example, there is the Great *Induna,* who is the chief's principal lieutenant in all his functions and who deputizes for him when he is ill or away. He is the intermediary between chief and tribe and his spokesman on many important occasions.[6]

Our glance at these modern examples of complex administrative systems developed by tribal societies — and there are many others available[7] — imperatively warns us against assuming that there was no substantive development of administration before writing made history possible. Indeed, it seems probable that administration, and particularly public administration, had already experienced a long phase of incubation before that invention occurred to increase its scope a hundredfold.

THE OLDEST PROFESSION?

It is clear that the official ranked early among the first professionals. The popular claim of prostitution to be the oldest profession is not therefore likely to stand close examination. Certainly the normal customs of tribal society lend little colour to this popular euphemism. Coon has another and much more plausible suggestion:

'The religious practitioner, the *shaman,* was the first specialist. His profession, not prostitution, is the oldest. There can be little doubt that Shamans existed in Late Pleistocene times, for they have been found among all living hunting peoples, even including the recently extinct Tasmanians.'[8]

Equally, when one considers the early emergence of government as a separate activity and the need of the governors for administrative assistants, there is surely a good case for the public official as the first professional. The widening of our knowledge of human activity by the discovery of cave and rock paintings going back into pre-cultivation ages, and thus providing evidence of very early concerted or communal activity, suggests that the public official must have emerged long before the dawn of history. The point is made by Arnold Hauser:

'The artist-magician, therefore, seems to have been the first representative of specialization and the division of labour. At any rate, he emerges from the undifferentiated mass, alongside the ordinary magician and the medicine-man, as the first professional and is, as the possessor of special gifts, the harbinger of the priestly class . . .'[9]

Really there is no disagreement between Coon and Hauser since at that early stage government and religion were not separable.

THE EARLY EVIDENCE

We know very little about the beginnings of mankind up to the invention of writing, and even less about the emergence of administration. Even though archaeological discovery and research are pressing back the boundaries of such knowledge into areas unsuspected, say, a hundred years ago, it is evident that man had walked the earth for the best part of a million years before his activities became recordable in any precise way. The discovery of early graves and the unearthing of an occasional human skeleton, or more usually part of a skeleton, and perhaps a few chipped flints, are about all we have on which to base our speculations. The latter, shaped into the first stone implements, indicate the development of high skills over long ages.[10] The degree of excellence achieved in similar uses of bone and especially wood, so readily available and so rapidly perishable, is a matter for conjecture.

How much more difficult then, is it bound to be, to figure out the impact of administration during these early stages. Fortunately it is not our object to outline the whole vast history, but to sort out such facts and incidents as illustrate the administrative theme running endlessly through mankind's more dramatic story.

As we have suggested in the Introduction, administration, the work of the official in his several capacities, is a subordinate activity, devised to implement and to co-ordinate the policy-decisions of leader and community. From the first its existence has been greatly facilitated by the techniques of writing and record-making, though the records themselves do not not usually say much about it. Even today, in an age of proliferating records, administration is an evanescent activity leaving scanty information about its inner working.

Nevertheless there are certain matters, both prehistoric and contemporary, that provide evidence of the existence of administrative activity before means were worked out of placing speech on record. In the prehistoric period we have the evidence of the sites and of the structural remains; subsequently we have the evidence of oral tradition, of language and, as we have already seen, of contemporary societies which are still today at a primitive stage of development.

ARCHAEOLOGY AS A KEY TO EARLY ADMINISTRATION

From the sites originally occupied by man, deductions may be drawn as to the activities of their occupants, especially from the objects accumulated about their living places, in refuse dumps and middens, in the form of chippings, discarded and half-shaped tools, bones, sherds and the like. Wherever such objects indicate a co-operative activity the essential contribution of administration — in planning, organizing and supervising — can be assumed.

It was apparently not until between 9000 and 6000 B.C. that man ceased generally to be a mere food-gatherer, gave up his rootless mobility and settled down to agriculture and the occupation of permanent sites. Yet before this, special conditions had led to the long occupation of certain sites and thus evidence of the existence of some sort of administrative organization can be traced much further back. The most spectacular of these sites are the caves in many parts of the world, particularly in southwestern France and northern Spain, where rock-paintings have been discovered which show that prehistoric man had already, perhaps as long as twelve to twenty thousand years ago, developed an art of considerable aesthetic beauty. The earliest significant discovery of this type was made at Altamira in Northern Spain, as recently as 1879.

Hidden away in the darkness of caves, sometimes high up in almost inacessible places, the mere existence of these paintings is evidence enough of an effective administrative organization to service the participants and provide security for the sites, or shrines as they often were. Kuhn points out how these prehistoric painted caves were sited to the south of the glacier fringe of the

Ice Age, the mobile hunters taking with them on their expeditions engraved bones, incised stones and female statuettes of the type that have been found in the excavation of such caves.[11]

Clearly, the cave pictures were not mere decorations. They appear to have had a practical purpose, a magical application, possibly to ensure the trapping of game. In some of the sites new paintings have been superimposed successively upon the older ones, clearly indicating the special, probably sacred, nature of the site itself. These bear witness to the development of advanced skills and presuppose the existence of schools with a corps of teachers, of local trends and traditions. There is ample evidence of such organizations, calling for a good deal of administrative talent, in the discovery in the caves of sketches, rough drafts and corrected pupils' drawings.[12] According to Hauser, the evidence points to the selection of these early professional painters from among the hunters themselves, as they would be the only persons capable of providing that realistic touch which convinces us today that the paintings were based upon the living experience of the contemporary trapper.

There was also the problem of obtaining and looking after the supplies of materials needed for the pursuance of this artistic activity. At Lascaux, for example, deposits of natural iron and manganese oxides provided the red and black, and carbonates of iron provided the yellow pigments which had to be finely ground with pestle and mortar.[13] Is it not feasible that the sites were serviced by lesser officials, subordinate to the artist-technicians, and responsible not only for the maintenance of supplies and the running of the schools, but also for the care and, possibly, defence of the sites, though the latter requirement may have been reduced to a minimum by a widespread fear of the consequences of sacrilegious trespassing upon such precincts?

The discovery of rock-drawings and paintings in Africa, particularly in the district of Tassili n'Ajjer in the midst of the Sahara, again indicates how such discoveries press back the boundaries of human history in places where the existence of settled communities was hardly suspected. A good deal has yet to be worked out in regard to the age and occasion of these paintings and certainly there is little that can be said about the administrative arrangements of such communities, though further examination of the sites could be revealing to the expert. Lhote has noted the existence of several art styles — he provisionally lists a dozen — which may well assist in interpreting the development of the sites.[14]

Artifacts of great value to the archaeologist are the sherds, already mentioned. These pieces of pottery disclose by their shape, substance, texture, design or markings, the epoch of their manufacture and thus on many sites successive layers, in which differing pottery pieces are found, provide clear evidence of the stages of development. As an activity pottery manufacture itself indicates the existence of administration, both in production and in distribution over wide areas by means of barter and other forms of trading. It has indeed been suggested that the pottery industry has a special tendency to develop a measure of organization even at modest cultural levels.[15]

Apart from pictorial and written records, about which more will be said later, some useful deductions about the administrative arrangements of early times can be drawn from the remains of structures of all kinds. A good example of this is provided by the remarkable prehistoric stone circles of Stonehenge and Avebury in south-east England, and Carnac in Brittany on the opposite side of the English Channel.

The most interesting of these is Stonehenge, whose standing stones and surrounding earthworks today still indicate the shape and grandiose nature of the original structure. This religious centre, which is estimated to date back to the period 1500-1400 B.C.[16] is partly built from immense stones not found in the vicinity but almost certainly brought from as far afield as the Prescelly Mountains in Pembrokeshire not far from the Irish Sea, which is the nearest spot where this type of stone is found. We are not concerned here with the several interesting theories of how the stones were transported so far with the primitive means available at the time. Certainly a considerable feat of engineering must have been involved, suggesting that the people of prehistoric Britain were not so intellectually backward as we are too prone to conclude. It is a common error to underrate the intelligence of our ancestors, and indeed of contemporaries whose material resources are limited, and one particularly to be avoided in our efforts to assess their administrative achievements. Such a feat of transportation over so wide an area, presumably occupied by different tribal communities, presuppose an organization to arrange the supply and supervise the whole operation, as well perhaps as a sort of Ministry of Works on the spot to see to the proper erection of the structure. It calls for no real stretch of imagination to visualize the existence of an effective supporting administration, although it is unfortunately less easy to clothe with flesh and blood the bones of a contemporary who may have ably represented the devoted public servant of the age.

The extent and purposes of early structures may automatically suggest the sort of administrative organization and services needed for their construction and subsequent servicing. For example, extensive irrigation works called not only for the recruitment, management and provisioning of large labour forces but also for the employment of considerable engineering skills. Matters of supply, law and order, and defence had to be provided for. Similar considerations applied to the large palace and temple buildings with perhaps even more complicated questions regarding design, supervision and servicing. From the planned layout, even when the entire superstructure has disappeared, the administrative purposes of certain rooms and compartments may be deduced. Evidence of their furnishings and contents may occasionally survive to fill the gaps, though it must be remembered that only durable substances usually survive. Furnishings of leather, fibre and wood and other perishable materials so widely used in administrative work, can usually only be imagined as the result of careful detective work. And all archaeologists are not interested in the administrative implications of their discoveries!

Certain basic administrative functions had to be catered for in these ancient buildings, even where the buildings themselves were not primarily intended for administrative uses, as they so often were. The scope of the administrative services of the time can therefore to some extent be deduced from the provision made for them. We should expect to find in surviving ground plans floor space for such functions as police and security, ceremonial and audience-giving, secretarial and recording, and the storage of foodstuffs, wine, arms and records. Thus the ancient buildings had their guard-rooms, their waiting rooms and their audience chambers. There were storage places and archives, and most certainly strong places for valuables and, much later, for moneys.

SETTLED COMMUNITIES IN THE MIDDLE EAST

The important surviving civilizations can be traced back to the river valleys of the Middle East, India and China, and the oldest surviving records to the first of these areas. This is of particular interest to us since the cradle of the European peoples is placed somewhere in the highlands of central Asia with their main migration routes leading through the very area with which this chapter is mainly concerned. The Middle East extends from the western borders of Persia (or Iran), across the Tigris and Euphrates valleys to Asia Minor as far as the Bosphorus, and southwards through Syria and Palestine to Egypt and the Nile valley. Thus it comprises two important river systems, namely the Tigris and Euphrates flowing southwards into the Persian Gulf, and the Nile flowing northwards into the Mediterranean. Formerly priority of incidence and importance was given to the Nile valley civilization, but, while the position is still highly controversial and liable to be modified by new discoveries, the balance seems to have turned in favour of the Tigris-Euphrates area centering on Mesopotamia (modern Iraq). At the moment we shall pay most attention to this area, sometimes known as the Fertile Crescent, but in view of the rich administrative contribution of Ancient Egypt the whole of Chapter 2 will be devoted to it.

The Sumerians have a good claim to be considered the initiators of history, both in point of time and creativeness.[17] Some time during the fourth millennium B.C. the first Sumerians drifted down from the high ground of western Persia into the gradually silting estuaries where the Tigris and the Euphrates entered the Persian Gulf. There the migrants were able to raise a surplus from the fruitful alluvial soil of the delta. Today these rivers meet far inland from the head of the Gulf. These peoples appear as the outstanding inventors of the ancient world, first users of the wheel and ox-drawn plough. They may well have brought such ideas with them; certainly early pottery remains suggest that their art at least came from Persia, whose potters had by 4000 B.C. developed a vigorous and abstract style not found anywhere else at that period.[18] In agriculture, mathematics, science, engineering, government, law and literature, to mention some of their outstanding fields of activity, the Sumerians made considerable contributions, and to support this sustained and varied effort there surely existed effective administrative machinery and means, even if administration received no recognition as a separate activity. Indeed, it may well be that the failure of others to develop so fruitfully as the Sumerians was due in some measure to a lack of administrative talents in management and co-ordination, which the Sumerians were able gradually to develop under the impact of their rich but challenging environment.

It must be remembered that the time-span of the civilization of the Sumerians and neighbouring peoples extended over three thousand years, from the dawn of settlement early in the fourth millennium, through the ascendency of Babylonia, to its absorption in the Assyrian Empire during the eighth century B.C. Assyria, in the high lands of the Tigris Valley away to the north, had developed concurrently and the whole intricate history of this area is involved in the struggles between these and numerous other peoples, notably the Akkadians and the Elamites. Another independently developing stream of peoples destined to be absorbed in the short-lived Assyrian Empire were the Hittites, whose history is still being gradually unfolded as a result of archaeological finds and research in the central plateau of Asia Minor. Altogether this long surviving and complex concourse of peoples provides a wonderful source of political and administrative experience. We are particularly interested, however, in the Sumerian contribution.

Little was known about these peoples until exploration of the ruins in the area was undertaken early in the nineteenth century, and even then the need to decipher their cuneiform inscriptions delayed progress for some time. Attention began to be paid to the mounds of earth which were characteristic of the landscape between the rivers and which were actually formed from the decayed brick-structures of the ancient cities. Within these outwardly unexciting rubble heaps the dry atmosphere had assisted in preserving a wondrous tale of human endeavour. The alluvial mud had been the only available building material. The hand-made brick dried in the sun had already been used in Persia, now it was to be used not only to provide shelter for a new civilization in Sumer but also to act as a handy recording medium for the same people. Agriculture took first place in the settlers' minds and they were immediately faced with the problem of drainage and protection from flooding. It has been suggested that reclamation of swamplands created the idea of property, which was firmly implanted in the new communities.[19] Certainly the development would have languished without important advances in engineering, which themselves presuppose administrative co-ordination on a communal basis. There gradually emerged an extensive system of canals which was to work efficiently over the centuries until its breakdown, with consequent agricultural decline, under the Seljuk Turks during the eleventh century A.D.

As a result of these developments the Sumerians became urbanized and their settlements formed into cities, each with its own agricultural domain. Even here history suggests that they were not the first to reach this stage, for recent excavations at Jericho, on the site of which archaeological research has traced a long succession of inhabited places superimposed one upon the other, have disclosed ruins of an early settlement dating back, it is thought, to 6800 B.C.[20] There is even evidence of earlier structures on the same site a full thousand years earlier, associated with temporary occupation, largely for ritual purposes, by Mesolithic hunters drawn by the existence of a spring.

The Sumerian cities formed independent communities, organized during the third millennium as small political units or city states.[21] At the centre of each state was the temple from which the main estate was managed, under the direction of the *Patesi,* who, as conjoint prince and priest, carried out the will of the god to whom the city and lands were dedicated. Cultivation was carried out by serfs and share-croppers who, together with the servants of the temple, formed practically the whole population. The city's government had something of the form of a corporation, under the *Patesi,* with a band of minor gods or divine servants acting as supervisors. Divine inspiration ensured efficient husbandry, while effective administration at that stage was synonymous with effective estate management.

Good agriculture called for peace, but the gods could fall out and war broke out between the city states from time to time. As a consequence there was a tendency towards the formation of larger units, sometimes of nationwide extent; but initially these experiments were not usually long-lived. Existing managerial skills effective in the cities were not yet able to cope successfully with larger units. All the activities of the state were carried out under divine command — for example, the construction of the temple, the waging of war, the conclusion of peace, the making of new laws — but the function of the city was mainly economic and it was a private rather than a public institution.

The idea of a more extensive unit as a political rather than an economic entity had still to emerge, and when it did it was still under the control of a god, a great god in this case. There was an assembly of gods, one of whom was selected as leader, working through his human steward. The role of the leader had become political; the idea of public service had emerged; the human head of this larger organization was well on the way to kingship.

The contents of surviving records, inscribed on baked mud tablets, consisted on the one hand of routine details of day-to-day administration and on the other of literary fragments — such as the celebrated poetic account of the epic struggle between Agga, ruler of Kish, and Gilgamesh, King of Erech — makes it difficult to separate fact from fiction. Indeed it was of the very nature of theocracy that the Sumerians themselves should be in a similar confused state of mind. In this epic poem there is a reference to an assembly of elders, a sort of senate, according to Kramer,[22] and an assembly of arms-bearing citizens, or lower house. The former declared for peace, while the latter opted for war, and the King in this instance agreed with the popular group. Kramer cites this as evidence that the Sumerians 'took the first steps towards democratic government by curbing the power of kings and recognizing the right of political assembly'.[23] This seems to be reading more into the evidence than the facts will support: it is a common practice of rulers — in tribal societies as in the more complex — to devise ways of obtaining the advice and consent of the ruled, and there appears to be little to suggest that the Sumerians broke new ground here.

Gradually the influence of theocracy waned, or rather concentrated more and more on the estate management functions, while the political inter-state aspect increased. The first city known to have gained leadership among Sumerian cities was Ur, where extensive and exciting discoveries have been made.[24] The city was under a king named Mes-anni-padda, who founded the First Dynasty of Ur. Already there were fine buildings, and the princes and nobles were buried in massive tombs together with members of their entourage, whose function no doubt was to minister to their needs in the other world. Whether or not this service was enforced or voluntary, as Sir Leonard Woolley thinks it was, it was an eventuality that must be considered as one of the unavoidable hazards of being an official in that age! City rivalries became more acute and eventually the King of Ur was overthrown by the King of Lagash, a neighbouring city.

Inter-city strife was destined to be overshadowed by the marauding of nomadic Semites who had settled in Akkad to the north. The southwards drift of the peoples was continuing. Somewhere about 2500 B.C., under Sargon, these Akkadians finally defeated the Sumerians and controlled all the riverine lands down to the sea. The warlike Sargon built up a powerful state and, as so often has happened in history, the nomadic conquerors learned almost everything from the conquered whose strange arts were necessary if the combined community was to be effectively administered. Within a couple of hundred years the Sumerian culture attained supremacy and Ur enjoyed a further period of prosperity and power under the Kings of Sumer and Akkad. With this flourishing civilization Babylonia had entered the pages of history.[25]

Pressures from without continued, by the Elamites from the east and by the Amorites down the valley from the north, whence previously the Akkadians had advanced. Eventually the Amorites were victorious and established a line of kings with their capital at Babylon, which they raised from an obscure village to an important centre of government. Outstanding among these Amorite kings was Hammurabi, who came into power in Babylon somewhere about the beginning of the second millennium B.C. (although authorities vary on this).

As military leader Hammurabi excelled, but it is upon his skill as lawgiver that his fame justly rests. The laws of Hammurabi survive on a diorite shaft nearly eight feet high around which the inscriptions occupy over 3,600 lines.[26] Yet he was not so much an innovator in this field as a rationalizer. Most of his laws stemmed back to earlier epochs, but in a very inexact and disjointed way. For the first time in history a comprehensive system of law was set down in writing, so that the judges could henceforth administer justice consistently in accordance with the code. No longer did they depend upon precedent based upon oral tradition. Legal authority was now centralized under the king, as law-giver, and the judges were brought more definitely under his control. This also presupposed a strong centralized administration.

In fact a professional official class was being established. Already a commercial society had emerged, with book-keeping, standardized measures, a system of bankers' cheques, and possibly the world's first real bourgeoisie.[27] Now this middle class was to be supplemented by a paid public service. The city *patesis* were replaced by royal officials and the local government became secularized. Deprived of their main governing functions the priestly class, who had gained adequate financial experience the hard way in managing the temple estates, assumed a financial role and acquired a virtual monopoly of banking.

The Laws of Hammurabi were mainly concerned with providing a working civil code, dealing particularly with property and contract. On the criminal side, which was not separately distinguished, it remained crude, based largely upon such *lex talionis* principles as 'an eye for an eye and a tooth for a tooth'. Thus savage mutilation was prescribed for specific injuries without reference to the particular circumstances under which they came about: as, when a surgeon, causing the death of a gentleman or loss of an eye, was sentenced under the code to have his hands cut off!

At about the same time the state system of the Hittites was developing, apparently independently, in the high lands of central Anatolia to the north-west of Syria. Here at Hattusus, the ancient capital, situated near Boghazkoy in modern Turkey, many important facts are still coming to light.[28]

A table of kings already existed in the second millennium B.C.[29]

At first the king's tenure seems to have been insecure, rival candidates being supported by the nobles, but this is hardly an unusual phenomenon in history. It has been suggested from such evidence that the early kingship was elective, but this is not supported by the only existing record of the royal act of 'designation', made by Hattusilis I towards the middle of the second millennium B.C. The ruler's right to settle the succession was finally regulated by law about a hundred years later, and a period of dynastic stability ensued. The Hittite king was not a god, though he might be deified after death. He exercised the normal powers of kingship as supreme commander of the army, supreme judicial authority and chief priest. He was a fully responsible head of state. Diplomatic dealings with other powers were in his hands. Normally, he would delegate his judicial duties to subordinates, but he was expected to retain direct control of his military and religious functions. He was obliged to give priority to the latter and might find it politic to hasten back from a campaign to his capital for the celebration of a festival. It was unwise to risk an accusation of having offended the gods! He was expected to visit periodically the main cult-centres of his realm, which he did, often accompanied by the queen and the crown prince. The queen had an independent position of her own, and if she survived retained her special importance as Queen Mother after the king's death.

Government in the localities continued under a sort of town council of elders, presumably an older institution which had now come under the control of centrally appointed provincial governors. Newly conquered territories were usually administered on behalf of the king through the agency of his own sons, but successful generals might also be given such responsibilities. Their duties included the dispensation of justice, the appointment of priests and the supervision of religious matters, and the construction and repair of public works. At first these appointments were informal and temporary, but gradually, as the extent and power of the empire grew, more permanent governors with a good deal of autonomy were appointed. They were bound to the sovereign power by solemn and explicit oaths of fealty. For associated territories less precise relationships were evolved, the vassal being required to undertake an annual act of homage and to render appropriate tribute. To the maintenance of these relationships the solemnity of the oath was fundamental and such customs as the taking of hostages, widely adopted in neighbouring lands, was not favoured by the Hittites whose outlook was particularly humane for the times.

Returning to Babylonia we discover that, following the great age of Hammurabi, a period of stagnation ensued. The Sumerians, having made their imperishable contribution were now to leave the stage. New masters were coming down into the land. The Assyrians had established their capital at Asshur away to the north and around this focus had gradually built up a strong military state. These people were ruthless warriors who developed a standing army and established firm sway over a wide territory which ceased to be distracted by inter-city rivalries such as had tended to weaken the regimes of Sumer and Babylonia. But the Assyrians did not neglect trade. Their merchants travelled widely and Asshur became an important trading centre. In fact they took full advantage of the business methods developed by the Sumerians.

By about 750 B.C. a powerful new empire stretched across the Tigris and Euphrates valleys. Under Sargon II (722-705 B.C.) this Assyrian Empire achieved its greatest military power. He built a new capital to the north-east of Nineveh, which he called Sargonberg, and inaugurated the earliest known system of roads by first linking these two places and later throwing out a network to cover the whole empire, a necessary basic communications system to support the army, whose maintenance was a military state's chief concern. The road system facilitated the flow of supplies, not least the produce of tribute and taxation. Along these roads travelled the royal messengers carrying their clay-tablet missives, while the king inaugurated a postal system by appointing officials in each of the more important centres to ensure the transmission of the royal correspondence. Here the basic mechanics of successful administration are laid bare. Letters and reports flowed in from over sixty governors, as well as from the subject kings who were allowed to continue in vassalage. Sargon was well-informed and controlled a communications system whereby his will could be conveyed with the utmost expedition that the knowledge of the time permitted. Among these letters have survived a number despatched by Sargon's son, Sennacherib, while the latter was crown prince[30]

Sennacherib, as ruler, continued his father's work; extending his military conquests; ruthlessly suppressing revolts, in the course of which he completely destroyed Babylon; and undertaking extensive constructional projects. He transferred his capital to Nineveh, to which he brought water from the northern streams by a canal along a magnificent aqueduct which is the earliest known to us.[31] The Assyrian state was a vast military machine administered centrally from the king's business office.[32] It made a real contribution by showing how, with good communications, numerous peoples could be welded together over a wide area, but there were serious defects. A too rigorous control appears to have been maintained over internal affairs: for example, surviving laws demonstrate the strict supervision of the state over marriage and property rights! The army was maintained at the expense of production and came to depend too much on the recruitment of foreign levies.

A new rival power arose when the Chaldeans mastered Babylon. In conjunction with the Medes they attacked and, after two years' struggle, captured and destroyed Nineveh towards the end of the seventh century B.C. Babylon was rebuilt on a magnificent scale and Nebuchadnezzar, the greatest of the Chaldean emperors, reigned there for forty years. Maps of the city survive, incised on clay-tablets. They suggest an early example of town-planning on a vast and luxurious scale. The magnificent roof-gardens of Nebuchadnezzar's palace were so widely famed that the Greeks included them among the Seven Wonders of the World. This was the Babylon of the Hebrews' captivity recounted in the Bible.[33] All the arts of the Sumerians and their business methods were cultivated anew, while the Chaldeans made an important contribution when they virtually founded the science of astronomy by undertaking regular observations of the heavens. But it seems that these new conquerors came to look too much towards the past. This attitude was certainly reflected in their administrative methods, for their 'scribes loved to employ an ancient style of writing and out-of-date forms of speech'.[34] After Nebuchadnezzar's death national decline set in rapidly and the peoples of the Mesopotamian lands ceased to take an important part in the development of our civilization.

THE COMING OF THE WRITTEN RECORD

History, as the story of mankind, depends upon the written record: without the written record administration would have lacked the one technique vital to its extension. After the development of speech as an unique human accomplishment, a development which made communal living possible to mankind, the next revolutionary step was the invention of writing.[35] But while the former event is shrouded in the mists of prehistoric time, the latter seems to have occurred during the fourth millennium B.C. in the time of the Sumerians, who may or may not have been its inventors.[36]

As in all such developments writing emerged only after a long period of experiment, of trial and error; but when the last step came to be made it appeared as the result of a special situation — a need created by the particular nature of the temple economy of the Sumerians, which called for the consistent recording of numerous daily transactions.[37] In other words, the final impulse to its invention was administrative, a point that needs to be pondered by all who debate whether the pen is mightier than the sword!

At a very early stage, as we have seen when considering the cave pictures, efforts were made by primitive man to pictorialize his ideas, the vital topic at that time — the hunt — being practically the sole subject-matter of his impulse to communicate on a permanent basis. But apart from the cave engravings and paintings, which may well have included, subsidiary to the main religio-magical set-pieces, marginal signs of directional intention, evidence has fortunately survived of much more ephemeral attempts by Stone Age man to make drawings in the earth with his finger tips, examples of which have been almost miraculously preserved at Pech-Merle and Tuc d'Audoubert in France.[38] Upper Paleolithic hunters (35,000 to 8,000 B.C.) are known to have used notched sticks, which may well have preserved counts of their kills, although, on the analogy of a custom of modern Australian Bush-men, these may even have been formal invitations to feasts or weddings, the notches indicating the number of days to the ceremony.[39] The existence of such aids in a surviving community provides an interesting commentary on the administrative methods that may well have been available in the pre-literate age. Knotted cords could also be used as a modest accountancy aid or for the transmission of messages.

Before a system of writing could be of much value a manageable medium for receiving the signs and a fairly simple means of making them were both essential. In those early days rock carvings and impressions could be made and the recording of important events in bas-relief afford early examples of the sculptor as historian. Pottery might have provided a valuable administrative material and indeed signs and designs on prehistoric pottery may well have been an early attempt at writing: indeed potsherds were used for record purposes, but surviving examples are usually of later date.

However, one important administrative article in this category, which had priority over the invention of writing, was the cylinder seal, many examples of which have survived, thanks to the permanence of the material of which they were often made. The seal was used for safeguarding possessions, sometimes for marking a package or jar already sealed with clay. In other words, it was an early forerunner of the personal signature. The seal itself was a small portable object made out of some hard substance, usually a locally available stone; but even metal, such as the commonly found haematite of Babylonia, could be used. These seals were often artistically designed and in such a way as to make copying difficult. The designs provide valuable evidence of the life and activities of the times.[40] After the invention of writing inscriptions were sometimes included. The importance of these cylinder seals to the historian is illustrated by the design found on an Akkadian seal of around 2400-2200 B.C.[41] This represents a *shaduf,* a counterbalancing attachment to apparatus devised to lift water buckets with the minimum of human effort, and thus an important agricultural invention which may well have gone back to a much earlier age.

As we have seen, in the sun-baked brick which formed the basic building material in Mesopotamia, there existed a potential medium for the receiving of impressions out of which writing could, with not too much difficulty, emerge. It would have its disadvantages, as we shall see, but its widespread availability would assist the Sumerians in devising an effective solution to their administrative problems. From the point of view of posterity the inscribed burnt brick had the virtue of being almost indestructible, indeed much more permanent than the vast soft-finished buildings in which they were usually kept. It is interesting to observe that dating of the buildings is sometimes facilitated by the early custom, employed with an eye to posterity, of burying inscribed cylinder stones in the foundations, or of inserting headed clay nails inscribed with the name of the ruler between the courses of brickwork.

The fine clay was well kneaded to form tablets on which the impression had to be made while it was still damp. This was a major drawback of the material, since the whole brick, or entry, had to be made quickly at one time. No doubt the scribe had ways of keeping the material moist while he worked on it, but a system of ledger entries made at different times could not be operated by this means. The first writing was pictographic, represented by a series of fine lines similar to those incised in stone, but made by a sharp reed-like stylus, of bone or hard bamboo. This did not readily leave a good impression and new types of 'pen' were introduced. Eventually a triangular stylus was invented by which wedge-shaped or, as they are called, cuneiform impressions and short strokes were easily made. At the same time the pictograph system, by which objects and ideas were represented pictorially, was gradually rationalized so that the new cuneiform writing was based upon a system of syllables. There were over 560 Sumerian signs, each representing a syllable, or word, and the system was not alphabetical.

Thus a fairly quick system of writing had emerged although the scribes had a difficult skill to acquire. The records thus produced, often consisting of lists or inventories, were handy enough purely for record and reference purposes, but they left much to be desired in regard to portability and did not therefore facilitate correspondence at a distance. Nevertheless, as will be seen, so urgent became the need for such correspondence in a new world of commerce and diplomacy that until something better could be invented the incised clay tablet was to have its day, and again a very important one in the history of administration. The work of the scribe was more often than not tedious and called for patience as well as skill. It was possible to duplicate impressions by using cylindrical or hexagonal rollers to obtain continuous impressions on longer tablets of soft clay, but in the main copies of documents had to be inscribed individually. This continued to be a basic characteristic of office work, at least until the invention of printing. The copying scribe, modest as was his status, was to remain for long one of the real mainstays of every administration.

While the Sumerians can claim priority, on present evidence, for the invention of writing, and the reasons for their success are plain to see, it would be a mistake to regard their system as the one original fount of all writing. There exists in fact evidence of at least seven such systems that can claim an independent origin. These are listed by Gelb as: [42] (1) Sumerian in Mesopotamia — 3100 B.C. to just before the Christian era; (2) Proto-Elamite in Elam — 3000 to 2200 B.C.; (3) Proto-Indic in the Indus Valley — around 2200 B.C.; (4) Chinese in China — 1300 B.C. to date; (5) Egyptian in Egypt — 3000 B.C. to 400 A.D.; (6) Cretan in Crete and Greece — 2000 to 1200 B.C.; and (7) Hittite in Anatolia and Syria — 1500 to 700 B.C. Among the several initiatory factors in these developments no doubt the administrative ones were important.

Large stores of incised tablets have survived, and much interpretative work upon them remains to be done. From the variety of their contents a good deal of valuable information about administration can be deduced and some of this should now be examined. Such tablets may turn up singly or in small quantities in almost any excavation in the area under investigation but probably the most interesting case is where the discovery of quantities denotes the existence of libraries, which had been accumulated at an early date. The Assyrians had such a library at Calash somewhere about 1300 B.C., but Sumerian booklists existed before this.[43] Probably the most important find of this sort was made at an early stage of Mesopotamian excavation in 1849, by Layard when he unearthed the royal library of Ashurbanipal (known to the Greeks as Sardanapalus), who reigned over Assyria in mid-seventh century B.C.[44] When the two large chambers were uncovered they were piled a foot deep or more in tablets and, together with a subsequent find, these totalled to more than twenty-six thousand, the majority of which are now in the British Museum, London. These tablets may be divided into five groups according to place or content: (1) historical literature; (2) the king's private library; (3) the library of the Temple; (4) correspondence; and (5) certain contracts. Sometimes large baked-clay prisms or cylinders were used, particularly for historical texts, but these were much more difficult to retrieve without damage. The bulk of the tablets came from the royal library which covered such subjects as mythology, medicine, chemistry, philology and astrology. In the scientific section there was an invaluable treatise on the components of glass and the glazes of pottery. Altogether this find emphasizes the importance at the time of library management as a function of public administration, while specifically the surviving correspondence throws light upon more general administrative methods.

A find, perhaps even more instructive to the administrator, was that of the diplomatic correspondence at Tell-el-Amarna in Egypt.[45] This included missives from Babylonia, but more will be said about this in Chapter 3. There is evidence that Asshurbanipal sent his agents abroad to collect outstanding written works or to make copies of them. His interest in the past is manifested by the importance he attached to historical texts. It would be interesting to know what were his reactions to the numerous ruins that already dotted the landscape, for these are mentioned in tablets dating back as far as 1500 B.C., although only in order to facilitate the location of fields and other features!

The close linkage between governmental and commercial administration is demonstrated by interesting finds at Atchana in the Turkish Hatay, on the site of the important trading port of Alalakh.[46] This was a centre of particular importance in the history of administration in virtue of its close commercial and diplomatic relations over a long period with the ancient empires of Sumer, of Babylon and of Egypt, with the Hittites, and with numerous less-known powers such as the Hurri and the Mitanni.[47]

Situated in the port of Alalakh were the business premises of merchants engaged in the import and export trade between Asia and the Aegean. Sir Leonard Woolley reports upon the remains of one of these entrepôt buildings which was burned down with its contents *in situ*:

'We could see that the whole of it was given over to goods, and these were stored in separate categories, a magazine-room being devoted to each class; one room was filled with great wine-jars, another with small oil bottles of local make, a third with imported Greek unguent-pots, a fourth with big bell-shaped mixing-bowls, and so on. Each of the large buildings in an *insula* was the business office of one firm; in the go-downs were stored the Asiatic goods ready for export, and the goods disembarked from incoming merchantmen were warehoused here for eventual sale to the land-traders whose caravans would transport them to the cities of the interior. The isolated room in the court was probably the office of the tally-clerk.'[48]

In the administrative offices of the more strictly public sector similar survivals can be examined, but usually administrative equipment, with the notable exception of the incised brick, is constitutionally destructible and not likely to endure. Nor was the administrative function yet sufficiently differentiated to leave its mark upon the general structure, except perhaps where the storage of records was involved. However, in the ruins described by Sir Leonard Woolley there were, in the official block of the palace-temple, a chamber of audience and several waiting rooms reserved for officials, with small rooms leading off which may well have been a secretariat and an archive.[49] At another level a secretarial office was discovered with an adjoining archive which had a shelf running all round it. With disappointment, Sir Leonard remarks, the shelves had been swept clean, although, on the analogy of a similar discovery at Ur, where numerous tablets were still lying on the shelves, the use of the chamber is quite clear.

Similar traders' accounts have been found at Kanesh, Kultope and Karatepe in Anatolia, where colonies of Assyrian merchants meticulously recorded their transactions in lead and fine clothing.[50] Law reports also figured among these archives. An interesting example found at Alalakh gives resumé of a lawsuit brought unsuccessfully by one Irib-Khazi, subject of Niqmepa, claiming to be actually a subject of the king of Mitanni.[51] There is also an instance of an intelligence report contained on a tablet also unearthed at Alalakh, which deserves to be mentioned. This report was obtained by an agent of Yarim-Lim, the local ruler, who was a contemporary of Hammurabi. It set out for the astute king's information the relative support forthcoming from neighbouring kings for Hammurabi of Babylon, Rim Sin of Larsa (who were the two outstanding rulers in Mesopotamia at the time) and Yarim-Lim himself. Each of the former were stated to have the support of fifteen vassals but, the report went on, 'twenty kings follow Yarim-Lim of Yamkhad'.[52] Certainly such secret service information, if reliable, was calculated to aid the king in conducting a middle-way policy between two such powerful neighbours.

These somewhat isolated examples indicate the range of information about the administration of the period that can be culled from the numerous clay tablets which have survived. There must be plenty of similar unpublished evidence to be extracted either from tablets which themselves were media of administration — as accounts, records, reports, inventories, and the like — or from others containing descriptive details of the organization and processes of the administrative agencies of the period. Something more may now be said about the officials themselves and the processes they employed.

THE EARLY PUBLIC OFFICIAL AND HIS WORK

Public administration has been touched upon from many angles in the course of the brief preceding survey, and even if the official himself must remain shadowy in light of the dearth of personal information, the results of his activities are almost all we have to tell of the history of his times, for were not the buildings whose ruins we examine the products of his planning and supervision, and the vital written records his very handiwork? Even in communities still based vitally upon agricultural production the ramifications of government were already considerable.

It has been seen how, as the numerous peoples flowed down into the valleys of the Tigris and Euphrates over thousands of years and contended, often to the death, among themselves, important developments in government and administration were going on all the time. It was in fact the major change which made historical records possible, namely the invention of writing, that also constituted the revolutionary change in administration, a change which thereafter was characterized by its stabilizing rather than its revolutionary nature. Thus, when the nomadic and warlike but ignorant Akkadians conquered the Sumerians, the first thing they had to do was to acquire the administrative skills of the defeated, the lack of which, had it persisted, would soon have rendered their victory futile.

During this long period we have noted the change in scale of government from the widespread but miniature theocratic city state, through the larger unions of such states or kingdoms, to the more extensive empires of Babylonia, Assyria and Chaldea. In each case the leader, wielder of the chief power, stands out as administrator among his numerous roles. But he invariably has close influential assistants who may even share the power. Below this top layer there is usually a class of experts of various types with, in the larger state organization, a host of menial workers at the base. Thus, at this very early stage the official world is already organized as a hierarchic pyramid with what appears to be a sort of tripartite class structure. In the small city-state under its temple corporation most of the community's activities came under official direction: in the larger states this was no longer practicable or indeed desirable and large agricultural and important trading interests remained outside, while the army tended to become a power of its own, eventually, in the case of Assyria, to the detriment of the state.

In the early city-state government and business management were one: it was a form of local government on a sovereign basis and the administration is not difficult to understand. At Ur such business was undertaken within the sacred area. Sacrifices and offerings in kind were the early equivalent of taxation. The temple scribe issued receipts for these items and listed them on clay tablets, which formed the basis of the simple accounting system from which lists could subsequently be built up and stored in the office, where they were destined to be uncovered four thousand years later. No doubt similar records were made when the offerings were passed into pantry or store for consumption in the temple, or otherwise issued to dependents of the estate. Factories and workshops were also sited in the temple precincts. At a factory unearthed at Ur, which produced a variety of woollen clothes, tablets were found listing the names of the women workers, the quantity of wool issued to each, the amount of cloth produced and the quantity of rations allotted. Significant is the title of the law court, also sited in the temple: it was called *Dublal-mah* or 'The Great House of Tablets'. Within the building clay documents were stored recording the decisions of the judges, whose practice it was to announce these decisions from the doorway.[53]

Detailed information also exists [54] about the organization of the main temple of the city state of Lagash, whose god was named Ningirsu. For the government of the temple-manor house and management of the temple lands there were two sets of lesser gods, often related to the chief god. To these were assigned such positions as Doorkeeper of the Holy of Holies, Chief Butler, Armourer, Divine Councillor, Body Servant, Divine Chamberlain, Coachman, Charioteer and Goatherd. There were also the Musician, the Drummer and the Ladies-in-Waiting at the court. In the fields we find the Bailiff, the Divine Inspector of Fisheries and the Divine Gamekeeper. A Divine Sheriff saw to the enforcement of the ordinances. The titles of this mythological hierarchy and their duties reflect clearly the administrative patterns of the city state. In fact the actual duties were carried out by human agents of various types, organized under specialist supervisors who formed an hierarchy of control with its apex occupied by the highest servant of the god, the *Ensi,* or manager. The *Ensi* was in fact the estate manager who was expected to uphold and fulfil the established order of the estate and to execute the specific commands of the owner (in this case made manifest through signs and omens). He was primarily an administrator responsible for all the manifold activities of the diminutive state. He had to keep close account of all daily transactions. But besides administering the estate he was responsible for law and order in the city and had to act when necessary as army commander. As a strong and successful leader the *Ensi* could be extremely powerful, but any failure or setback could be interpreted as reflecting the will of the gods, in which case his position could indeed be unenviable. He had always to watch his step and the priests would be constantly on the look out for breaches of religious protocol. The *Ensi* had every reason to ensure efficient management.

With the emergence of larger kingdoms a two-level pattern of administration began to take shape. The *Patesi* or *Ensi* of the city-temple was replaced by a royal nominee, at first presumably a family connection. Under the Hittites a pattern of government existed which was very similar to that at Ur and Lagash just mentioned.[55] The king's kinsmen, known as the Great Family, occupied most of the important offices of state, whose titles again indicate their close connection with the court as the main centre of administration. For example, there were the Chief of the Bodyguard, the Chief of the Courtiers, the Chief of the Treasurers, the Chief of the Wine-pourers, the Chief of the Sceptre-bearers, the Father of the House, and the Chief of the Overseers of One Thousand. With such posts army command often came to be associated. As yet there was no functional division between the business of the royal household and public business in a more general way. No such distinction could in fact have existed at the time. Under the high officials in charge of the various branches of activity there were numerous lesser officials, whose existence and functions remain somewhat shadowy in the absence of detailed information. However, they included courtiers, body-guards, golden-grooms, cup-bearers, tablemen, cooks, sceptre-men, chamberlains, and 'overseers of one thousand'. The latter, whose Chief has already been mentioned, are significant as an early specialized class of supervisors.

King Telepinus (circa 1525 B.C.) referred to these various officials as *pankus,* which is thought to mean 'whole community', although there were no doubt also numerous craftsmen, peasants and serfs in the background. Indeed, these are mentioned in connection with a general assembly of citizens, who in earlier times had met as a court of law. Nothing is heard of this assembly after the time of Telepinus, and it is clear that the Hittite system of government had become an absolute monarchy of the normal type, controlled by the king through his own officials.

The organized office had come into existence at an early date. One can already visualize rows of scribes, each with his pile of wet clay beside him, using his stylus rapidly and probably employing some means of keeping the clay damp during the process of inscribing the tablets. The scribes would usually be males although there might be females among them, for women were held highly in Babylonian society, where they were per-mitted to engage in business on their own account.[56]

The ruler himself was still chief administrator and Breasted provides an interesting picture of Hammurabi conducting his official business. This information is based upon Hammurabi's letters, many of which have survived. We see him sitting in his executive office, his secretary at his side, an administrative relationship that has hardly changed right up to the present day. Using his reed stylus, which he carries habitually in a leather holder at his girdle, the secretary writes down in cuneiform syllables the short clear sentences which the king is dictating in the form of letter-instructions to his city governors. Incoming tablet-letters are enclosed in thin clay envelopes. These are broken by the secretary in the presence of the king, who then dictates his replies to the enclosed messages. In this way decisions on current problems are issued. Possibly these include admonitions to delinquent tax-gatherers, orders to punish officials guilty of bribery, or for the arrest of others who have fallen under the king's displeasure. He may also deal with appeals from the rulings of the courts.

There are other duties for the office to perform. Outgoing correspondence has to be baked in a furnace. Envelopes of clay have to be provided. The letters may be listed. The confidential messengers who convey them to their destinations have to be briefed and sent on their way.

To ensure the safety of documents of special importance — for example, contracts and other business agreements — enclosure in a special envelope might be prescribed. The original document having been inscribed on a tablet and duly marked with the seals of the scribe and/or contracting parties, it was enclosed in a thin envelope of clay shaped precisely as the original and the contents of the enclosed document were for a second time inscribed on the outer surface, which was also properly authenticated. Any suspected alterations in the document could be checked by destroying the outer cover and examining the inner original, a procedure which would no doubt be performed in the presence of a magistrate. A forger could not change the inner tablet without first destroying irrevocably the outer one, while any attempt to replace the outer envelope with a revised text was rendered impossible by the fact that a clay covering placed on the original after that had dried would inevitably break through shrinkage during the process of drying.[57] By the general rules of business many transactions called for the provision of documentary evidence. Thus there was plenty of work for the professional scribe.

Recent discoveries at Ras Shamra, the ancient Ugarit, on the coast of Syria, where the ruins of the royal palace have been uncovered, add further interesting details to our picture of public administration in the middle of the second millennium B.C.[58] The King of Ugarit was a dependent of the Hittites, and Ugarit was an important diplomatic and trading centre. In the palace, upon which catastrophe appears to have fallen suddenly, numerous clay tablets have been found which formed part of the archives of several offices. They included correspondence between the king and surrounding rulers, among whom were the Pharaoh of Egypt and Hammurabi of Babylonia. In a courtyard near some enclosures, which may well have been the workplace of the scribes, an oven was discovered containing cuneiform tablets in various stages of baking. It was a simple oven about three feet high by four feet wide, similar to the open-air bread ovens used by the Arabs today. This highly interesting find shows that the offices were in full operation at the time of the disaster and thus emphasizes the suddenness of the event. Archives of the same period were unearthed in three separate parts of the palace, the positioning suggesting the existence of separate administrative departments: possibly those of the Interior and Treasury, of the Governor of the City, and of the Foreign Minister, in addition to those of the King's Chancery. The tablets in the oven had come from different offices, indicating that the baking process was carried on as a common service.

The correspondence ranged over a period of three hundred years. The documents, which are partly in Ugaritic and partly in Babylonian, the international language of the time, dealt with a wide range of subjects. Some texts listed such matters as the towns of the kingdom, the contingents they had to contribute to the army, their dues in taxes or in labour: some listed the corporations and the dependencies outside the kingdom. There were diplomatic exchanges and documents dealing with the affairs of the City of Ugarit. There were contracts and other business documents. Among the diplomatic texts were instruments designed to ensure equal diplomatic status for the commercial attachés to be exchanged by the King of Ugarit with the immeasurably more powerful King of the Hittites. The scripts are generally brief and to the point, but an occasional human touch appears; as, for example, when an official asks his senior to explain why he is angry with him. The reply would have been of special interest. The 'handwriting' is often finely inscribed and frequent inclusion of the scribe's name renders it possible for characteristic styles to be identified and compared. The tablets are impressed with the seals of individual officials and, of course, where appropriate the royal seal appears. A fact of exceptional interest is that in addition to the ruling monarch's personal seal, there is also a dynastic seal (of the founder of the dynasty) which continued to be used over a number of reigns. This suggests that the idea of the state as an impersonal institution was emerging. Furthermore there was more than one royal seal in current use. This may be explained by attributing their use to different officials to whom authority had been for the time being delegated.

Altogether these discoveries at ancient Ugarit give us a picture of a thriving centre of both public and business administration, with a large staff of competent administrators and clerks, operating procedures sufficiently advanced not to fear challenge from the administrative activities of much later ages.

It has already been suggested that the art of cuneiform writing

was difficult to acquire. Training was necessary and the existence
of schools in Sumer at an early date is well established. This
development must have begun with the invention of writing, for,
as we have seen, there were hundreds of syllables to be learned.
At first the schools would concentrate upon the training of
scribes concerned with official business — an early example of
staff training. Eventually the craft would expand and there
would be various categories of scribes: junior and senior, general
and specialist, official and others. Out of these schools a system
of general education would develop, covering various current
branches of learning and the study of past texts. Breasted
mentions a school-house of the age of Hammurabi which has
survived. The pupils used an 'exercise book' consisting of a soft
clay tablet from which signs could be erased by smoothing the
surface with a flat edge of wood or stone.[59] From the tablets
which have been salvaged can be pieced together the developing
stages of this process of instruction, from the making of rows
of single wedge-shapes to the forming of syllables, and on to the
formation of words and sentences. At that time, as today,
proverbs were popular among teachers and one surviving example
that is particularly apposite reads 'He who shall excel in tablet-
writing shall shine like the sun.'

By 1000 B.C. an important change was beginning to have its
influence on the administrative pattern as a result of the introduction by the Aramaeans of the earliest system known of
alphabetical writing, which greatly simplified the process by
radically restricting the number of signs required. For a time
Assyrian and Aramaic were used concurrently and there is an
interesting clay-tablet of the eighth century B.C. which pictures
such a process in practical use.[60] It shows a stream of captives
with sheep and cattle being brought into captivity before an
official, who is directing records of the booty to be made. There
are two scribes in the picture: one is using a stylus to make
incisions in a clay-tablet which he holds in his left-hand, the
other has spread out in his left-hand a roll of papyrus on which
he is writing in ink with a pen. Here we have visual evidence of
the impact of an important invention which came out of Egypt
and which will be described in the next chapter. Aramaic was
widely used in business and for a time parallel texts had to be
kept in government offices but eventually it became a *lingua
franca,* particularly for state business, over the whole area from
the borders of India to Egypt.[61]

Individual officials have left impressions of their personal
cylinder seals, but the nature of the records did not lead to their

leaving much information about themselves. There is certainly an inscription on a statue of King Idri-mi, found at Alalakh, which is an autobiography of the king written by a scribe named Sharruwa, who Woolley suggests,[62] was probably an 'elder statesman' of the kingdom, for not only does his name appear on a document of an earlier reign, but in the present example he speaks with the sort of self-assertion that would only be excused by high rank. Sharruwa uses his own dialect and 'unfortunately neither the scribe who made the copy for the mason, nor the mason who cut the inscription was very skilful, and the text is therefore difficult to read'.

Because he makes reference to administrative skills Ashurbanipal of Assyria, who in his inscriptions often refers to his education and to his intellectual as well as to his military achievements, deserves to be quoted here as the First Administrator of his realm. He 'writes':

'I, Ashurbanipal, learned the wisdom of Nabu, the entire art of writing on clay tablets . . . . I learned to shoot the bow, to ride, to drive and to seize the reins.

I received the revelation of the wise Adapa, the hidden treasure of the art of writing . . . . I considered the heavens with the learned masters . . . . I read the beautiful clay tablets from the Sumer and the obscure Akkadian writing which is hard to master. I had my joy in the reading of inscriptions on stone from the time before the flood . . . . The following were my daily activities: I mounted my horse, I rode joyfully, I held the bow . . . . I drove the chariot, holding the reins like a charioteer. I made the wheels go round . . . . At the same time I learned royal decorum and walked in kingly ways.'[63]

PUBLIC ADMINISTRATION BECOMES IMPERIAL

By the middle of the first millennium B.C. the foundations of our modern civilization had been truly laid in the Middle East, and most of the ingredients needed for the administration of extensive realms had been devised. The invention of writing had made possible the intricate communications system on which all effective administration depends. Remarkable advances had been made in the development of business methods. A workable calendar, monetary system and standards of weights and measures had been introduced. River transport had been widely supplemented by a network of roads along which an official postal service was being effectively operated. In the sphere of public administration taxational methods had been improved and effective central control, through executive agents, had been rendered practicable. There were libraries and schools. Everything was ready for the movement of civilization's centre of activity westwards into a Europe whose vigorous inhabitants were still steeped in pagan ignorance and quite unaware of the wonders that man had already fashioned for himself.

Already there had been successful experiments in wide unified control under such leaders as Sargon, Hammurabi and Sennacherib, and now, as the power passed away from the confines of Mesopotamia, there was to be a brief flowering beyond the eastern frontiers in which all their hard-won experience was to be marshalled to organize what has a good claim to be entitled the first great imperial administration outside the Far East. Although this means switching our interest beyond the main area surveyed in this chapter it seems desirable to do this before we turn to consider the parallel developments that had been taking place in the Nile Valley.

By the sixth century B.C. the Medes had formed, along the north-eastern boundaries of the Chaldean Empire, a realm which extended to the borders of India. Shortly after the death of Sennacherib Cyrus, the prince of a small Persian tribe, by sheer military prowess defeated the Medes and laid the foundations of the vast Achaemenian Empire which was shortly to stretch all the way to the Mediterranean and the shores of the Black Sea. But Cyrus was not only a military genius, he also had a flair for administration, and while the military arm remained the backbone of state power the allegiance of the provinces was obtained by fair treatment. Unlike the earlier Assyrian conquest, which had engendered hatred of the central power, the leaders of the Achaemenian realm were held in great respect by their subjects. A maximum amount of autonomy was left to the conquered peoples whose several civilizations were permitted to continue and indeed to contribute to the new state, which was centred on a community that recognized itself as inferior culturally to most of its constituents. In this sense the first Persian Empire differed from the Roman Empire, in which the conquering people were to take their own culture to the conquered. Cyrus's aim was to build a great realm throughout which an era of peace should reign.[64]

After conquering the Lydian Empire and thus incorporating in his dominions the Greek cities of Asia Minor, Cyrus turned southwards and captured Babylon, which was allowed to continue under the new rulership. An early act on his part was to release the Hebrews, who were still in captivity there, and to arrange for them to be accompanied back to Palestine by a high

Persian official who was commissioned to see that the royal orders were properly carried out.[65] During the brief reign of Cyrus's son Cambyses, whose outlook was much more autocratic, Egypt was conquered and added to Achaemenian Empire. However, the previous liberal policy seems to have continued: Cambyses assumed the mantle of the Pharaohs, paid homage to the Egyptian gods, and placed the administration of the country in the hands of a high Egyptian official with instructions that changes in the interests of the people should be introduced.

Towards the end of the reign the country ran into a period of unrest and, with the king's death, Darius rose to power. The Empire was now to enjoy its greatest glory. The new ruler realized that Cyrus's liberalism had been carried too far and that a stronger form of government must be introduced if the diversity of peoples was to be held together. Each people was still to retain its own individuality, religion and institutions, but in future its central government was to be represented by a Persian responsible to the Great King. For this purpose the Empire was divided into twenty provinces under a *satrap* or 'protector of the realm'. These *satraps* were usually selected from the royal family or Persian nobility. The system was probably not new — administrative reforms invariably have their forerunners — but it was now made universal. In each province the armed forces were under a commander-in-chief who was similarly appointed by and directly responsible to the king. Thus the civil and military powers were separated and the government of the provinces took the form of a diarchy. But this was still not the sum total of the checks and balances devised by Darius. In each province there was a high official responsible for the collection of taxes, a proportion of which had to be paid into the royal treasury on a fixed anual basis. Each *satrap* had a secretary who supervised his actions and acted as liaison between him and the central government. There was also a corps of travelling inspectors with full powers, and often their own armed force, to look into anything and everything and to report back to the king on the conduct of affairs. Thus was perfected an institution which was subsequently to be copied by many other rulers.

The construction of extensive administrative routes to the confines of the Empire was energetically undertaken. This road-network facilitated the organization of the messenger system which was essential to the effective maintenance of central control over such wide areas and at the same time facilitated the mobility of a court that was continually on the move. Other important constructional work was also undertaken. A surviving text of an important state document, which provides an authentic picture of the Empire at the time, contains a detailed account of how the palace of Susa was constructed.[66] A flourishing system of trade was built up with the aid of the banking methods that had been developed in Mesopotamia. The system included private banks, whose records have survived and whose functions were devised to meet the diverse needs of a widespreading commercial system. The advanced nature of some of these arrangements is shown by the special attention given to shipping. Ships' papers were already in use and sailors were graded according to skill.

Public administration in Persia was not merely concerned with the servicing of the State: it was involved in the success of the national economy, and the needs of the workers were not forgotten. Many of the modern types of taxation seem already to have been levied on goods and flocks, on land, on trade and even on sales. The great constructional activity called for the organization of an Imperial Public Works Department and there is evidence of the existence of labour exchanges to deal with workmen who came to Persepolis, the new capital, from all parts of the Empire.

Clearly, there was much that is very modern in the administrative system of Darius and it is probable that a modern man walking through the streets of his flourishing capital would have found much to admire, much to surprise him and nothing to suggest that all this was to be little more than a historical flash-in-the-pan. The liberal elements in the Persian system were admirable, but the methods and institutions available for obtaining the co-operation of the subject peoples were, despite their benevolence, incapable of inducing constructive developments. Ultimately the government was an autocracy and no means had yet been devised to ensure the spontaneous participation of the people. Continued success depended too much on the power and wisdom of the ruler and on a lucky concatenation of circumstances over an extensive and diverse political realm. The political invention of those early Achaemenians had insufficient roots but their administrative structure provided a remarkable blueprint for the future.

THE BIBLE AND PUBLIC ADMINISTRATION

Apart from its celebrity both as a work of religious inspiration and high literary art, the Bible has always been of great interest to historians, even when many of its chronicles have appeared to be concerned more with the legendary than with the factual. With the increasing corroboration of so many of the reported events through the discoveries of archaeology [67] the historian's interest has greatly extended and the political scientist is bound to ask himself how far the evidence of the text assits him in his interpretation of the government and administration of the age. As one can see, most of the Biblical characters, either as leaders or because of their impact upon the leaders, were acting within the context of government, the detail of which however is usually taken for granted by the contemporary analists. It is hardly surprising therefore that the purely administrative aspects only come to the fore when such activities have an important impact in the sphere of policy.

There is indeed a good deal about government set down in the Bible, since its chief protagonists were the kings and leaders of the people, and the prophets whose object was to control the people's destiny. Their greatest political inspiration, such as the promulgation of the law by Moses, was the outcome of religious involvement, while their most awful crimes, as recorded in the Old Testament, can often be attributed to compulsive political policies. Throughout the Hebrew saga of tribal development, of exile in Egypt, of wandering in the wilderness, of discarding nomadism for settled cultivation, of captivity in Babylon, and of subsequent national regeneration, the kaleidoscopic developments of government are evident. And although administration is not prominently featured, one is confronted at every turn by the appointment of officials and their functioning in accordance with the directions of kings and priests. Even at this early stage the processes of the census are well documented, and the people's immemorial criticism of the tax official is already being manifested on numerous occasions. Here surely is a theme for a whole book. The aim of this section is the dual one of placing this vital subject in the historical context of our study and to select one or two administrative incidents to illustrate further the ubiquity of the public official's metier.

The celebrated story of Joseph, who was sold by his brothers into slavery [68] introduces us to the world of Egyptian officialdom. Joseph was brought down from Canaan into Egypt where he was purchased from the Ishmaelites by Potiphar, an officer of Pharaoh; in fact, his Captain of the Guard. This occurred, it has been suggested,[69] some time during the Hyksos period (c. 1750-1580 B.C.), for which records are still defective. His reward for spurning the advances of Potiphar's wife, as is well known, was to be cast 'into the prison, a place where the king's prisoners were bound'. 'But the Lord was with Joseph, and shewed him mercy, and gave him favour in the sight of the keeper of the prison.' Among his fellow prisoners were two members of the Royal Household, the Chief of the Butlers and the Chief of the Bakers, who had fallen foul of Pharaoh. Joseph was in the habit of interpreting dreams recounted by the prisoners and in consequence he prophesied the release on the third day of the Chief Butler and the death of the Chief Baker. And so it happened, for the third day was Pharaoh's birthday, a day on which it was customary for all his servants to be feasted. During the ceremonies the Chief Butler was restored to favour, while the Chief Baker was hanged!

Some time later by a stroke of good fortune the Chief Butler, who had such good reason to remember Joseph's wisdom, had occasion to tell Pharaoh what had happened. The latter had had a disturbing dream which all the wise men of Egypt had failed to explain satisfactorily. Joseph was sent for and again proved an effective soothsayer, an office well established in early societies. Pharaoh was so pleased with him that he straightaway made him his deputy, a ceremony which is vividly described:

'And Pharaoh said unto Joseph, See, I have set thee over all the land of Egypt. And Pharaoh took off his ring from his hand, and put it upon Joseph's hand, and arrayed him in vestures of fine linen, and put a gold chain about his neck; and made him to ride in the second chariot which he had; and they cried before him, Bow the knee: and he made him ruler over all the land of Egypt.'

Thus was Joseph inducted into the high office of Vizir by the exercise of Pharaoh's despotic power. His status was immediately raised by Pharaoh's giving him as wife, Asenath, the daughter of the influential Poti-pherah, priest of On (Heliopolis). In this way his rank in Egyptian society was effectively assured. Joseph turned out to be an efficient administrator and Pharaoh's capacity as a chooser of men was fully endorsed. He steered the country through difficult times, conserving and storing excess produce during years of good harvest, against the years of famine which he had foreseen. His foresight enabled Pharaoh to build up his demesne, like any good capitalist: for Joseph, because of the famine was able to buy all the fields of Egypt for Pharaoh and to arrange with cultivators for a fifth of the produce to go to him. 'Only the land of the priests bought he not.'

Because they had heard that there was corn in Egypt Jacob sent Joseph's ten brethren to purchase supplies. As a result of their forgiveness by their now powerful brother, whom they had unwittingly raised to fame and fortune by selling him into bondage, they were invited by Pharaoh to migrate to Egypt from Canaan with all their households and flocks. This they did, accompanied by Jacob, and were given good land to settle upon. Joseph flourished in Egypt to a ripe old age, as a respected member of the official class.

'Now there arose up a new king over Egypt, which knew not Joseph . . . . Therefore they did set over them taskmasters, to afflict them with their burdens. And they built for Pharaoh treasure-cities, Pithom and Raamses.'[70]

Thus the Israelites became involved in the building activities of Pharaoh, in this case Rameses II, and were subjected to the rigours and injustices of forced labour. Such measures, after a long peaceful sojourn in Egypt, provided a sufficient social impulse to cause these aliens to look longingly towards the promised land. It happened that their predestined leader, the Egypt-born Hebrew Moses who had been brought up at the royal court, at this critical moment killed one of the guards whom he saw ill-treating a kinsman. Officials had special protection under Egyptian law and to escape unavoidable punishment Moses decided to flee eastwards, only to return later to intercede with Pharaoh who had refused permission for the Israelites to leave the country. The Egyptian administrators had no desire to relinquish such a valuable labour force. It is not the place here to repeat the much told story of *Exodus*, which is thought to have occurred about 1290 B.C.[71] In passing, however, it should be remarked that the nomadic movements of such a large body of people together with their livestock and effects, harried for part of the way by the Egyptians who at the last moment had again changed their minds, must have involved feats of organization and informal administration of no mean order.

At this stage, however, we come upon perhaps the first recorded lesson in the 'science' of administration and certainly a Biblical text that has been much quoted not only by modern teachers but at least as early as Chichele, Archbishop of Canterbury, in a sermon to the Parliament of A.D. 1422.[72] It describes 'hierarchy' and 'delegation' in terms which, though basic and simple to grasp, are still often not fully understood by occupants of the seats of executive power. It all happened after Jethro, priest of Midian and Moses's father-in-law, joined him in the wilderness:

'And it came to pass on the morrow, that Moses sat to judge the people; the people stood by Moses from the morning unto the evening. And when Moses' father-in-law saw all that he did to the people, he said, What is this thing that thou doest to the people? Why sittest thou thyself alone, and all the people stand by from morning till even? And Moses said unto his father-in-law, Because the people come unto me to enquire of God: when they have a matter, they come unto me; and I judge between one and another, and I do make them know the statutes of God, and his laws.

And Moses' father-in-law said unto him, The thing that thou doest is not good. Thou wilt surely wear away, both thou, and this people that is with thee: for this thing is too heavy for thee; thou art not able to perform it thyself alone. Hearken now unto my voice, I will give thee counsel and God shall be with thee: Be thou for the people a God-ward, that thou mayest bring the causes unto God; and thou shalt teach them ordnances and laws, and shalt show them the way wherein they must walk, and the work that they must do. Moreover thou shalt provide out of all the people able men, such as fear God, men of truth, hating covetousness; and place such over them, to be rulers of thousands, and rulers of hundreds, rulers of fifties, and rulers of tens: let them judge the people at all seasons: and it shall be, that every great matter they shall bring unto thee, but every small matter they shall judge: so that it is easier for thyself, and they shall bear the burden with thee. If thou shalt do this thing, and God command thee so, then thou shalt be able to endure, and all this people shall also go to their place in peace.

So Moses hearkened to the voice of his father-in-law, and did all that he said.'[73]

In *Exodus* and the following books there is much that is of interest to the administrator — the giving of the law by Moses on Mount Sinai, and its setting down in the book of the covenant; the promulgation of rules for the priesthood and on the conduct of religious rites; the listing of conquered kings and the division of Canaan among the twelve tribes of Israel — but the recurrent theme that deserves special mention is the taking of the census.

Excavations during 1933 near an unimportant modern place named Abu Kemal, on the banks of the Euphrates between Damascus and Mosul, led to the identification of the country of Abraham, which was formerly known as Hurran, although its whereabouts had hitherto remained a mystery.[74] The actual excavations were made on the remote hillside of Tell Hariri and the place discovered was the royal city of Mari, also widely mentioned in earlier texts. Successive operations laid bare the lower walls and the rooms of an extensive palace, as well as other buildings, and brought to light large numbers of inscribed tablets. These tablets attest the effectiveness of the political and administrative organization of the kingdom of Mari during the eighteenth century B.C. One problem that worried administrators

of that age was the defence of the kingdom against the attrition
of nomadic tribes who pastured their flocks on the frontiers.
Military posts had to be established and a desert police force
organized. In this context frequent references to the Benjamites
are of special interest, particularly on a clay tablet which contains
a police report:

'Say to my lord: This from Bannum, thy servant. Yesterday I left
Mari and spent the night at Zuruban. All the Benjamites were
sending fire-signals. From Samanum to Ilum-Muluk, from Ilum-
Muluk to Mishlan, all the Benjamite villages in the Terqa district
replied with fire-signals. I am not yet certain what these signals
meant. I am trying to find out. I shall write to my lord whether or
not I succeed. The city guards should be strengthened and my lord
should not leave the gate.'[75]

These references to the Benjamites led to further researches into
the records, the result of which has been to corroborate much
of the information in the Bible about the family of Abraham,
to link Huran with Mari, and to establish the fact that Abraham
lived about 1900 B.C., which agrees with the Biblical evidence.

Another problem of the local officials of Mari connected with
the Benjamites arose from the desire of the palace officials that
these tribesmen, against their own wishes, should be included in
the census. In this case the local officials, basing their case on
the undesirable effects of such an operation, were to carry the
day. In Mari itself the census, taken as a basis for taxation and
military recruitment, was already a long-established practice.
The population was summoned by districts and the names of
those eligible for military service were listed. During the proceedings, which lasted several days, bread and beer were
distributed by the officials.

However, the Israelites appear to have learned by this experience. The taking of the census was to be operated by them during
their subsequent wanderings and thereafter, strictly in accordance with the methods adopted by Mari. The first recorded
occasion was at the camp in Sinai:

'And the Lord spake unto Moses in the wilderness of Sinai, in the
tabernacle of the congregation, on the first day of the second month,
in the second year after they were come out of the land of Egypt,
saying, Take ye the sum of all the congregation of the children of
Israel, after their families, by the house of their fathers, with the
number of their names, every male by their polls; from twenty years
old and upward, all that are able to go forth to war in Israel: thou
and Aaron shall number them by their armies.'[76]

After their sojourn in the wilderness, when they had come to the plains of Moab by the Jordan near Jericho, the procedure was repeated almost in identical terms, now under the direction of Moses and Aaron's son, Eleazar.[77] In their settled kingdom the taking of the census continued whenever the situation called for it. According to the Bible[78] this was done on at least two occasions under King David (c. 1000 B.C.). It is clear from the Biblical account of the later of these operations that the people resented them as a threat to their liberties, an example of the age-old evils of officialdom. On this occasion, Jacob, Captain of the Host, who had been given responsibility for the census, took nine months and twenty days to travel throughout the land and to return to Jerusalem to report the results to the King. The figures indicated that Israel and Judah could muster respectively 800,000 and 500,000 men of military age.

To round off this brief account of the Biblical census, and ignoring for the moment that this will take us some hundreds of years beyond the scope of the present chapter, it is interesting to note that other powers, including the Romans, adopted similar methods. In fact it was to meet their obligations in connection with the tax-collecting census that Joseph and Mary were travelling down to Bethlehem at the time of Jesus' birth:

'And it came to pass in those days that there went out a decree from Caesar Augustus, that all the world should be taxed. (And this taxing was first made when Cyrenius was governor of Syria.) And all went to be taxed, every one unto his own city. And Joseph also went up from Galilee, out of the city of Nazareth, into Judea, unto the city of David which is called Bethlehem; (because he was of the house and lineage of David:) to be taxed with Mary his espoused wife, being great with child. And so it was, that, while they were there, the days were accomplished that she should be delivered. And she brought forth her firstborn son, and wrapped him in swaddling clothes and laid him in a manger, because there was no room for them in the inn.'[79]

Enough has now been said to illustrate the numerous references to administrative matters that appear in the Bible and the supporting evidence from archaeological excavation, but it would take us too far from our main theme if we explored this interesting field much further. It goes without saying that there are important phases and events such as the rulership of David and the deportation to Babylon, which have their interesting administrative aspects. For example, there are references to important officials:

'And David reigned over all Israel; and David executed judgment and justice unto all his people. And Joab the son of Zeruiah was over the host; and Jehoshaphat the son of Ahilud was recorder; and Zadok the son of Ahitub and Ahimelech the son of Abiathar, were the priests; and Seraiah was the scribe; and Benaiah the son of Jehoiada was over both the Cherethites and the Pelethites; and David's sons were the chief rulers.'[80]

In a later reference many of the same officials are mentioned but there are changes and additions. The scribe's name is now given as Sheva, and Abiathar, not his son, is shown as Zadok's priestly associate: 'Ira also the Jairite was a chief ruler about David.'[81]

The Biblical text itself may be corroborated by the discovery of administrative materials, such as court inventories, receipted accounts, ordinary book entries, and the like which are normally of interest as indicating the way the business of daily life was conducted. Thus, a receipt for stores issued to one, Jehoiachin, by a steward of the commissariat in Babylon, somewhere about 593 B.C., was the first evidence to come to light of the existence of this king who, as a result of the revolt in Judah against the payment of tribute to Nebuchadnezzar, was with all his people deported to Babylon.[82]

We may well wonder what points of general and administrative interest may yet emerge as further pieces of this vast archaeological jig-saw are brought to light!

REFERENCES

1 I. Schapera, *Government and Politics in Tribal Societies*, (Watts, 1956), especially pp. 40-6.
2 M. G. Smith, *Government in Zazzau*, (Oxford, 1960).
3 Smith, *op. cit.*, p. 6.
4 Smith, *op. cit.*, p. 6 and Appendix A, pp. 333-43.
5 Smith, *op. cit.*, p. 47.
6 Schapera, *op. cit.*, p. 46.
7 For example, L. A. Fallers, *Bantu Bureaucracy*, (Heffer) and Lucy Mair, *Primitive Government*, (Penguin, 1962).
8 Carleton S. Coon, *The History of Man*, (Cape, 1955), p. 105.
9 Arnold Hauser, *The Social History of Art*, (Routledge, 1951), Vol. I, p. 40.
10 E. R. Leach on 'Working Stone, Bone and Wood' in *A History of Technology*, (Oxford Univ., 1954), Vol. I, pp. 128-9.
11 Herbert Kuhn, *Rock Pictures of Europe*, (Sidgwick & Jackson, 1956), p. 48, and Annette Laming, *Lascaux: Paintings and Engravings*, (Penguin, 1959).
12 Arnold Hauser, *The Social History of Art*, (Routledge and Kegan Paul, 1951), Vol. I, pp. 39-40.
13 L. S. B. Leakey on 'Graphic and Plastic Arts' in *A History of Technology, op. cit.*, Vol. I, pp. 148-9.

14 Henri Lhote, *The Search for the Tessili Frescoes*, (Hutchinson, 1959), pp. 205-6.
15 Lindsay Scott on 'Pottery' in *A History of Technology, op. cit.*, Vol. I, p. 405.
16 R. J. C. Atkinson, *Stonehenge and Avebury and Neighbouring Monuments*, (H.M.S.O., 1959). Both the date of construction and the provenance of the stones have recently been challenged by evidence which, if corroborated, would radically modify the deductions in the text.
17 S. N. Kramer, *History Begins at Sumer*, (Thames & Hudson, 1958).
18 R. Ghirshman, *Iran*, (Penguin, 1954), pp. 33-4.
19 Robert Brittain, *Rivers and Man*, (Longmans Green, 1959), p. 74.
20 Kathleen Kenyon, *Digging Up Jericho*, (Benn, 1957).
21 T. Jacobsen on 'Mesopotamia' in *Before Philosophy*, (Penguin, 1949).
22 Kramer, *op. cit.*, p. 66.
23 Kramer, *op. cit.*, p. 67.
24 Sir Leonard Woolley, *Ur of the Chaldees*, (Pelican, 1938).
25 J. H. Breasted, *Ancient Times*, (Ginn, 1944), p. 166.
26 F. R. Hoare, *Eight Decisive Books of Antiquity*, (Sheed & Ward, 1952),
27 Hoare, *op. cit.*, p29.
    p. 29.
28 O. R. Gurney, *The Hittites*, (Penguin, 1952), and Seton Lloyd, *Early Anatolia*, (Penguin, 1956).
29 Gurney, *op. cit.*, p. 63.
30 Breasted, *op. cit.*, p. 198.
31 Breasted, *op. cit.*, p. 197.
32 Breasted, *op. cit.*, p. 196.
33 *II Kings*, Chapters 24-5.
34 Breasted, *op. cit.*, p. 215.
35 I. G. Gelb, *A Study of Writing*, (Routledge & Kegan Paul, 1952), and D. Diringer, *Writing*, (Thames & Hudson, 1962), pp. 35-7.
36 Gelb, *op. cit.*, p. 62.
37 See p. 14 above.
38 L. S. B. Leakey, in *A History of Technology*, pp. 144-5.
39 Carleton S. Coon, *The History of Man*, (Cape, 1955), p. 95.
40 D. J. Wiseman and W. & B. Forman, *Cylinder Seals of Western Asia*, (Bletchworth Press, 1959).
41 Brittain, *op. cit.*, p. 60.
42 Gelb, *op. cit.*, p. 60.
43 Kramer, *op. cit.*, pp. 256-9.
44 Seton Lloyd, *Foundations in the Dust*, (Penguin, 1947), pp. 154-6.
45 Edward Chiera, *They Wrote on Clay*, (Univ. of Chicago, 1938), Paperback edition, pp. 201-11.
46 Sir Leonard Woolley, *A Forgotten Kingdom*, (Penguin, 1953).
47 Woolley, *op. cit.*, p. 15.
48 Woolley, *op. cit.*, p. 177.
49 Woolley, *op. cit.*, p. 74.
50 Seton Lloyd, *Early Anatolia*, (Penguin, 1956).
51 Woolley, *op. cit.*, p. 126.
52 Woolley, *op. cit.*, p. 67.
53 Jack Finegan, *Light from the Ancient Past*, (Princeton, 1946), p. 44.
54 T. Jacobsen, 'Mesopotamia: The Function of the State', in *Before Philosophy, op. cit.*, pp. 202-4.
55 Gurney, *op. cit.*
56 Breasted, *op. cit.*, p. 170 *et seq.*
57 Chiera, *op cit.*, pp. 71-2.

58 Reports in *Manchester Guardian*, 1952-6.
59 Breasted, *op. cit.*, p. 176.
60 Breasted, *op. cit.*, p. 188.
61 Ghirshman, *op. cit.*, p. 163.
62 Woolley, *op. cit.*, p. 124.
63 Finegan, *op. cit.*, p. 180.
64 A. J. Toynbee, *A Study of History*, (Oxford), Vol. VII, (1954), pp. 580-689, Annex on 'The Administrative Geography of The Achaemenian Empire'.
65 Ghirshman, *op. cit.*, p. 132.
66 Ghirshman, *op. cit.*, pp. 165-6.
67 See, for example, Werner Keller, *The Bible as History*, (Hodder & Stoughton, 1956).
68 *Genesis*, Chapters 38-50.
69 Keller, *op. cit.*, p. 102.
70 *Exodus*, Chapters 1 and 8-11.
71 Keller, *op. cit.*, p. 121.
72 E. F. Jacob, *The Fifteenth Century, 1399-1485*, Vol. VI, (Oxford, 1961), pp. 214-5.
73 *Exodus*, Chapter 18.
74 Keller, *op. cit.*, Chapter 5.
75 Keller, *op. cit.*, p. 66.
76 *Numbers*, Chapter 1.
77 *Numbers*, Chapter 26.
78 *Samuel II*, Chapters 18 and 24.
79 *St. Luke*, Chapter 2.
80 *Samuel II*, Chapters 8 and 15.
81 *Samuel II*, Chapters 20 and 23.
82 Keller, *op. cit.*, p. 273.

CHAPTER 2

ANCIENT EGYPT : 3400 to 525 B.C.

It was somewhat disconcerting to historians when discoveries in the river valleys of Mesopotamia challenged the priority of Egypt as the accepted progenitor of civilization. Compared with the somewhat incoherent diversity of human endeavour in the former sphere, whose complicated pattern has been summarily surveyed in the preceding chapter, the story of Egypt is admirably homogeneous, long-lived and comparatively well documented. It provides an eminently suitable starting point for a study of civilization and government.

The reasons for this are not far to seek. Egyptian civilization shares with those of Mesopotamia, Hindustan and China a basic siting in a river valley, providing the essential boons of fertility and communication. But the geography of Egypt had added advantages over that of its rivals. The long narrow Nile Valley was flanked on both banks by deserts which were a natural defence system in an age of limited mobility. Only in the spreading delta on the Mediterranean to the north and in the wild Ethiopian hills to the south was extensive attack likely to develop with success. The long valley itself was fruitfully and regularly irrigated by the Nile, whose strenuous and sometimes destructive bounty provided a decisive initial challenge to human ingenuity. A dependable climate with a minimum of rain meant also that the sands amidst which human settlements were raised provided an almost perfect medium for the preservation of anything that got buried — and in a sandy terrain it requires constant vigilance and effort to prevent this happening. Unfortunately inherent human selfishness has tended to cancel out this great asset to posterity. Then — as often thereafter — tomb robbers were quickly at work to despoil those caches of treasure and goods that had been laid down by human design.

Worship of the Sun-God provided a universal inspiration to men and an effective basis to government: the Nile provided the essential means of existence and an admirable challenge to the engineering ingenuity of a vigorous people; while the sands themselves provided the means both to protect and, unexpectedly, to preserve the fruits of human effort. Among all the suitable locations for the growth of civilization during those last-prehistoric millennia the stage was surely set in the Valley of the Nile for the rise of a flourishing community.

Whether there were primary links between the civilizations of Egypt and Sumer, or of their progenitors, is difficult to decide. Evidence is still needed and may well await discovery under some unimpressive mudheap or sandhill that has not yet attracted the curiosity of the archaeologist. That there are interesting parallels between the customs and governmental arrangements of the two peoples soon becomes apparent from even a perfunctory examination of their histories, but such instances may of course have arisen spontaneously out of similar situations and not require any evidence of inter-communication to explain them. An interesting example of this sort was forthcoming with the uncovering of early burials in Egypt, as in Ur, in which the ruler has been accompanied on his last journey by an entourage of relations and officials, whether compulsorily or voluntarily sacrificed it is not possible to decide.

HISTORY AND GOVERNMENT

The story of Egypt begins sometime during the fourth millennium B.C., when separate village settlements appeared in the Nile Delta, and continues steadily for the best part of three thousand years to the conquest of Egypt by Cambyses in 525 B.C. and its incorporation in the Persian Empire. This is a very long time for a system of human institutions to endure. Nor does even this set the limits for, despite subsequent dynastic vicissitudes and conquests, Egyptian ways and methods of administration were to continue well into the Christian era.

Egyptian history is derived from archaeological evidence mainly connected with tombs, and from literary survivals usually also associated with burials, often indeed in the form of inscriptions on the outsides or inner walls of tomb structures. Pictorial records existed long before the first political union of the country, which occurred about 3200 B.C. The development of a hieroglyphic, or representational, system of writing out of these pictographs and the invention of a writing medium in the form of papyrus, greatly facilitated the growth of organization and of the business methods essential to the support of a political system sufficiently wide-spreading to dominate the Nile Valley as a whole. In conjunction with the dynamic character of the people, already fully extended through having to grapple with the engineering problems of Nile irrigation, the new challenge drew forth the needed response.

The country fell naturally into two divisions, known generally as Upper Egypt and Lower Egypt, the former consisting of the long narrow river-valley stretching far up to the First Cataract near the Island of Elephantine, the latter of the much more compact but wide-spreading delta area on the Mediterranean. Integration, which was taking place probably between 3400 and 3200 B.C., proved more difficult in Lower Egypt where many city-states, already thriving in the Delta, were jealous of their local traditions and autonomy. The unification has been ascribed to Menes, the first Pharaoh, during that period although the dates are the subject of controversy. The long line of rulers are listed in the ancient records which group them in thirty-one dynasties, each extending over several reigns, stretching from the age of Menes to the second conquest by the Persians in 341-333 B.C.

The first, or Archaic, period lasted till 2660 B.C. and covered the reigns of Dynasties I and II. It was a time of great intellectual activity and technical endeavour, and by no means its least achievement from the administrative point of view, was the invention of papyrus and other aids essential to the conduct of government. Exploitation of the copper mines of Sinai and the production of metal tools opened the way to stone architecture.

The fruits of these advances were manifested in the growth of monumental building and the emergence of the pyramid tomb, which left its indelible impress upon the Egyptian landscape. This took place during the Old Kingdom (Dynasties III to VI) which continued until 2180 B.C.

Under Dynasties VII to X, which lasted for a hundred years, Egypt was divided against herself, and it was not until the Middle Kingdom (Dynasties XI to XIII) from 2080 to 1640 B.C. that the two lands were reunited and another phase of construction ensued. The powers of the feudal nobles were curtailed, and expansion abroad both by conquest and trade, was actively pursued.

There now followed another period of recession which lasted for seventy years (Dynasties XIV to XVII). It was during this period that the Hyksos, a vigorous but uncultured Semitic tribe from the uplands, furnished Egypt's rulers. Just how this transfer of power came about is not clear, but there can be little doubt that the advent of these vigorous outsiders brought rejuvenation to a system that was showing signs of age. They introduced the horse and working in bronze, but wisely continued to make use of the culture and administrative competence of their subjects. It required a hard-fought war of liberation to restore Egypt to her ancient glory in the form of the New Kingdom (Dynasties XVIII to XX) which endured for a record spell, from 1570 to 1075 B.C.

This was indeed an age of flowering and expansion. An aggressive policy extended the sway of Egypt into Palestine and Syria, but such advances were checked by the growing power of the Hittites, with whom Pharaoh Rameses II wisely made a treaty, copies of which survive.

Towards the end of this long golden age the inevitable symptoms of decay were appearing. The frontiers were retracting, the kings losing interest in affairs, the internal economy deteriorating, and unrest becoming widespread. This seems to have been the heyday of the tomb robbers, whose depredations are said to have been aided and abetted by the responsible—or should one not write 'irresponsible'—officials. The period of decline and eclipse, stretching from 1075 to 332 B.C., through Dynasties XXI to XXXI, is usually known as the Late Period. Powerful and competent rulers arose from time to time to stop the rot, although the day had long passed when a new forward trend could be sustained. Invasion had to be endured from the Assyrians during the eighth century B.C, and the Persians twice imposed their control, in 525 and 341 B.C.

Despite the many vicissitudes of a history extending over such a long period, the outstanding characteristic of Egyptian government was its stability, and particularly the continuance of the Pharaoh-ship, even under foreign control. The rule of the Egyptian king was based firmly upon religion and embodied consistently in an absolutism, which, if generally benevolent, found no place for democratic participation. The Sun and the Nile were worshipped, for obvious reasons, and the State from the outset belonged to the Sun-God, whose chief agent was Pharaoh, meaning 'The Great House', a term applied to a human agent entitled to such reverence that he must not be directly mentioned. In these circumstances it is no surprise that the all-powerful ruler should himself be treated as god and that his priests should wield tremendous power. There could be no distinction between church and state: the two were not merely inseparable, they were one. A basic idea was the continuance of life after death, an idea that permeated the whole corpus of Egyptian statecraft, especially in the early formative stages. The surplus resources of the community were appropriated by the state and concentrated upon preparation for death. Practically everything Egyptian that has survived was linked in one way or another with burial. Not that this prevented the ruler and his chief assistants from taking excessive steps to ensure their own wellbeing during the indefinite waiting period!

This powerful religious urge was not monotheistic. Although

the doctrine of the Sun-God was accepted, there was room for lesser-gods, many of whom held local sway and were usually represented by animals. Among the more important of these we may single out Thoth, the inventor of writing, who acted as Scribe to the Gods. Religious writing emanated from Thoth, albeit through the agency of some sacred scribe, and among such attributions is the celebrated *Book of the Dead* whose text, first inscribed upon the sides of coffins and later written down in a papyrus roll for inclusion within, provided for the dead man's soul in the after life.

The awe in which Pharaoh was held was reinforced by a carefully laid down court ceremonial, calling for the ministrations of numerous officials whose functions were religious rather than administrative in the normal sense, while the ruler himself tended more and more to be subjected to a closely regulated routine which left him little time to devote to the ordinary affairs of state. In the beginning Pharaoh was High-Priest and King, Chief Administrator, Chief Judge, Chief War-leader, Chief Treasurer and Controller of all Property, all rolled into one. Not that these separate roles were distinguishable, since they were all implied in his status of god. But practical considerations soon led to delegations of responsibility which fell within the ruler's powers. At first no doubt these went to relations and nobles, but with increasing specialization of function and expansion of offices it soon became necessary to bring others into the field of administration. By the time of the Old Kingdom a complex administrative system had been worked out to serve the king and to relieve him of burdens that would otherwise have been insupportable. At an early stage a form of bureaucracy had begun to emerge that was to develop into an impressive power within the Egyptian system.

Pharaoh had overwhelming legal power and all were subject to his authority. Yet within court and temple intrigue was ever-present to erode this power. Much would depend upon the character of the ruler and his capacity, not to say vigilance, in ensuring loyalty within the royal halls.

Control of the localities from such a power-centre was always a problem. From an early date the country was divided into local units, called *nomes,* each under a *nomarch,* who was the royal representative. The underlying pattern seems to have been based upon irrigation needs. Co-ordination and control was difficult owing to indifferent accessibility, and inspecting officials were soon being appointed to ensure that the royal government was being properly executed in the provinces. But the balance of power tended to fluctuate between the two spheres of administration. By the time of the Middle Kingdom a feudal system had emerged under which the governors of the *nomes* had become petty princes, rivals of the central power. The matter came to a head under the vigorous rulers of Dynasty XII who set to work to compel the provincial leaders to return to their old allegiance to the central government. It is an interesting point that one of the methods of accomplishing this was the transfer of the capital from Memphis to Ithet-Tawy which was better situated to ensure the effective administration of a widespreading realm. To canalize the vigour of the local leaders into more orthodox and profitable channels the rulers of Dynasty XII adopted an expansionist policy and used the military ardour of their governors by appointing them militia commanders in their foreign campaigns.

Egyptian society was shaped both by the religious power pattern on which government was based, and by the technical needs of the agricultural system and of the state building programme, the latter itself being determined by basic religious requirements. The sciences of irrigation, tomb building and embalming received great attention from scholars, while the productive resources of the country were used up in their practical accomplishment.

The leadership group, apart from Pharaoh and the nobles to whom he delegated executive and administrative responsibilities, included also an influential body of Scribes, assisted by other technicians and craftsmen. The Army, securely under royal leadership, constituted something of an independent power. At the base of society were the farmers and peasants, including numerous slaves, and on these the productivity of the community absolutely depended. The slaves and peasants also furnished the immense regiments of workers who provided the massed-man-power needed to raise the colossal monuments to the dead, which have so far survived time's inexorable annihilation of all man-made constructions.

PICTURES AND WRITING

Apart from the three important techniques already mentioned, all of which of course had important formative influences upon Egyptian public administration, there is the art of writing without which the advances in other fields could have amounted to little. The Egyptians, from their very beginnings, evinced a prominent pictorial sense which made it natural for them to record their daily activities in diagrammatic form on rock and stone. An inveterate sense of display led them, with the development of building techniques, to reproduce pictorially, on the sides of tombs and the walls of ceremonial structures, intimate details of their daily life — much to the benefit of later scholarship.

With the habit of thus representing life and events so well-developed it was a mere matter of course that a system of writing should be devised, and the decisive impulse arose from the need for records to facilitate the conduct of an expanding system of government and business. Pictures had been transformed into phonetic signs and the well-known hieroglyphic system of writing had been evolved before the end of Dynasty II. Each sign represented a syllable and words were formed by combinations of signs. Egyptian writing eventually comprised over six hundred such signs, setting a formidable task to the scribal apprentice. This form of writing was used for public display purposes and continued practically unchanged until the production of the last hieroglyphic texts as late as 307-314 A.D.[1] At the same time forms of cursive writing, corresponding to our handwriting, were developed for the conduct of ordinary business, and an alphabet of twenty-four letters had been evolved by the twenty-fifth century B.C. But the sign-group habit was by this time so firmly engrained in the minds and practices of the scribes, who constituted something of a vested interest, that the perfection of the alphabet was left to an entirely different civilization.

The disadvantages of rock and stone as a base for writing were manifest long before the need for portable records had been plainly recognized. The use of pieces of bone, wood or pottery, which was the obvious and universally adopted alternative, left much to be desired, and in the absence of the mud-brick medium which had so facilitated the changeover in Mesopotamia, the Egyptians were compelled to look about them for an alternative. It is one of the fortunes of history that such an alternative was abundantly available in the reed of the papyrus plant which flourished in the swamps of the Delta. The importance attributed to this plant is shown by the considerable part it plays in Egyptian art. Columns in architecture were formed to represent its stem and their capitals were shaped as papyrus flowers. In domestic circles crowns of papyrus were widely used for decoration.[2]

The manufacture of writing material from papyrus was first described by Pliny (A.D. 23-79) in his *Natural History,* (Volume XIII). The stem was divided into strips, on which it was found that writing could be easily imprinted. To provide larger surfaces sheets were formed by laying a number of strips side by side with slight overlaps and superimposing a second layer similarly arranged but at right angles to the first. The two layers were then pressed and beaten together, and dried under pressure: finally the surface was polished with some rounded object. The next development was the production of a longer and stronger surface by pasting a number of sheets together with overlapping edges and strengthening the resulting roll by pasting other sheets behind the grain at right angles. In this way the first effective paper writing roll, precursor of the book, was invented and gradually came into use throughout the Western World.

Actual fragments of accounts in papyrus date back to Dynasty V, but it seems probable that the invention coincided with the introduction of hieratic writing. Representations of papyrus rolls and writing media are known as early as Dynasty I. Black ink was made from carbon, scraped from cooking utensils and mixed with a thin solution of gum. Writing was executed with a brush made from a kind of rush. Later, red ink was brought into use, made out of red ochre mixed with gum and water. The reed pen had first been used by the Greeks some time before the Egyptians.

The scribe carried a case of brushes and a palette of wood or ivory tied with string to a small pot for holding water. His equipment was completed by a small grinder for preparing ink. He wrote standing when a small piece of papyrus sufficed, but sitting with crossed-legs in the Oriental fashion when writing on a roll, as depicted in the celebrated sculpture of a scribe preserved in the Louvre, Paris. The scribe holds the roll in his left hand with sufficient length unrolled and writes with his right hand, proceeding from right to left. A table is not used, the roll, palette and other materials being laid conveniently on the ground, although the scribe may keep his writing brushes behind his right ear. Sheets of papyrus were used which varied in size according to current custom and purpose. The scribe wrote on the inside of the roll, for in this way his work was best protected. For added safety, rolls were sometimes stored in pots or glass jars. It is not known to what extent the Egyptians produced a number of copies concurrently by dictation, as later became the Roman practice, but there is some evidence of dictation to be deduced from the kind of recurrent errors which have been observed in numerous manuscripts.

It would be difficult to over-rate the importance of the invention of papyrus. Without a portable writing medium of this kind advances in the techniques of administration would have been extremely difficult if not impossible. Without such advances the scope for social co-operation would have been restricted and consequently the development of civilization would have been immeasurably retarded. With the production of the papyrus sheet one of the few major inventions in administration had taken place.

THE SCOPE OF EGYPTIAN
PUBLIC ADMINISTRATION

A despotic system of government concerning itself with all sectors of the country's economy, such as that of Ancient Egypt, could not have operated successfully without the services of a massive and efficient public service. In fact the bureaucracies of Egypt and China have been compared as the two outstanding institutions of this type in all history. That an organization exercising so much power, even though it was delegated power, should have evinced bureaucratic tendencies would hardly be surprising, but it is doubtful whether the Egyptian system ever formed a bureaucracy in the organizational sense. It was a series rather than a single public service. On the other hand, as will become evident, the activities of the scribal profession came to permeate the whole of Egyptian society.

Over such a long period there were many developments in public administration in Egypt, various phases of expansion and of contraction, of success and of failure. A continuous story would be difficult to sketch out. Specific administrative details, culled from the records, can relate only to particular periods and situations, although it is the comparative stability of the general pattern that impresses, rather than the changes rendered necessary to meet new needs, created, for example, by extensions of territory or advances in constructional methods.

There were various spheres of public administration, among which may be listed:

(1) The royal court and household, involving estate management, supply services and ceremonial organization;

(2) the nation's productive machine which, while depending largely upon individual agriculturalists, called for extensive state planning in the sphere of hydraulic engineering;

(3) service of the cult of the dead, eventually developing into a colossal programme of pyramid building and other constructional work;

(4) the local government areas, closely affected by (2) and involving a wide delegation of executive powers; and

(5) the conduct of foreign relations, ranging from the normal practices of diplomacy to the imposition of imperial rule.

None of these administrative spheres was clearly separated from the others, nor is there any evidence that the modern division of functions into executive, legislative and judicial was in any way developed, or even theoretically visualized.

In the beginning Pharaoh did everything, although in practice some delegation of responsibility soon became necessary. The sacred origins of his powers meant that in the first instance such duties would be confided to members of the royal family. The nobles were the chief officials, as in all such governmental situations. Offices tended to become hereditary. Many offices came to acquire a purely honorific significance — the court sinecure had already appeared. It even became the practice to grant sinecure posts to keep certain difficult characters about the court where they would be under observation and easily prevented from causing trouble! The sons of officials were brought up to follow in their fathers' footsteps and, as the need extended, it became possible to bring in others by a process of adoption. The idea of a more general public service only gradually emerged.

The funerary texts, which are detailed in their accounts of the dead person's numerous posts and responsibilities, provide ample information on the wide range of posts that existed, while their titles may suggest the sort of duties they had to perform. From the early royal tombs and seals we learn, for example, of the Royal-Sealer-of-the-Wine and the much more important Superintendent-of-the-Inundation; also a First-Peer, a Royal Constructor, a Follower-of-the-King, and a Master-of-Ceremonies. Among the less onerous positions the Overseer-of-the-Cosmetic Box can surely be listed. Turning to a much later period, namely the reign of Tuthmosis III of Dynasty XVIII, we find serving under the celebrated Vizir Rekhmire, officials with such titles as the Fanbearer-at-the-King's-Right-Hand, the Eyes-and-Ears-of-the-King, the Messenger-of-the-Country, the Tutor, 'making-excellent-of-the-King', the Scribe-of-Horus, the Strong-Bull (a pseudonym for the King) and the Chief-of-the-Guard.[3]

Obviously some of these were purely personal posts, but others would need numerous assistants and no doubt some amounted to highly organized departments. Breasted instances the centralization of irrigation administration in the hands of the King, under what was no doubt the equivalent of a Department of Irrigation, as the first great administrative machine in the history of human government.[4] The several Superintendents-of-the-Inundation were no doubt on its establishment.

However, while specialization would soon be imposed by the march of events, whatever might be the wishes of the chief participants, there was always in the Pharaonic system a leaning towards the generalist. It was of the very essence of his own position of omnipotence that Pharaoh should prefer the all-rounder. Organizing ability was more valuable than specific technical knowledge. An interesting example of this was the high official Weni of Dynasty VI, who, trained as a steward, held in turn the posts of judge, general, master of works and hydraulic engineer. Shortly after the reign of Tutankhamun a general named Harmab rose to the kingship and inaugurated the notable Dynasty XIX. He had begun as a royal scribe and his statue in that capacity survives to show him in the normal scribe posture, sitting cross-legged on the floor and holding in his lap a papyrus roll which contains a hymn to Thoth, God of the Scribes, whom we have already mentioned. Indeed Harmab's career was to substantiate the rightness of his apprenticeship, for he proved an able administrator and gave Egypt an efficient administration.[5]

At an early stage Pharaoh adopted the practice of appointing a deputy in the form of a Vizir, that perennial power-under-the-throne of most oriental monarchs. For such a position the King would prefer a man of parts, one with wide experience who could turn his hand to many tasks. The Vizir could be powerful, although for many reasons his tenure of office and even his life could prove precarious. Intrigues at court could undermine his position as favourite of the king and, in a system in which succession to the throne led through the Royal Consort but could be challenged by the designs of other favoured ladies of the harem, such intrigues had to be accepted as normal. The Vizir would have to be a ruthless diplomat to keep his head above the scandalous waters and would probably run his own secret service to keep himself informed on the underflow of court opinion. In addition to this the Vizir often took over the entire burden of being political head, while Pharaoh retained the religious and ceremonial functions, albeit without relinquishing the ultimate power by which he could visit upon the Vizir the consequences of failure. In this way the Vizir's position was not unlike that of the modern Chief or Prime Minister before the kingship became constitutionalized, taking responsibility for the practical conduct of affairs but subjected to a much higher penalty for failure to maintain his acceptability with the powers-that-be. Yet, despite the hazards of power, the surviving tombs of a line of successful first ministers stand witness to the great ability of many of Egypt's Vizirs and of the capacity of the Pharaohs, whatever their failings, for choosing the right man for this outstandingly onerous position.

Of certain of these great public administrators more will be said in the next section. For the moment we are interested in the general functions and structure of the vizirate. The Vizir would certainly be both Chief Judge, which might involve little more than the application of common sense in deciding important pleas to Pharaoh, and Chief Architect, which would certainly require more than a nodding acquaintance with the technicalities of an activity upon which all the surplus products of the realm were expended. Next to Pharaoh the Vizir was the chief power from whom all executive authority was drawn. Within a system, of which public administration was not just a limited sector, the scope of the Vizir's powers could extend to the confines of society. Egypt was conceived as the estate of Pharaoh and the Vizir as his Chief Steward. He was really Minister-in-Chief, holding the combined portfolios of Justice, War, Internal Security, Agriculture and Public Works. He worked directly through a large number of officials and received periodic reports from local officials of all kinds. He had a daily duty to report upon his stewardship to Pharaoh, although this might not always be possible, for the court was very mobile. Pharaoh might be away on tour or even conducting a campaign, while the Vizir's own duties often took him far afield. The Vizir also made himself responsible for certain routine administrative matters, the care of important documents such as wills, records of land suits, lists of criminals awaiting trial, and even scientific information, such as observations on the rising of Sirius, which had a bearing on the incidence of the annual inundation.

Much of this is picturesquely authenticated on a tomb of Dynasty XVIII in which a Vizir is described as

'Chief of the six courts of justice, a mouth giving satisfaction in the whole land . . . . judging justly, not showing partiality, sending two men forth satisfied, judging the weak and the powerful, not bringing sorrow to the one who petitioned him: satisfying the heart of the King before the Two Lands, prince before the people, companion approaching the sovereign, favourite of him who is in the palace . . . . going forth over the land every morning to do the daily favours, to hear the matters of the people, the petitions of the South and the North, not preferring the great above the humble, rewarding the oppressed, bringing the evil to him who committed it'[6]

It seems that at this time the vizirate was rising to its peak, for it has been suggested that the institution passed its heydey with the end of Dynasty XX, when Egypt split in two.[7]

Although the Egyptians did not leave a treatise on the philosophy of statecraft the officials no doubt had a code whereby their administering was regulated and an etiquette prescribed which determined their personal conduct. It was the custom of Pharaoh at his inception to address a traditional homily to his Vizir and other high officials, enjoining certain principles which they were to follow and defining their duties. Thus the Vizer was impressed with the weight of his responsibilities and told that he was the mainstay of the entire land. He must be scrupulous in administering the law, neither favouring his friends nor judging them more harshly because they were his friends.[8] In a book from the early period advice is given to an official on the principles of success in the public service. He is advised how to get on with his superiors, his equals and his inferiors. In fact the art of holding the candle to the devil is unemotionally expounded without reference to morals, and one could well imagine from a perusal of this human document that the spirits of Machiavelli and Sir Henry Taylor had already permeated the atmosphere of officialdom. 'He who sits at the table of a superior is urged to maintain a sedate countenance, to take only what is offered, and to laugh only when his host laughs; thus the great one will accept whatever one may do.' Thus, the art of 'yesmanship' is fully developed while the civilization to which it ministers, and often defiles, is yet young, but it would be wrong to deduce that the text was completely opportunistic and materialistic. Our novice is even urged that honesty is the best policy, albeit not as a matter of precept so much as a result of hard experience, for a success visible to all men was the great good.[9]

It need hardly be said that over such a wide period as we are now surveying there ruled men of varying capacities and differing outlooks. Some were highly efficient and capable of interpreting the needs of the age, but many, as at all times, were inadequately equipped to grapple with the grave responsibilities of power. Surviving records are more likely to dwell upon their successes than their failures, while periods of recession and decline usually endorse the adage that silence is golden.

In an interesting comparison between the attitudes to life in the early and late phases of Egyptian civilization, Wilson compares the tomb pictures of Vizirs of around 2400 and 600 B.C. respectively, buried within a few hundred yards of one another near the Step Pyramid at Sakkara.[10] In the first the walls are literally crammed with scenes of vigorous life, which show the Vizir as participant in all the activities of the day: hunting hippopotamus, spearing fish, roping and butchering cattle, ploughing and harvesting, working at trades and building boats for his funeral services, presiding over the punishment of tax delinquents, as well as engaging upon all the normal activities of home life with his wife and children. His vision of the good life by which he wants to be remembered is one of vigorous creative activity. On the other hand the man of the late period is not much concerned with such mundane activities, vigour and lust are no longer in the ascendent. The walls of his tomb are covered with ritual and magical texts, sparsely illustrated and then mainly with scenes from the underworld and the genii who dwell there. His is a life of philosophy, of contemplation, of preparation for death.

There were a number of officials appointed by Pharaoh who, although they reported to the Vizir, were almost as important in their own spheres. Among these the Chief Treasurer is of particular interest. As Overseer of the Treasury he was head of the most important department next to the Judiciary and although he followed the Vizir in precedence at court and in actual power, the latter had to report to him on his daily transactions. Thus the idea of a separate check upon finance operated in Egyptian public administration. It is to be remembered, however, that there was as yet no monetary system. So that accounting had to be carried out in terms of actual supplies. Taxation took the form of collection of a fraction of the product, which had to be transported and stored, and subsequently distributed. One of the tax official's most complicated tasks was to estimate the yield of the harvest. Land measurement and economic assessment were basic skills of the public service. Efficient financial organizations had already emerged by the time of Dynasty I in the shape of separate treasuries for the two parts of the kingdom. That of Lower Egypt was known as the Red House from the royal colour and similarly in Middle Egypt the treasury was known as the White House. For administrative purposes this double organization was long to continue and to be reflected in different branches of the government.

Efficient administration at the centre depended largely upon efficient organization in the localities. As we have already seen, for this purpose the kingdom had been divided into *nomes,* each under a *nomarch* appointed by the king. It was in these local government areas that irrigation and production were actively cared for and the practical tax collecting operations carried out. The *Nomarch* was responsible not only for the royal administration in his area and for the community's welfare, so far as it had any separate existence, but also for control of the local militia, and he officiated as district judge and clerk of works for the temples and other public structures in his area. For this purpose

he employed a large staff of officials, including scribes, technicians and workers and such special appointees as the assessor
who acted as clerk in the district court. The *nomarch* was
'assisted' by two royal deputies, whose presence could have been
far from welcome. They embodied the idea of inspection which
was another common characteristic of Egyptian administration.
Appointed from the centre and posted to each end of the *nome*,
their job was to keep an eye on the activities of the *nomarch* and
to ensure that the interests of their master in the capital were
properly attended to. Ostensibly the *nomarch's* assistants, they
were regarded, and indeed hated, as the king's spies.

Effective administration, then as now, depended upon reliable
statistics of population and manpower. It is not surprising therefore that the Egyptians were undertaking censuses at an early
date, but fortunate for us that there is a reference on the so-called
Palermo Stone to a census that was carried out during Dynasty I,
which reads 'in the following year we have the numbering of all
the people of the *nomes* of the west, north and east'.[11] The
fragment of this important monument in black diorite, which is
preserved in the museum at Palermo, Sicily, contains an inscription which includes a list of the kings of the early dynasties,
constituting the oldest surviving year-list in history.

An important and, in many respects, unique branch of Egypt's
public administration developed and had its finest phase during
Dynasties III and IV with the building of the monumental
pyramid tombs. Whatever one may think of the ends in view,
the designing and planning of these colossal structures and their
servicing called for an imaginative effort of the highest calibre
and for organizing and administering efforts that were indeed
worthy of a better goal. Little is disclosed in the tomb texts of
the constructional methods employed in the engineering of these
monster memorials[12] and even less of the administrative processes
entailed. We do know however that they came to make excessive
demands upon current resources and eventually provided an
automatic brake upon their own further development. The mere
organizing and provisioning of the colossal gangs of workmen and
slaves needed for the work assume an administrative effort of
outstanding magnitude and quality. No doubt these early architects, engineers and other officials of the Royal Egyptian Works
Department would have had a good deal to teach us on the
subject of human relations. For long it was argued that only by
ruthless use of power could such results have been achieved and
the existence of a slave community was adduced in support of
this thesis. But for such an effort all the surplus labour of the

realm needed to be mobilized and, as it happened, there were times of the year during the great inundation when the agriculturalist was idle. Then his labour could be channelled to other purposes and there is no reason why the Egyptians should have remained unaware of the sort of human relations approach that was best calculated to obtain continuing co-operation in this great national undertaking. It is not impossible that they were already aware of the psychological precepts that it remained for our own industrial society to rediscover.

The important subject of general army organization, which could at that time very well be considered as a specialist sector of public administration and certainly one from which valuable lessons can be learned by the administrator in the public field, is not one for discussion in this present study. Nevertheless it is of interest here that the Egyptian army was well cared for on the administrative side. The army scribes were an influential branch of the wider scribal profession. Pay and supply services were efficiently organized under administrative officers of various ranks and the administrative side was responsible for conscription of young men, which puts it squarely within the governmental field. These specialist officers had such general titles as Army Scribe, Scribe of the Infantry, Scribe of the Assemblage, and Scribe of Distribution. One of these army scribes, who was named Hori, has left a vivid account of the campaigns in Syria and also a letter addressed to one of his subordinates, Amenemope, in which he replies effectively to the latter's boastings by quoting from his own past experience in various campaigns. In effect the old soldier-become-bureaucrat, sitting in his office, deals decisively with the inexperienced front-line soldier who is impatient with the pen-pusher at headquarters.[13] The eternal strife between fighting soldier and staff officer is already well under way by the middle of the second millennium B.C.

With the expansion of trade and the growth of Egyptian imperialism during the time of the New Kingdom there was obviously a great deal of scope for Pharaoh's Foreign Office, although in the nature of things, since conquered peoples who have regained their freedom are ever eager to destroy all records of the good that has been done them by the foreign administrators, this phase of Egyptian public administration is not very well documented. However, pictures on a tomb at Beni-Hassan (situated between Memphis and Thebes) provide instructive evidence of a well-organized system of immigration control. These engravings depict a group of nomadic Semites, reminiscent of the Biblical tale of Abraham's arrival with his family in Egypt.

All persons entering the country were subject to careful examination by frontier guards and officials. These were concerned no doubt, as are their counterparts today, with the number of the party, the reason for the journey and the probable length of their stay. All these particulars were noted down on a papyrus roll in red ink by a scribe who then transmitted them by messenger to the frontier officer for decision as to whether an entrance permit should be granted. These higher officials worked in accordance with precise directives issued from time to time by Pharaoh's central office. It was important that the grazing lands to be placed at the disposal of such nomads should be carefully designated, and controlled.

Countries under direct administration were cared for as in the case of Nubia during Dynasty XVIII, by a Viceroy directly appointed by Pharaoh, whose rank was even superior to that of Vizir. Diplomatic relations were maintained with the neighbouring states, such as Cyprus, the Aegean cities, Anatolia and Babylon. A chance find by a peasant woman at Tell-el-Amarna, site of one of Egypt's capital cities, brought to light a small section of the diplomatic archives of Amenhotep III and Akhnaton of Dynasty XVIII. These letters, totalling over three hundred in all, were in cuneiform on clay tablets. They came from various kings in Western Asia and formed the oldest international correspondence that has survived. Chiefly pleas from vassal kings for assistance against troubles that were assailing both Syria and Palestine from within and without, these were, as we know today, destined to be in vain, for Egypt's power fell shortly in eclipse before the rival might of the Hittites.

PUBLIC OFFICIALS

So much for the leaders and their tasks. Although the world of officials was vast, few have left their own records, for only the mighty could afford their personal tombs. Yet many appear as officials in action, more or less anonymously, among the *dramatis personae* of the tomb pictures that have survived. Apart from the important servants of Pharaoh, whom he directly appointed, there was all the multitude of servants of court and temple, of central offices, of constructional works and of the *nomes*. Egyptian officialdom was all-pervasive: its size, its efficiency and long life place it in a category on its own. As we have already suggested, although in some ways bureaucratic the term 'bureaucracy' is misleading in this connection. There was no impersonal state in the modern sense. Officials were servants of Pharaoh, or of the nobles or other dignitaries of state, and certainly did not regard themselves as public servants with a mission to further the public weal, although efficient organization and working would often have this very result. Many posts became hereditary and, as such, personal property which could be transferred by purchase. The inevitable inefficiencies of such a system were mitigated by the exercise of arbitrary power from above. A strong Pharaoh could ensure that efficient officials occupied key positions. It was possible too for the same person to hold a number of posts by delegating their actual operation to efficient deputies.

An important unifying factor, however, was the need for all holders of important religious and official posts to be competent scribes: in other words they had to be able to read, write and count. To acquire a competent knowledge of hieroglyphics was difficult and took time: consequently the scribes needed a long education. The acquirement of essential skills tended to produce a vested interest and encourage the growth of a natural degree of professionalization. This in its turn led to the adoption of standardized methods and routines, with the result that public business was carried on everywhere in the same way and general rules were evolved and accepted. Safeguards to prevent errors and misappropriations meant the adoption of numerous checks and roundabout ways.

Red tape, as it would be called today, already existed and called forth protests. The duplication of offices and creation of sinecures became a scandal. Young men were advised to obtain an official job if they wanted an easy life. 'Put writing in thy heart, so that thou mayest protect thine own person from any labour and be a respected official.' Officials received fees or took a rake-off: they were often accused of extortion. 'The land is diminished, but its rulers are increased . . . . is bare, but its taxes are heavy. The grain is little but the grain measure is large and measured to overflowing.'[14] It was ever thus: the public official was never popular. Yet behind the scenes there must have been many dedicated and hard-working scribes; otherwise the effective management of Pharaoh's vast realm would never have been possible. That Egypt's officialdom had its long periods of success is amply proved by the high achievements of the government.

The widespread need and active demand for scribal knowledge led to the establishment of an effective system of education to which all aspirants for posts of responsibility and power submitted their children. In the villages the humbler scribes taught their own children, together with those of their neighbours, in small classes. The widespread survival of school exercises on potsherds and flakes of limestone proves the existence of such informal establishments. But there were more formally organized schools attached to government offices, temples and the royal court. To the latter privileged establishment the children of nobles with court appointments and others of non-royal rank might be added, an association with royalty that no doubt could have profitable consequences in later life.

The basic curriculum of these schools covered reading, writing and arithmetic, as the three essential scribal disciplines, but by careful selection of set examples for reading and reproduction general information about the country and society could be art-fully inculcated. Copybook maxims were already widely employed by the teachers and good manners were instanced prominently among the graces to be acquired. The composition of letters was taught and, in the schools attached to the public offices, the production and handling of official correspondence, the use of forms and the processes of calculation required for the completion of tax returns. Here we have a first example of a system of staff-training in operation.

The classes used to assemble early in the morning before the heat of the day. Methods of memorizing by repetition were employed, the laggard being urged forward by the use of the stick, as is evidenced in the statement: 'The ears of a boy are on his back, he hears when he is beaten.'[15] The pupil had to become efficient by using cheap materials for his exercises before he was allowed to practice on the expensive papyrus. Most of the scholars were boys, but girls were not precluded from becoming scribes. After graduation from school the scribe might choose from among a number of careers, although such choice would usually be determined by any specializing tendencies of the school he had attended and especially by the occupation of his father. Other than a career in the temple, the army, the palace or the public offices, he might choose the profession of medicine or art or possibly to enter one of the crafts, or even to become a modest village letter-writer or petty attorney. Thus the scribe's sphere was not confined to the public services though it was essentially public service. Opportunities in the public services were indeed varied and excellence in clerkship could enable a humble entrant to climb to the top of his profession, even to the office of Pharaoh's Private Secretary or Vizir. Under the Middle Kingdom in particular it is on record that an expanding administration called widely upon the resources of the middle class, which by this time had become prominent, to augment the personnel of the public offices.[16] The Egyptian educational system was essential to the existence and the efficiency of the Egyptian public services.

It may now help us to fill in some of the detail of our general picture of these services if we look briefly at the careers of some of the outstanding among Pharaoh's servants whose stories have come down to us. For it was another of Egypt's contributions in the field of public administration to hand down the first biographies, frequently autobiographies of officials, ever to survive.

We must be forewarned that these early life-stories, depicted or reported on tombs, sometimes their own but frequently their master's, are in the main uncritical success stories, presenting the subject's life as he wished it to be known after his death, but they do provide evidence of achievements that were worthy in themselves, even if little acknowledgment is made to the many others who must have participated in their attainment, and they certainly demonstrate a professional pride that speaks well of the Egyptian public services in their heyday.

First in this notable line was Imhotep, who, in the thirteenth century B.C., built for his master King Zoser of Dynasty III the first real stone building above ground at Sakkara, known today as the Step-pyramid. Zoser's fame as a great student, mighty builder and lover of literature may well have rested largely upon the considerable capacity of the wise man he took as counsellor, chief executive and master architect. Imhotep was one of that select band whose fame is destined to rise to even greater heights after their death. His wise sayings came to be quoted and as philosopher, scribe and physician he figured among Egypt's great men. The powerful scribal class looked upon him as their patron and scribes were in the habit of pouring out a libation to him before beginning an important piece of writing. A temple was raised to him at Sakkara near to his architectural masterpiece and eventually he came to be deified by the Memphite sect as Son of God, offspring of Ptah the Greater-God of Memphis by a mortal mother.[17] This is a success story of a public official surely unequalled in history and one undoubtedly grounded upon a record of practical achievement.

Another famed and perhaps more typical official of the period, namely Methen, servant of Snefru of Dynasty IV, was also buried at Sakkara, where his tomb preserves his own life story. His services began in the preceding reign, when he rose from a comparitively modest position to numerous posts of great importance in the Delta Administration, which provided his field of operations. His story begins with his inheritances: 'There were presented to him the things of his father, the judge and scribe Anubisemonekh: there was no grain or anything of the house, there were serfs and small cattle.' He was made chief scribe of the provision magazine and overseer of the things of the provision magazine. But his success was soon manifested in the acquisition of higher offices and in becoming local governor of Xois and inferior field judge of the same area. His career surges upwards step by step until we find him occupying a regular galaxy of high offices. He was 'Ruler of Southern Perked; Ruler of Perwersah; Ruler and Local Governor of the Stronghold Hesen in the Harpoon Nome; Palace Ruler and Local Governor in Sekhemu of Xois; Palace Ruler and Local Governor in Dep, as well as in Miper of the Saite Nome, and also in the Two Hounds of the Mendesian Nome; Palace Ruler of the Con-stronghold; Local Governor in the Desert and Master of the Hunt; Ruler of Fields; Deputy and Local Governor in the Sekhemite Nome; Nomarch Administrator and Deputy in the Eastern Fayum; Field Judge and Palace Ruler of the West of the Saitic Nome, Leader of . . . .' and so on.[18]

While it seems unlikely that Methen held so many posts at one and the same time, there was clearly a good deal of overlap and he can be accounted as the arch-pluralist among public officials of all ages. His posts covered a wide geographic field, calling for a good deal of mobility on his part. The ability of his many deputies must have been beyond question for there seemed to be no limits to Snefru's favour, which must have been based on deep trust in his servant's integrity and capacities. Are we not justified therefore in deducing that Methen had excellent judgment of men and a wide understanding of the art of supervision which enabled him to exercise delegation of responsibilities on a scale sufficient to procure effective administration in such a diversity of spheres? His personality must have been felt throughout the Delta and in many fields of public activity.

That Methen's rewards, as favoured official of omnipotent Pharaoh, were commensurate with his contribution, and probably more, is confirmed by his own admissions. He details some of the returns of office. 'There were conveyed to him as a reward 200 stat of lands by numerous royal decrees; a mortuary offering of 100 loaves every day from the mortuary temple of the mother of the king's children, Nemaathap, wife of Zoser; a house 200 cubits wide and 200 cubits long built and equipped; fine trees were set out, a very huge lake was made therein, figs and vines were set out . . . .' and so on. He did well for himself even if he lived within the insecure shadow of arbitrary personal favour which could, and often did, though not in his case, turn overnight into discard and utter ruin. As the representative of a long-lived class of high officials we receive from Methen also a picture of the realm of officialdom by which the temples and palaces of Ancient Egypt were surrounded — a super villadom reminiscent of the equally artificial constructions of modern Texas, with pleasant gardens and amenities second only to those of Pharaoh himself.

Our next example in Nekhebu, who himself tells how, during Dynasty VI, he rose from small beginnings to high office. He began in the footsteps of his brother who acted as his trainer. 'When I was in the service of my brother, the Overseer of Works, I used to do the writing, I used to carry the palette. When he was appointed Inspector of Buildings I used to carry his measuring rod. When he was appointed King's Architect and Builder I used to rule the city for him and did everything excellently. When he was appointed Sole Companion, King's Architect and Builder in the Two Houses, I used to take charge of his possessions for him. When he was appointed Overseer of Works, I used to report to him concerning everything about which he had spoken.' Modesty was not a natural virtue for the embellisher of tombs! Anyway the reward of all this strict and detailed tutelage is set out by Nekhebu himself 'His Majesty found me a common builder and His Majesty appointed me to the offices of Inspector of Builders, the Overseer of Builders and Superintendent of a Guild. And His Majesty placed me as King's Architect and Builder, then Royal Architect and Builder under the King's supervision. And His Majesty appointed me Sole Companion, King's Architect and Builder in the Two Houses.'[19] Nekhebu, too, was a man of parts but he certainly specialized and it would perhaps be fair to designate him one of the first of the Professional Civil Servants.

At about the same period we hear of an even more impressive official, one Weni, Minister of Pepi I of Dynasty VI. He began as a modest crown-bearer, graduated to a minor post in the Royal Treasury and was from thence promoted Inspector of the State Woods. Pepi's great favour is indicated by his accession to the office of Inspector of the Prophets of the Funerary Pyramid and later to the important post of Auditor. Further success in his official career brought him the nomination of Friend of the King and of Steward of the Queen's Household. Into his hands gradually accumulated the direction of all business, including the quarries of Sinai, in which, under his inspiration, up-to-date management methods and a proper system of inspection were introduced. Weni's achievements did not end with administration: as warrior he established the power of Egypt in Nubia,

Libya, and Palestine. His high abilities and great power place him among the great men of history.[20]

Our next example of a successful Egyptian high official is Ptahshepses, whose story has often been quoted as that of the most permanent of permanent officials of all time. He found favour under no less than nine monarchs and, as far as the records show, must have worn official harness for at least eighty years! When it is borne in mind that he began his incredible career during Dynasty IV, as husband to the daughter of King Shepseskaf, and continued in office under the Kings of Dynasty V, which displaced its predecessor, probably with violence, it seems obvious that, apart from his other abilities, Ptahshepses was an expert trimmer. He knew how to please his masters, was an adept at currying favour, which has ever been an understandable, if not admirable, characteristic of the successful bureaucrat. His good fortune in marrying the King's daughter, a theme to embellish the annals of romance throughout the ages, must have appeared in a very doubtful light when the Dynasty began to totter. But in the hour of decision Ptahshepses was not only wise enough to evade the rather obvious step of becoming a claimant to the throne himself but sufficiently cunning to be able to commend himself to the successful claimant who could well have considered his elimination an essential preliminary to the building of his own security. Possibly Ptahshepses had a hand in bringing about the change-over, though, as king-maker, he would still have had to demonstrate consummate diplomatic skill in maintaining his indispensibility, as he so obviously did.

Ptahshepses was another who was not in the least modest about his success and while his personal statement, incised on his sepulchral stele, adds little to our knowledge of the art of public administration, it affords conclusive evidence of the sort of man he was. Dr. James Baikie's translation is quoted:

'(Who was born) in the time of Menkaura: whom he (i.e. Menkaura) educated among the king's children, in the royal harem; who was honoured more before the king than any child; PTAHSHEPSES. . . . . in the time of Shepseskaf; whom he (i.e. Shepseskaf) educated among the king's children in the palace of the king, in the privy chamber, in the royal harem; who was honoured before the king than any youth; PTAHSHEPSES.

His Majesty gave him the king's eldest daughter, Maatkha, as his wife, for His Majesty desired that she should be with him more than with anyone; PTAHSHEPSES.

(Attached to Userkaf, High Priest of Memphis), more honoured by the king than any servant. He descended into every ship of the court; he entered upon the ways of the southern palace at all the

Feasts-of-the-Coronation; PTAHSHEPSES.

(Attached to Sahura, more honoured by the king than) any servant, as privy councillor of every work which His Majesty desired to do; who pleased the heart of his lord every day; PTAHSHEPSES.

(Attached to Neferarkara, more honoured by the king than) any servant; when His Majesty praised him for a thing, His Majesty permitted that he should kiss his foot, and His Majesty did not permit that he should kiss the ground; PTAHSHEPSES.

(Attached to Neferafra, more honoured by the king than) any servant; he descended into the sacred barge at all Feasts-of-the-Appearance; beloved of his lord; PTAHSHEPSES.

. . . . attached to the heart of his lord (Ra-en-user or Nusserra), beloved of his lord, revered of Ptah, doing that which the god desires of him pleasing every artificer under the king; PTAH-SHEPSES.'[21]

In this paen of self-praise, composed with an almost poetic fervour, Ptahshepses certainly discloses one skill which the public official usually goes out of his way to disclaim, namely an infinite capacity for self-advertisement. However, Ptahshepses's attitude was a natural product of Egyptian culture and it has to be mentioned that he was servant of no mere ruler: his masters were gods who called for the observance proper to a god from all those around them. The most exalted were expected to grovel before Pharaoh on their bellies. How right then was Ptahshepses to dilate upon the great privilege granted to him by Neferarkara in this respect! In the East, obsequiousness was ever an official's virtue and no doubt Ptahshepses's almost mythical success must have enshrined him as doyen of his profession.

One of the best-known among Egypt's officials is the hero of a fictional work *Memoirs of Sinuhe* written sometime during Dynasties XII-XIII, which was so popular that it was repeatedly copied. Three manuscripts have survived.[22] Although fictional in form this story was factual in content and almost certainly a true biography. Sinuhe, prince and count, flourished during the reign of Amenemhat I of Dynasty XII, whose death was announced while Sinuhe was away with the King's son, Sesostris on a punitive expedition against the Libyans. The event is described in poetic terms:

'In the year 30, on the ninth day of the third month of the Inundation the god entered his horizon. King Amenemhat flew away to heaven and was united with the sun, and the god's body was merged with his creator. The Residence was hushed, hearts were filled with mourning, the Two Great Portals were shut, the courtiers sat head on knees and the people grieved.

Now, His Majesty had sent forth an army to the land of Temehu, and his eldest son was captain thereof, the god Sesostris; and even now he was returning having carried away captives of the Tehenu and all manner of cattle without count.

And the Chamberlain of the Royal Palace sent to the western border of the Delta to inform the King's son of the event that had befallen at Court. And the messengers met him on the road and reached him at eventide. Not a moment did he tarry; the hawk flew away with his henchmen, and did not make it known unto his army.'[23]

When Sinuhe heard of this, he was frightened and, for reasons not disclosed, decided to leave without delay in search of sanctuary beyond the confines of Egypt. He probably feared the intrigues of a rival power under the throne or had grave doubts about the policies of the new Pharaoh. In any case his reasons must have been compulsive to make him give up so much without further ado. His journey up the Nile, across the Isthmus of Suez, across deserts and inhospitable lands as far as Syria — 'the land of Retenu' — is described in vivid detail.

Nenshi, Prince of Upper Retenu, who had heard of his fame, was eager to befriend him. The words in which Sinuhe explained his presence deserve quotation:

'And I said again, dissembling: "I came from the expedition of the land of the Temehu, and report was made unto me, and mine heart trembled and mine heart was no longer in my body. It carried me away upon the pathways of the wastes. Yet none hath gossiped about me, none hath spat in my face; I had heard no reviling word, my name hadn't been heard in the mouth of a herald. I know now what brought me to this land. It was like the dispensation of God".'

Somehow there is a ring of truth about this apparently far-fetched statement which throws a devastating light upon the atmosphere of abject subjection in which even the most influential servants of Pharaoh lived their lives.

Sinuhe stayed long at the court of Nenshi and proved his abilities afresh. He married the King's eldest daughter and raised a family. Travellers from the Egyptian Court on their way through Syria to more distant lands often stayed with him. King Nenshi made use of his services and, as successful captain of the King's hosts, he rose to fame in his adopted country. There is the inevitable tale of the powerful champion who, jealous of the success of a foreigner, came against him before all the people. But Sinuhe did not differ from the heroes of romance. He vanquished his powerful enemy in single combat and Nenshi embraced him.

After many years among people whom the Egyptians considered barbarians, Sinuhe yearned to return home and wondered whether it would now be safe to do so. The Egyptian King sent him a kindly message telling him that he had nothing to fear. There is a touching scene at his homecoming as he grovels before the throne in his ragged barbarian attire. He is raised up and welcomed by Pharaoh, introduced to the queen and the royal children, clothed in fine robes and given a sumptuous house in which to spend his declining years and, more important even, orders are given for the construction of his pyramid out of stone in the precinct of the pyramids. The story ends 'And so live I, rewarded by the King, until the day of my death cometh'. Humanity was not, then, a complete stranger at Pharaoh's court?

We should not leave this selection of notable Egyptian officials without mentioning Vizir Rekhmire, whom Leonard Cottrell has used as a focus around which to reconstruct a picture of the daily life in Egypt during the reign of Tuthmosis II of Dynasty XVIII.[24] In this we are introduced to Rekhmire's daily routines as administrator on the basis of details from his tomb inscriptions at Thebes. Evidently Rekhmire was an important man, deep in the confidence of his Pharaoh and of similar calibre to the predecessors with whom we have already become acquainted.

Two incidents are of special interest in our present context. In the first Rekhmire is on his way back in his official launch on the Nile from one of his periodical tours of inspection in the provinces. He has been busy receiving reports from district inspectors, attending to provincial boundaries and allocations of land, issuing instructions about such matters as the crops, the inundation, tax arrears, and robberies, and attending to complaints from governors in the *nomes*. He is Pharaoh's representative in all branches of government, the chief co-ordinating authority in the royal administration. As the boat, driven forward by benches of rowers under the command of its captain, comes steadily up the river, the Vizir, seated in solemn splendour under his awning amidships, dictates to scribes who sit around him cross-legged with the papyrus rolls on their knees. This office-work in which Rekhmire is immersed is characteristic of the administrative system needed to ensure that the Egyptian scheme of government should work effectively. It is a constant preoccupation leaving the Vizir little leisure while away on tour. They reach Memphis, once the capital but now just the chief city of the surrounding *nome,* although an important centre as such.

There Rekhmire stays with the Governor, with whom he engages in close conference on the affairs of the district. The following day there is a special session when local officials come and go for interrogation, during which, we may be sure, there are some heated altercations, for Rekhmire is not an easy man when dealing with his master's business. He knows all the means and subterfuges that are habitually employed to falsify the census of cattle, the estimates of crops and the tax dues. Even when he has done his utmost there will be outstanding queries for the governor to clear up, and no doubt in time messengers will come with reminders from the responsible central office. Rekhmire will be concerned with arrangements for the provision of adequate labour for the construction and repair of irrigation works and will need to consult the officials responsible for the *corvée*. Direct reports made by the district inspectors appointed by Pharaoh will enable the Vizir to check up statements made by the local officials who are appointed by the Governor, to whom they owe personal allegiance. The widespread use of inspection in Egyptian government is notable and the Egyptian definition of the inspector as 'eyes-and-ears' of his master is still widely quoted today. No doubt when Rekhmire, his mission at Memphis completed, repaired to his floating office his erstwhile host was as relieved that the ordeal was over, at least until the next time, as any modern manager who courteously bids farewell to his modern counterpart from head office.

The second incident is of a quite different type. Rested after his return from his official travels Rekhmire decides to throw a party to celebrate his homecoming. At the party we meet not only his family and other close connections but also numerous officials and their relations. This will ensure that the conversation, while not overlooking the social graces, will not entirely ignore official affairs. Many will want to glean something of what the Vizir saw and heard during his travels. In those days before the press or even a public postal system every traveller was a messenger from the wider world. Among the important guests we should expect to find the Mayor of Thebes and his family, the Fanbearer to the King (a sort of Grand Chamberlain), the Chief Priest of Amun, who happens to be accompanied by his wife and daughter, the Keeper of the Royal Garden, the Royal Tutor and the Royal Scribe. The latter is accompanied by his Son, Senmut, who is an Officer of Chariotry and suitor for the hand of Rekhmire's daughter. There is a strict order of precedence in the seating arrangements for the more important guests. Such social gatherings, whether he finds them pleasurable or not, will no doubt be of great value in enabling the Vizir to keep his finger on the less formal pulse of Court opinion, although he will be ever awake to the blanketing effect of the sycophancy to which his position at the right-hand of Pharaoh inevitably subjects him.

REFERENCES

1 Jean Yoyotte, *Encyclopedie de la Pléiade: Histoire Universelle, I,* (Paris, 1956), pp. 262-3.
2 Jaroslav Cerny, *Paper and Books in Ancient Egypt,* (University College, London, 1952).
3 Leonard Cottrell, *Life under the Pharaohs,* (Evans, 1955), pp. 31-2.
4 Breasted, *Ancient Times,* (Ginn, 1944), p. 57.
5 Finegan, *Light from the Ancient Past,* (Princeton, 1946), p. 102.
6 J. A. Spender, *The Government of Mankind,* (Cassell, 1938), p. 22.
7 Margaret A. Murray, *The Splendour That Was Egypt,* (Sidgwick & Jackson, 1938).
8 Cyril Aldred, *The Egyptians,* (Thames and Hudson, 1961), p. 169.
9 J. A. Wilson on 'Egypt: The Function of the State' in *Before Philosophy,* (Penguin, 1949), pp. 99-101.
10 Wilson, *op. cit.,* pp. 103-4.
11 James Baikie, *A History of Egypt,* (Black, 1929), pp. 83-4.
12 J. E. S. Edwards, *The Pyramids of Egypt,* (Penguin, 1947), p. 206.
13 Cottrell, *op. cit.,* p. 102.
14 Wilson, *op. cit.,* p. 97.
15 Murray, *op. cit.,* pp. 105-9.
16 Yoyette, *op. cit.,* p. 160.
17 Baikie, *op. cit.,* pp. 96-7.
18 Baikie, *op. cit.,* pp. 110-12.
19 Murray, *op. cit.,* pp. 105-9.
20 C. F. Jean in *European Civilization,* (Oxford, 1935), Vol. I, p. 287.
21 Baikie, *op. cit.,* p. 161.
22 Jean, *op. cit.,* p. 308.
23 Cottrell, *op. cit.,* p. 128 *et seq,* quoting translation by Erman.
24 Cottrell, *op. cit.,* p. 31 *et seq.*

CHAPTER 3

THE MEDITERRANEAN CITY STATE :
circa 2000 to 146 B.C.

Concurrently with the development in Egypt of a comparatively stable and long enduring system of public administration, which had important tendencies towards professionalism and large-scale organization although it remained a personal rather than an objective or bureaucratic system to the end, a multifarious experiment in small-scale and decidedly amateur public administration was under way in the rest of the Mediterranean area, particularly among the cities of the Greeks, widely scattered along its shores.

While the classic age of the Greek City State may be placed in the middle of the first millennium B.C. its traditions go back to a much earlier period. The origins of the Greeks are still obscure and until recently their history from the third millennium onwards depended largely upon oral tradition. Discoveries at Troy in Asia Minor, at Minos in Crete, at Mycenae and Pylos on the Grecian mainland have altered all this, so that our picture of these early millennia, when so many important developments were already taking place in Mesopotamia and Egypt, is being progressively re-focused. Nor were the Greeks and their successors, the Romans, the only peoples to develop the city state as the predominating system of government and administration. The comparatively easy sea-communications between otherwise isolated communities in the great land-enclosed Mediterranean sea undoubtedly facilitated the migration of peoples and the transmission of their ideas. The process must have begun at a very early age, as the existence, often unexplained, of Megalithic remains on such islands as Sardinia, Minorca, Crete and Cyprus clearly indicates. In a general way the conditions were then favourable to the emergence of the type of political community that so often appears at a particular stage in development of peoples from the family and tribe to the much more extensive political union. In the present context the Phoenicians, Mycenaeans and Etruscans are notable among the peoples who contributed to this development.

THE PHOENICIANS

Phoenicia consisted of a narrow strip of coastland, on shores now occupied by Syria, Lebanon and Israel, which was settled by probing Semitic invaders some time about 2000 B.C. These invaders, assisted by their geographic situation, became skilled seamen and traders who, using the whole Mediterranean basin as their field of operations, passed well beyond the Pillars of Hercules into the uncharted Atlantic to the Scilly Isles and Cornwall in search of tin. They may even have penetrated as far north as the Baltic!

The Phoenicians do not appear to have formed a united people, but to have continued as a group of loosely linked city states, with names such as Arvad, Gebel (the 'Byblos' of the Greeks from which the word 'Bible' is derived), Beirut, Sidon and Tyre. They were under Egyptian control from the fifteenth to the thirteenth centuries B.C. and later fell successively into the orbits of Assyria, Babylon and Persia. Their story ended with the fall of Tyre, after an historic siege by Alexander, in 332 B.C.

In their heyday the Phoenicians planted colonies throughout the Mediterranean. Notable among these was Carthage, near modern Tunis, which is said to have been founded in 814 B.C. by Dido, sister of the King of Tyre, as a sort of staging base between the home city and the Phoenician colony of Tartessus in far Andalusia. Carthage, favoured by its central position, was destined to become a power great enough to challenge, during the third century B.C., the rising might of Rome. Carthage conquered large areas on the north coast of Africa, in Spain and in Sicily, which she wrested from the Greeks, but she remained essentially a city state concerned in trade and compelled to expand mainly to protect her commercial interests.

There is a dearth of information on Phoenician institutions, but it is clear that Carthage[1] was dominated throughout her career by a noble class resting upon birth and wealth and that the people were subject to a tyranny, which was suspicious of any individualist tendency. The priests, who served a number of gods, formed a powerful hierarchy which was within the patronage of a few important families. However, it is on record that, to keep an eye on the priestly class, a collegium of ten members was eventually appointed.

There appears to have been an Assembly but this had little power, the main authority having rested with an aristocratic Senate and a Committee of Five. Outwardly, therefore, the Carthaginian constitution appears to have differed little from that of other city states of the period, but an original feature was introduced during the fifth century, when a body of non-political magistrates, known as 'the Court of the Four Hundred', was appointed to impose a rigorous civic and moral discipline upon both executive and people. The executive power was divided between two magistrates, or *shofetim,* who had replaced the earlier kingship. These *shofetim* acted as political and military leaders of the state. Warmington, who uses the term *sufet* for these chief magistrates, states that in the third century the office was filled annually and provides a good deal of information about the government and administrative system.[2] There was an interesting institution in Carthage in the shape of clubs, or *hetairiai,* which had corporational status. Their members met for communal meals and they may have been financed by the leaders of their association who depended upon them for political support.

Little is known of the Carthaginians' administrative methods but they were certainly good, as one would expect from their wide trading activities. If the well-known diplomatic texts found at Tell-el-Amarna and Ras Shamra do not tell us much about Carthage they certainly afford evidence of the ability of the Phoenicians in diplomacy. No doubt for the same reasons a good deal of attention was given to effective correspondence. In any case, in seeking improved methods of communication, the Phoenicians superseded the cumbersome cuneiform and hieroglyphic systems of writing by inventing a twenty-two letter alphabet, which later, through the Greeks and the Romans, became the basis of all modern Western alphabets.

THE MYCENAEANS AND MINOANS

Archaeological discoveries during the present century on the Island of Crete, (Minos) especially at Knossus, have brought to light abundant evidence of a civilization which goes back as far as the Late Stone Age. In the ruins of the vast palace at Knossus, uncovered by Sir Arthur Evans, dating back to 2000 B.C., decorated pottery and wall-engravings and paintings have been found which indicate the high cultural level attained by the Minoans. These Minoans were a sea-power who had close contacts with Egypt. By 2000 B.C. they had already adopted a hieroglyphic system of writing and by 1600 B.C. this had been replaced by a linear system. Catastrophe fell upon Knossus somewhere about 1700 B.C. but there followed a brilliant revival and a phase when Crete through her overseas influences linked up with the states of the Greek mainland under the leadership of Mycenae. The palace of Knossus was rebuilt on a vast scale, only to be consumed by fire a couple of hundred years later when the whole of Cretan civilization seems to have been destroyed, apparently by an invasion organized for this sole purpose, since there is no evidence that the invaders lingered upon the scene of their depredations.

Before these discoveries at Knossus the inspired German archaeologist, Heinrich Schliemann, had been at work from the late 'sixties on the sites of Troy, Mycenae and Tiryens and startling discoveries had brought the world of Homer into the frame of history. Our picture of that important epoch is being continually broadened by new discoveries, particularly at Pylos.

Clay tablets inscribed with a well-developed system of writing have come to light not only at Knossus, but also at Pylos and Mycenae. The earliest are inscribed with hieroglyphics, but these were followed by others with two types of script which Evans named 'Minoan Linear A' and 'Minoan Linear B'. The former and earlier is in a language which has not yet been deciphered. Translation of the latter, however, has been rendered possible through the research of a young London architect, the late Michael Ventris. From this it has been concluded that the language then used at Knossus and on the mainland was one and the same, an archaic form of Greek which was thus in use five hundred years before Homer's day. A wonderful new page had been added to the history of Mediterranean civilization.

It is fortunate that the nature of these epoch-making discoveries disclose a good deal about the government and particularly the administration of the period. The political pattern appears to have consisted of a group of small kingdoms, each centred about a leading city, though the control of Knossus itself may well have extended throughout the island of Crete. The state was under the autocratic rule of a monarch, while the outlying places were under princes or nobles owing a feudal duty to the king. The King was his own chief official, administrator as well as ruler, but little has been gleaned about his assistants. There is a reference to a 'Leader-of-the-People', ranking next to the King. His title does not appear to have had any democratic significance:[3] he was probably a sort of Vizir, or perhaps Heir-apparent. There were members of the royal household, with such titles as King's Armourer, King's Fuller, and King's Potter. There were heralds, inspectors and obviously scribes, though no specific description for the latter has yet been deciphered. Over the villages there were Under-kings or Mayors who exercised a good deal of power in the King's name.

The magnificence of the palace of Knossus, with its advanced drainage and bathing amenities and its art establishments and wall decorations, indicates a place of great regal ceremony, while its numerous offices and workshops prove that it was planned as a focus of public administration. There are not only chambers used for the filing of records and, no doubt, as working offices, but workshops for the artists and numerous storage vaults to contain 'income' in the form of gifts or tribute and ordinary taxation and extensive enough, at least in the case of oil-storage, to suggest that the palace was also a vast trading centre.

The tablets were dried but not baked, stored away in wooden boxes or wicker baskets which were sealed with lumps of clay impressed either with the seal of an official or marked with the name of the contents. The containers were filed on shelves round a room assigned for the purpose, a regular archive. In the case of Pylos this Archive Room was connected with the main gate of the palace where it was convenient to supervise the incoming and outgoing of goods. This arrangement appears to explain a reference on tablets found elsewhere which runs: 'written at the door of the palace gate'.[4] The officials were expert in arithmetical calculation, a decimal system being in use. There was also a system of weights and measures, which seems to have had some links with Babylon, and pieces of gold, silver and bronze may have formed metal currency.[5]

All the tablets so far found are of an administrative nature and it is probable that other less permanent but more convenient media were used for literary and historical records. On the other hand such records may have been stored separately in other parts of the city which have not yet been uncovered or may have been completely destroyed, for even the surviving tablets at Knossus only escaped destruction because they were baked hard in the general conflagration. Some of the tablets are of a peculiar form, having a close resemblance to a palm-leaf, which may well represent other media already familiar and in general use, such as papyrus or even skins. There is evidence too that the tablets which have survived were intended merely for current transactions, since precise years are not mentioned, and it is possible that careful administrators kept more permanent ledgers, for which more expensive but less durable materials were probably used. Presumably after the annual summaries had been made, sometimes from large tablets on which the contents of smaller tablets had been listed, the constituent tablets were destroyed, as rough drafts are destroyed today.

These tablets deal with such matters as tribute, religious offerings, and stores. They include assessments of the several districts with an indication of the progress of payment or collection. Movements of personnel were indicated, e.g. the allocation of rowers to a ship or of masons to build walls, while there are many entries relating to individuals which show their occupation and suggest a well-developed division of labour, which could only have existed to meet the needs of a highly civilized community. The Mycenaean and Minoan public official was already professionally involved in those fundamental record-making activities that have formed the core of office work right into the twentieth century of our era. There is clearly much more to be gleaned from material already available.

THE ETRUSCANS

The origins of the Etruscans, traces of whose civilization have survived to this day over large parts of Italy, are still a mystery. They appeared on the scene somewhere about 1000 B.C. and arose to prominence during the three following centuries.[6] With the rise of Rome their power waned, although their influence upon the shaping of Roman institutions was surely important. Apart from references in Roman literature and from numerous inscriptions, a fairly complete picture of the externals of Etruscan life has survived in the ruined towns and numerous deeply dug tomb chambers in which carvings, inscriptions, wall paintings and domestic articles have been preserved, very much as a picture of Egyptian living was preserved in the pyramids and other tombs. They had an alphabet of twenty-six letters which, however, has not yet been made to solve the mystery of their language.

The political system of the Etruscans is already fairly familiar from other early civilizations. Ancient Etruria consisted of a loose group of city states each claiming full autonomy within its surrounding territory. There is no evidence that they ever consolidated themselves into a single kingdom, although a high degree of co-operation was undoubtedly achieved among the cities, in virtue of similar sentiments of fraternity, race and religion. This was essentially an urban type of civilization which at its height achieved a high standard of living for the ruling class. A loose confederation was apparently formed by twelve tribes, deriving their names from the principal cities, who met together annually in an Etrurian Council at Voltumna to discuss matters of peace and war.

In the beginning the states were under powerful kings, but gradually these were replaced by aristocratic oligarchies with annual magistracies and a senate of leading citizens. Little is known about the detailed working of the Etruscan city state. Evidently it was essentially aristocratic and from the remarkable art objects that have survived it is clear that its leaders, who appear to have concerned themselves mainly with government and administration, led a life of ease and high culture. The free craftsmen, the peasants and the slaves leave a dim picture in history. There were a number of foreigners, among whom Greeks figure prominently. Executive power was placed in the hands of magistrates, whose titles can often be deduced from the tomb inscriptions although their functions are not determinable. These magistrates, some of whom operated as colleges, had names such as *zilath, purthene,* and *maru,* and the inscriptions indicated a *cursus honorum,* or order of precedence, although their relative importance is not clear.

THE GREEKS

From the *Iliad* and the *Odyssey* an outline of the government of the early Greek city state can be derived.[7] There was a king and a series of sub-kings or nobles and a system of classes. The king consulted his leading subjects in council and decisions would be announced to the people assembled in the Agora. Administration at the summit was still household administration carried out by a band of domestic servants with specific functions, but these were supplemented by the *therapontes,* a group of higher servants recruited from the noble families. They were arranged in ranks, those at the top assisting the King in his religious duties, or as heralds representing him at all public functions, carrying his sceptre or insignia of power. The *therapontes* served at the royal feasts, acted as messengers endowed with the royal power, convoked the council, made proclamations to the people, carried the royal orders in battle, and bore the royal authority on missions abroad. Lower down the hierarchy junior *therapontes* were assigned lesser responsibilities, such as control of the stables or armoury. Already we can see the emergence within the Homeric King's household of a group of Ministers or an Administrative Class and of lesser officials. In a broader sense administration was based upon the *phratry,* or tribe, to which the individual belonged. Recruitment of the army, provision of ships and of supplies to meet the public expense were all allocated according to tribe, each of which made its contribution as commanded by the king through leaders who held their hereditary titles from the King.

THE GREEK CITY STATE IN THE CLASSICAL AGE

During the first millennium B.C. the Greeks planted city colonies throughout the Mediterranean, each of which took with it the governmental pattern of the colonizing city. Despite the large number of such cities it is nevertheless necessary only to examine two, which represented opposite conceptions of government, to gain a reasonable picture of state administration at the time, namely Athens and Sparta to which the histories have given full attention. It is not necessary to go into detail on the government here but sufficient information must be given to discern broadly how Greek public administration was conducted.

By this time the Homeric Kingship had declined in power. Only in Sparta had it survived as a system of two Kings, deriving from the two royal houses out of which the state had emerged. These acted jointly and conveniently exercised a check upon one another. They continued to wield the authority of high priest and army commander but had lost most of their judicial power, an interesting exception being judgment on all matters concerning public roads.[8] In Sparta the *Gerusia,* or Council of Elders, consisted of the two Kings and twenty-eight members of noble families who had to be over sixty years of age. Their selection was acclaimed in the *Apella* or Assembly, as the 'prize of virtue'. The *Gerusia,* although advisory, exerted a good deal of political influence and also acted as a court of criminal justice. Every Spartan citizen of over thirty years of age sat in the *Apella* as a duty rather than a right. Originally summoned by the King this function was transferred to the *Ephorate,* probably the most characteristic part of the Spartan system. The *Apella* did not debate: it met merely to acclaim proposals put before it by the kings and the *Ephors.*

The *Ephorate* consisted of five citizens chosen by lot, who held office for a year. They began as administrative assistants to relieve the kings of onerous responsibilities which were getting beyond their personal control, but as a result of some internal upheaval they became guardians of the rights of the people with the task of watching over jealously the conduct of the kings. They accompanied the kings on all official occasions and had the power to call them to account, a sort of perambulatory censorate! They also administered civil justice and were responsible for order and discipline within the state.

It was, however, the Spartan social system which gave this city state its distinctive stamp. The people formed a military caste devoted to the service of the state, subject to a strict discipline and living communally. They formed a privileged class whose lives were devoted to the service of the State; indeed they were the state and its administration. Production was left to the *Helots,* the original inhabitants who had been reduced to the status of serfs. The threat of revolt was met by the institution of the *Krypteia,* or secret police, to keep the Helots under constant surveillance and control. The devotion of the Spartan to the service of the state was widely admired by the other Greeks, although gradual degeneration came to deprive the system of its original quality.

A more flexible system, suitable to the needs of growing trading states was being sought elsewhere, where trends were steadily in the direction of more democratic forms. At first the kings were replaced by tyrants whose popularity depended upon their ability to curb the power of the aristocracy and to provide much needed public works. The golden age of the tyrants occurred during the sixth century B.C., but doing good by arbitrary methods did not satisfy the Greeks who soon sought ways of curbing the tyranni-cal proclivities of prominent citizens. One of the fruits of the movement was the invention of the peculiar Greek institution of ostracism. The Athenian leader Cleisthenes introduced a law in 500 B.C. that annually the people of that city should have an opportunity to vote against any prominent citizen whom they considered dangerous to the state and call for his banishment for a term of years. An easy administrative method of operating this scheme was devised. All the citizen had to do was to pick up one of the many pieces of pottery, known as an *ostracon,* that lay about the market place, to write upon it the name of the citizen he wished to have banished and to put it in the voting urn placed there specially for the purpose. To be effective at least six thousand citizens had to be present at such a vote.

So much has been written about the government of Athens that it is unnecessary to repeat more than a few important facts here. At an early stage the King, diminished in power as one of three magistrates with the title of *Basileus* or religious leader and judge in religious causes, was replaced by the *Archon* who, as supreme judge in all civil cases and defender of the property rights of the citizen ranked first among the magistrates. There was a third magistrate known as the *Polemarch,* who was judge in all cases involving non-citizens, as well as commander-in-chief of the army. These magistrates were elected annually. The governing power rested in the hands of the Council of the Areopagus, or Elders, who had certain jurisdiction and controlled the selection of the magistrates. Some time during the seventh century six judges were elected to control the judicial system and these, shortly associated with the three magistrates, came to form a magisterial college of Nine Archons.

Administration was based upon four tribes, each divided into three *phratries,* and having its own officials. With the growing importance of the navy the four tribes were further divided into forty-eight *naucrariae,* each of which was responsible for the supply and manning of the ships. The *naucrariae* were represented by an administrative council which was responsible for the organization of the fleet, an interesting example of grass-roots administration. It was Cleisthenes who, after numerous attempts at reform, recast the tribal basis by dividing the whole of Attica into three geographical regions — of city, coast and hinterland — each of which was to consist of ten *trittyes.* He then took one *trittys* from each of the three regions and formed it into a tribe which, further divided into *demes,* was to form a basic administrative division with its own officials, assembly and corporate property. The president of the *deme* kept a list of citizens from the age of seventeen, while the organization of the army depended upon the tribe. The *trittyes* had no independent existence. The aim of this artificial combination of three different areas was to stop the jealousies and unrest between the wider areas that had caused so much dislocation in Athens. The solution appears to have had greater success than one might have expected.

Reforms introduced between 592 and 594 B.C. by Solon, poet and wealthy citizen elected *Archon* for this very purpose, laid the foundations of the Athenian democracy. The citizens were to meet in the *Ecclesia,* or general assembly, and to participate in the election of the magistrates. All citizens were also eligible to sit in the new popular court, or *Heliaea,* which, beginning as courts of appeal, gradually took over the judicial functions of the *Archons.* At the same time the Council of the Areopagus was deprived of its deliberative functions and therefore ceased to participate directly in administration and legislation, but assumed the new role of protector of the constitution, with wide powers over the magistrates and censorial authority over citizens.

A Council of Four Hundred was established to prepare the business of the *Ecclesia,* consisting of one hundred members from each of the four original tribes, probably selected by lot, a method on which Solon placed considerable store as embodying the impartial judgment of the gods, and therefore more reliable than human choice! Forty candidates were selected for the Archonate, ten from each tribe, the final nine being chosen by lot. With Cleisthenes's reforms of the tribal system each of the ten tribes selected fifty members of the Council which now became the Council of Five Hundred. This Council changed annually, all candidates for the new council being sifted by the outgoing Council as to the integrity of their public and private lives.

The work of this interesting Council in conjunction with the magistrates was essentially executive and it represented therefore an attempt to place the management of the state in the hands of ordinary citizens. The *Archons* and other magistrates were bound to report to it and to see to the execution of its orders. It was responsible for most matters concerned with public works, foreign affairs and war, except that only the *Ecclesia* could approve the declaration of war or the making of treaties. The Council was also concerned with the preparation of new laws which were then placed before the *Ecclesia* for approval. Finance was under its control, though the actual administration was delegated to ten finance officers or *Apodektai,* selected from the ten tribes. It exercised judicial powers in matters of finance, including the power to fine officials.

To facilitate the working of an executive of five hundred it became the practice to resolve it into ten tribal committees, each of which functioned on its behalf for a tenth of the year. A *prytaneis* of ten was selected weekly from the tribal committee to act as a sort of corporate president of the council.

THE ATHENIAN EMPIRE OF THE FIFTH CENTURY

Following the defeat of the Persians at the battles of Thermopholae, Salamis and Cithaeron in 480 B.C. the Greeks for a time achieved a high degree of unity, but the genius of the city state was against the permanence of such a development. For the purpose of sea defence the Confederacy of Delos was formed, each city being expected to contribute a quota of ships to the combined navy. Many cities belonging to the Confederacy, which totalled over two hundred at its height, preferred to contribute money in place of ships and this money was collected by ten *Hellenotamiae,* or 'Treasurers of the Greeks', who were all citizens of Athens. The money was paid into the Treasury at Delos where the Council of the Confederacy met to decide a general policy. Each member state had one representative on the Council irrespective of size but Athens, in virtue of her wealth, came to sway the votes of the smaller states and thus to dominate the Confederacy. What had begun as a naval union was soon developing into an empire. Gradually the states became absorbed, leaving only the three remaining ship-contributing cities of Lesbos, Chios and Samos with any real autonomy. In 454 the Treasury of the Confederacy was transferred to Athens, and Athenian overlordship had become an accepted fact. But the mere idea of empire, irrespective of whether its results were good or bad, was anathema to the spirit of the Greeks and within fifty years the Athenian Empire had ceased to be.

This was the period in which the constitution of Athens was further democratized and, under the leadership of Pericles whose name first appeared in an official document in 473 B.C., Athens achieved her greatest glory. But the principle of democracy seems to have been pushed too far, with the reduction of the *Aeropagus* and *Archonate,* the payment of magistrates who were no longer confined to wealthy citizens and even payment for attendance of the citizen-judges at the *Heliaea.* Their expert speech-writers were able to sway the untutored judges and justice became a farce. Nor is our respect for the system heightened by the knowledge that slaves could be forced to give evidence before these courts under torture!

However, the advent of democracy did not mean that public expense was laid upon the poor citizen, except in times of crisis. Instead of the state levying taxes, wealthy citizens were expected to undertake onerous financial responsibilities. Thus the system of *trierarchy* had been introduced, whereby wealthy citizens in turn accepted responsibility for fitting and launching a galley — the hull and certain rigging having been supplied by the state — for training the oarsmen, for keeping the ship in good repair, and, indeed, as *tetrarch,* sailing with his ship during his period of office. Although sums of money were allocated from the public treasury to equip deputations sent on some religious errand or to a Panhellenic festival, such moneys were insufficient to equip the deputation with the magnificence worthy of the occasion and again a citizen was appointed to make up the difference and take responsibility for results. Annually each tribe deputed a wealthy member as *choregos* with the duty of providing a chorus and skilled trainer to teach them the dances and songs of the drama to be performed. Rivalry among the *choregoi* for the honour of achieving success in the artistic competitions encouraged generosity on the part of these citizens, and certainly increased the great contribution to art and literature made by the Greeks during this notable era.

Athens's age of glory was short-lived. In 431 B.C. the Peloponnesian War broke out and her fate was sealed. Two years later Pericles died. To Thucydides was left the task of writing the historical epitaph to the age. Much can be gleaned from this notable chronicle[9] about the weaknesses of Greek public administration in the conduct of such a military enterprise: for example, the influence on leaders like Nicias of a belief in divination which was strong enough to negate vital policy decisions, as when he fatally delayed the withdrawal of the ships from Syracuse because of an eclipse of the moon.[10] One cannot understand the problems of public administration of the time without taking into account the effects of such superstitions upon its participants.

THE CITY STATE OF PLATO AND ARISTOTLE

We now reach the age of outstanding writers, like Thucydides, Xenophon, Plato and Aristotle, who were particularly concerned with the affairs of the *polis,* or city, and were therefore the first to treat politics as an art and science. Plato was concerned more with the philosophical aspects, with the discovery of the ideal society designed to ensure the good life. In such works as the *Republic* and the *Laws,* in which he delineates successive versions of his utopia, there is a good deal that throws light upon the administrative mechanism which the great philosopher regarded as necessary for the implementation of his ideas, but it will surely be the *Politics* of Aristotle to which we shall turn to understand the actual practice of the age. The latter in his encyclopaedic survey of existing branches of knowledge was much more the exponent of the scientific approach. It should be remembered that these notable contributions were made during the fourth century B.C. after the defeat of Athens, and that both philosophers were concerned about the decline of the city and involved in the discovery of ways to eliminate the ills that beset the body politic.

In the *Republic* Plato was thinking in terms of the city state which was the practical ideal of every Greek politician. In devising the discipline for the governing class of the ideal state, which was to ensure its complete dedication to the public interest, Plato was much influenced by the Spartan system. Leadership was to rest in the hands of philosopher-kings, citizenship was to be divided into classes resting securely on the inherent abilities of the individual, and children were to be educated — we should say 'indoctrinated' today — so as to develop effectively within the sphere to which they had been called. The idea of leadership by a group of dedicated Guardians, who have been specially selected and educated for their high mission, has appeared again and again in history, though the fulfilment of such an ideal has never come within a mile of achievement. Administrators have never been so blessed as to receive their policy-directions from such ideal leaders!

In the *Laws* the realities of life seem to have had their effect upon Plato and his ideal state is now rather closer to earth. His philosopher-kings, originally conceived in the plural, are now changed into a philosopher-king in the singular. Plato had obviously been influenced by the failure of his personal missions to Syracuse to persuade the tyrant Dionysius to adopt the principles of the *Republic,* and his new scheme attempts to combine the virtues of monarchy and democracy in a mixed polity. There is less communism in his revised system, but the state is still concerned with almost everything, except that foreign trade, which is a despised occupation, is to be left to the aliens who always formed an important non-citizen class in Greek cities. The Assembly of all citizens was to be replaced by a Council of 360, elected from four different property classes, a provision which, as Spender remarks,[11] is a deviation from direct democracy towards representative institutions. In the selection of the higher executive age was important and a continuing educational discipline was necessary to fit the citizen to undertake high responsibilities. Thus the Nocturnal Council, which was to be the ultimate guardian of the constitution, was to consist of old men, as was also the council in charge of the arts. To introduce the new institutions and choose the first executives a special council was to be established, and thus the constituent assembly appeared on the political stage.

Although progressive development to meet inevitable change was not an idea that commended itself to the Greek mind, Plato did not bar the possibility that there might exist in other lands practices from which Athens might profit, and the Nocturnal Council was to have power to send missions abroad to inquire into the methods of other states so that improvements could be embodied in existing institutions. Such research was even more acceptable to Aristotle who is reputed to have collected information about the constitutions of as many as 158 Greek states, although only his *Constitution of Athens* has survived. This came to light as recently as 1890 in a papyrus discovered in Egypt.[12]

The democratization of the Athenian Constitution continued. An interesting method of financing the additional payments and doles was introduced, when a special fund was set up under the management of its own minister to receive taxes from the wealthy. A property tax, levied on one fifth of the capital of each citizen inscribed on the register, was imposed and for its administration the citizens were divided into twenty *symmories*. Responsibility for payment of the tax to the Treasury was placed upon the richest citizens in each *symmory*. This system of joint responsibility was found to work more expeditiously in practice and with less friction than the normal method of collection by state officials. At about the same time the old Attic alphabet was replaced for official purposes by the improved Ionic alphabet.

The executive side of the government of the city rested with the Council of Five Hundred, through the *prytanies,* but these were responsible for general policy, specific administrative responsibilities being placed in the hands of magistrates, often grouped in boards representing the ten tribes. In the *Politics*[13] Aristotle classifies these magistrates and examines their functions. To begin with he excludes, as being in a special category, priests of public cults, heralds, persons concerned with the production of plays, and others elected to undertake embassies. Then he distinguishes three main types of official duties: namely the political, the economic, and the subordinate or menial. The duty of the magistrates was to deliberate, to decide and to issue instructions, and these seemed to cover the political group. As an example of the economic group he cited citizens elected to measure corn for distribution, but the description is vague and may have covered important officials below policy-making level. The third class included the public slaves.

Aristotle examined the way the executive functions of the state were distributed among the magistrates and concluded that the allocation could be made according either to the subject dealt with or to the persons served — an obvious pointer to the Haldane Committee over two thousand years later! [14] His practical scheme paid little attention to his second heading. The assignment of one subject to one authority was favoured, but Aristotle agreed that the size of the state made a difference and that in small states a single magistrate or board would necessarily deal with several subjects.

It is, however, in Aristotle's discussion of specific offices that we are given the most illuminating picture of the functions of Greek public administration.[15] Aristotle now divides the important offices into two levels. In the top level he includes:

   (i) Those who are concerned with general control of the whole range of public offices and responsible for convening and introducing matters to the Assembly.

(ii) The generals or commandants charged with the defence of the city, including the superintendence of the city gates and walls, and the inspection and drill of citizens; and

(iii) The financial officers who receive and audit the accounts of other offices, known variously as auditors, accountants, examiners or advocates of the fisc.

Of considerable interest to us are the six types of magistrate of the second level, which Aristotle characterizes as absolutely indispensible though not so important and indeed discusses before he turns to consider the top level posts.

(i) First, there was the *Agoranomos* charged with the care of the market place, and responsible for supervision of contracts and the maintenance of good order.

(ii) A second type, closely associated with the first, was the *Astynomos,* or City-superintendent, who exercised oversight of both public and private property in the city centre, the maintenance and care of derelict buildings and roads and similar matters, as well as superintendence of the boundaries, all with the object of preventing disputes. In a large city this function might be distributed among several departments, each responsible for specific duties.

(iii) The third type, almost a duplication of the second, were the *Agronomoi,* or Rural Inspectors (sometimes Forest Wardens) who performed similar duties outside the city.

(iv) The fourth type were the Receivers of Accounts, or Treasurers, who had the task of receiving and holding public revenues and disbursing moneys to the several departments.

(v) The fifth type was concerned with the registration of private contracts and court decisions, and dealt with indictments. These magistrates had various names, such as Public Recorder or Master, and again in larger cities the work might be departmentalized.

(vi) The sixth and last type, which follows from the foregoing, had to do with the execution of sentences on offenders, with the recovery of debts and the custody of prisoners. In view of the odium attaching to this office Aristotle held that it should be shared among representatives from the various courts, and that it was desirable that responsibility for inflicting penalties and for their enforcement should be disassociated.

These six types of magistrate surely constituted the executive management of the city state. Their task was to see that the day-to-day affairs of the city were conducted in good order.

Aristotle also mentioned a special class of office which had to do with the cult of the civic deities: priests, superintendents of sacrifices, guardians of shrines, stewards of religious property. Where it was the custom to conduct public sacrifices in the city's common hearth this office was not legally assigned to the priests but to an Archon, or King, for whom this was the chief remaining function.

Finally, Aristotle drew attention to certain offices more common in richer states or those concerned with good discipline: such as supervision of women, enforcement of obedience to the law, supervision of children, control of physical training, superintendence of athletic contests, of dramatic competitions and similar spectacles. He agreed that some of these, such as supervision of women and children, were out of place in a democracy: others, as we have seen, were assigned to selected wealthy citizens.

The Greek magistrate was not a specialist, since circulation of office was the rule, as well as tenure for short terms, usually a year. Offices were often assigned to a board, usually numbering ten on the tribal basis. Selection was usually by lot but, despite the belief that such choice depended upon the wisdom of the gods,[16] it is significant that it gradually became customary for certain offices with responsibilities of a high order to be the subject of election. Thus according to *The Constitution of Athens* the following magistrates were elected: Treasurer of the Military Chest, Disburser of the Theatrical Dole, Curator of Fountains, and the *Strategoi* or Military Commanders. Citizens chosen for Diplomatic Missions were also elected, for it was recognized then, as now, that personality, skill in speaking, and good social qualities were essential to the success of such missions. Selection by lot was obviously not sufficiently discriminating in this case! The field of selection depended upon whether the state was an oligarchy or a democracy, but even in the latter case much might depend upon the esteem in which the office was held or upon the burdens it imposed. Where services were voluntary it was still possible to draft a citizen if there were no offers, while some offices, as we have seen, depended very much upon the wealth of the holder and had to be confined to the wealthy.

A significant characteristic of the system was the way the magistrate's activities were subject to critical review at all stages.[17] At the outset it was his character and reputation, not his potential competence to carry out the duties of the post, that were under examination. After being chosen by lot or otherwise, the magistrate-elect came under scrutiny and had to prove at the *dokimasia,* as it was called, by the production of witnesses, such matters as his descent, the performance of past duties and military service, payment of taxes, family conduct and fulfilment of religious obligations. It was possible for a citizen to show cause before the court why the magistrate-elect should not be confirmed in his office. After passing the *dokimasia* the new magistrate had to take the oath of office. Even now impeachments by citizens could be taken before the Council. On relinquishing his post his conduct while in office and his accounts were subject to an elaborate scrutiny by a special board whose report had to go to the courts, either for specific charges to be laid or for discharge to be approved. Even in the latter case, the special board having given a clean bill, it was still possible for a citizen to bring charges and show why the discharge should not be granted. When we bear in mind the existence not only of this continuous system of public inquest but also the close supervision which the Council was able to exercise both directly and through the ruling *prytanies,* it is hardly surprising that the conduct of Greek administration has often been characterized as unenterprising.

The lack of expertness was often made up by the fact that the citizens as a whole were well-informed upon the conduct of affairs, since they participated at every turn throughout their adult lives, but there were two devices which helped to broaden the basis of experience available to particular posts. One was the widespread custom of operating collective responsibility through the board system, as we have already mentioned, and the other was the practice of appointing assessors to magistrates and other officials, whose function was to assist the office-holder and indeed to share responsibility, for they too were subject to scrutiny at the termination of their office. The magistrates were also assisted by public and personal slaves who no doubt often supplied scribal ability and a type of basic administrative expertise acquired by experience, the sort of assistance that administrators the world over need for the efficient performance of their duties.

During their period of office magistrates wielded considerable power and were entitled to legal immunities. In a system of government that places responsibility for administration directly in the hands of the citizenry there is much to admire, and when such a system allowed the repeated selection and dominance of such an outstanding leader as Pericles it had a good deal to commend it. Nevertheless there is some evidence to suggest that in the case of Greece theory was often better than practice, for there can be little doubt that the virtues of the system tended to be cancelled out by the constant apprehensions of all but the most courageous of magistrates that they could be called to account not merely for their administrative faults but for any wise action that was adversely received by a majority group in any of the councils. Moreover, a system of government in which policy was likely to be unstable through the influence in the *Ecclesia* of the brilliant rhetoric of popular but unstable politicians, was hardly calculated to draw forth initiative from administrators who had so much to lose from one false step. This point is admirably illustrated by Thucydides, reporting upon Nicia's predicament before Syracuse in 414 B.C.

'He had before sent [*to Athens*] frequent reports of events as they occurred, and felt it especially incumbent upon him to do so now, as he thought that they were in a critical position, and that unless speedily recalled or strongly reinforced from home, they had no hope of safety. He feared, however, that the messengers, either through inability to speak, or through failure of memory, or from a wish to please the multitude, might not report the truth, and so thought it best to write a letter, to insure that the Athenians should know his own opinion without its being lost in transmission, and be able to decide upon the real facts of the case. His emissaries accordingly departed with the letter and the requisite verbal instructions; and he attended to the affairs of the army, making it his aim to keep on the defensive and to avoid unnecessary danger.'[18]

ALEXANDER'S BRIEF EMPIRE

The political leagues founded by Athens, ostensibly for defence purposes, had been short-lived, and ideas of a Greek union were not popular, but it was at last dawning upon some Greeks that the city state was becoming an inadequate form of government to cope with the political situation of the fourth century B.C. Isocrates (436-338), for example, dreamed of a United Greece, marching shoulder to shoulder against the might of Persia, although his idealism seemed to be rooted in visions of a past Golden Age rather than in any progressive idea of a better future.

It was away to the north, in Macedonia, a land of the outsider to the Athenian, that the one short-lived Greek attempt at imperial domination was destined to be born, a brilliant last throw that marked the final breakdown of Greek democracy. This is not the place to recount the well-known story of Philip II of

Macedonia, who conceived the grand design but was murdered by an obscure assassin just at the moment when he was ready to march eastwards. But his son Alexander had been well tutored both by Aristotle and by his father. He astutely ensured his election by the Confederacy of Corinth as General of Greeks and, having secured his rear, in 334 B.C., he set off upon his unprecedented career of conquest. Within ten years Asia Minor, Syria and Egypt, Babylon, Persia and large parts of Central Asia and India were subject to his rule.

Altogether this spectacular rise of one man to world dominance was very much a *tour de force,* depending not only upon the genius of Alexander's leadership (supported, be it remembered, by his father's far-sighted preparations) but also upon the chronic weakness of the Persian realm and of the oriental system of government generally, a weakness already demonstrated in 401 B.C., to all who could read the signs, by the epic march of the Ten Thousand under Cyrus, as recounted by Xenophon in his *Anabasis.* Apart from his undoubted military genius and his personal valour, often so foolhardy as to demand an almost unbelievable run of good fortune, Alexander must have had a genius for organization. There is room for fruitful research here. His vast dynamic campaign obviously called for organizational gifts of a high order. He was wise in leaving the rulership of the conquered territories in the hands of native governors whom he could rely upon. In Egypt, for example, he took upon himself the mantle of the Son of Ammon in order to establish his legitimacy in the line of the Pharaohs, and at Memphis he reorganized the government of the country, placing it in the hands of two native *Nomarchs,* but at the same time confiding the adjoining provinces of Arabia and Libya to Greek governors, who could keep an eye upon their Egyptian neighbours. He divided the military command in Egypt among several generals and appointed a special minister, Cleomenes of Naucratis, to take control of all finances. A notable act was the foundation of Alexandria at a strategic point in the Nile Delta.

Alexander's vast realm lacked an enduring *raison d'être.* No sooner had some ordinary illness struck down the conqueror at the early age of thirty-three than his lieutenants, amidst unprecedented controversies, set about carving up his realm into a series of successor states. Alexander had even failed to secure the succession to the throne. No doubt he had thought there was still plenty of time! His Empire dissolved even more quickly than it had arisen. Only in Egypt was the system to continue, for there Alexander's commander, Ptolomy, through controlling the

Mediterranean by means of his fleet based upon Alexandria, was able to found a dynasty modelled not upon Greek practices but upon the well-rooted methods of the Pharoahs which we have already examined.

THE HELLENISTIC AGE

During the next three hundred years Greek ideas flourished in Egypt, the Middle East and far into Asia, under the impact of an impressive inflowing of Greek colonists. Homeland Greece, however, was in decline and efforts to attain greater unity by the formation of leagues of cities were destined to achieve only limited success. Chief amongst these attempts at greater unity were the Achaean and the Aetolian Leagues operating on either side of the Corinthian Gulf. Each League elected annually a General to command its combined army and there were other officials to attend to defence and foreign relations, but the individual states continued to be responsible for their own affairs and for the collection of taxes. The Achaean League appears to have approximated most closely to a modern federation.[19] Its General was furnished with a Cabinet of ten ministers, elected at the same time, and there was a Secretary of State, an Under-General and a General of Cavalry. The relationship between General and Cabinet is not clear, but no doubt city representation exercised a good deal of influence. Unfortunately these two leagues remained hostile to one another and both Athens and Sparta remained outside.

Throughout the Hellenistic world the city state continued as the normal local government unit within the mainly despotic kingdom which extended over the area. Despite the wide range in size and wealth these city states were remarkably alike in appearance and operation. This was an era of great artistic flowering and the cities became storehouses of culture. One effect of this was to extend the range of services for which the city was responsible: such matters as education and food-control were actively undertaken. Although democratic forms were generally maintained, by the election of magistrates, actual power tended to fall into the hands of the wealthy whose resources were needed for the effective provision of public services.

Little is known about the arrangements for the fulfilment of the first duty of government, the maintenance of law and order.[20] There is certainly reference to a Commander of the Night Watch in Ptolemaic Alexandria and there were frontier guards whose functions included the arrest of runaway slaves, but no doubt the military commander was generally responsible. Separate police forces were to appear in the Roman period.

General municipal services, such as the care of roads and bridges, seem to have been assigned to a special board of town controllers, but information about such services has usually to be deduced from later developments which were better recorded. Massive building programmes covered the construction of colonnaded streets and markets, of great ceremonial buildings and impressive aqueducts, as well as the essential administrative offices of the magistrates and boards. Construction of such edifices rested mainly upon the voluntary contributions of rich citizens, under the direction of special commissioners appointed on an *ad hoc* basis. These commissioners were expected to fulfil such technical tasks as quantity surveying and to submit detailed accounts of expenditures. The repair and servicing constantly needed were probably the concern of the town controllers. In some cities an official architect was employed to advise on public buildings.

Cities began to appoint commissioners to deal with the distribution of imported grain. This was to grow into an important municipal service in Roman times, as we shall see. Some cities maintained salaried public doctors to give medical attention to citizens, either for a fee or freely where the citizen could not afford to pay. They also acted as police doctors to certify the cause of death. Provision and management of the public baths was always a heavy item in the cities' budget, for these required plentiful supplies of water and the services of bath-attendants and stokers, usually public slaves. Here again fees were charged but these were moderate, usually covering only part of the cost.

Thus social services were coming increasingly within the scope of these cities. Education particularly began to figure among their functions. Before the fourth century education had been left largely to private effort. State participation often began with the setting up of a gymnasium centre, about which other activities gathered. The centres were controlled by *Gymnasiarchs,* who were responsible for the upkeep of the fabric and again might contribute out of their own pockets. They often took over responsibility for other public duties, such as the running of the public baths and the management of the public slaves. The *Gymnasiarch* sometimes also saw to the supply of oil, which was a very costly business, calling upon others to share the expense. Gradually magistrates were appointed to look after the education service, although actual instruction might still be left to private enterprise. Such arrangements varied widely. 'At Miletus there were to be four schoolmasters and four athletic trainers, who were elected annually by the people and paid forty and thirty drachmae a month respectively.'[21]

Greek city finance had ever been a haphazard affair, and there was little improvement in the period now under review: radical changes were to come later. For example, there was little idea of a formal budget and the departmental accounts were so numerous and complicated that expert knowledge was required for their understanding. Usually the Council was responsible for supervision but was much too large to exercise effective control. This was usually delegated to Treasurer-magistrates of low standing, who made payments, kept the books and had the custody of the monies. In some cities elected bankers were made responsible for the latter duty. The accounts were audited by magisterial boards, who usually reported to the Council. Large sums of money could be involved in running the city: on such items as wages for a considerable body of menial employees, prize money and pensions for public games, heavy expenses to maintain in appropriate style envoys to the Emperor or Governor or on other missions, the cost of litigation to which the cities were much addicted, as well as the general running and upkeep of the city and services already mentioned.

The pattern of public service was not therefore much altered during the Hellenistic period. Elected magistrates continued to be responsible for political administration and for the major technical tasks, although with the extension of services the specialist technician was now beginning to appear. At the same time the number of subordinate and menial officials was increasing. The amateur element remained important but the professional sectors were extending. More and more records were needed and it was becoming the practice to appoint a secretary or clerk to assist the higher magistrate or board. The secretary might in his turn be assisted by a band of permanent employees and public slaves. Council minutes, copies of decrees and treaties and other documents had to be kept in the city archives. Publication was arranged by posting notices temporarily with chalk on a wooden notice-board or convenient wall, and by incising others more permanently in stone. Papyrus was now available from Egypt. State libraries began to appear in Greece. The first recorded under a Greek government was formed shortly before 350 B.C. at Heracleia on the Black Sea. But it was at Alexandria, under the Ptolomies, that the most magnificent library was assembled and a centre established where accurate copies of famous works could be obtained. The accumulation of large collections of manuscripts called for a new art of librarianship, which comprised the care, classification and indexing of books. in addition to the official archives the Hellenistic cities maintained a registry of private documents covering important transactions of various types. It is said that in some cities births, adoptions and marriages were thus recorded. Taken all round their administrative ideas were well in advance of most ages before the present.

THE CITY STATE OF ROME

While all these things were happening in Greater Greece the stage was being set on a geographically suitable site on the Mediterranean shore for the birth of a great world power and the shifting of the centre of political gravity westwards. In the middle of Italy, already the focus of Etruscan power and of a number of coastal colonies of the Greeks which dated back as far as 1000 B.C., a collection of Latin village communities coalesced, no doubt for defence purposes, into the first city of Rome. This event appears to have occurred somewhere in the latter half of the seventh century B.C.

The city was under a king, an office already well established in the neighbouring cities of Etruria and Latium. It was a free community of artizans with a limited slave element, but political leadership was firmly held by a group of aristocratic families who formed a distinct patrician class. The division of the citizens between patricians and plebeians (plebs) was already fore-shadowed. The state religion, based upon a multiplicity of cults, was politically important, since *auspicia* had to be taken before certain acts of state could be embarked upon and the interpretation of the signs was left to a board of expert *augures*. We must include these among the first Roman officials. The family was the basic unit, the *paterfamilias* exercising autocratic legal power within his miniature realm. It is not surprising therefore that public administration was based upon tribal units as in the case of Greek and other contemporary communities. The main governmental purpose of the tribes was the levying of soldiers and money under the orders of the king, by the *tribuni*, or tribal, officials. Originally there were three tribes, divided into thirty territorial *curiae,* whose chief function was the admission of their members to the citizen body. The joint meeting of these groups in *Comitia Curiata* constituted the first Roman popular assembly, whose main task was to ratify the choice of a new king and to certify their allegiance to him in a *lex curiata de imperio.* They could be called together by the king at other times, but were merely an assenting body without even the power of discussion. A more effective influence rested with the Council of Elders, or *Senatus,* drawn from the leading patrician families, but even this important body was only advisory, although its collective opinion carried great authority. However, at the death of a king the power passed back into the hands of the Senate, who then appointed an *Interrex* to aid in the appointment of the next king. Thus the king had unlimited power, but his office was not hereditary. He was executive head of the state, with special religious functions, which he delegated to officials selected by him from among the patricians. First among these, empowered to conduct the more important ceremonies, were the *flamines,* who were assisted by six maidens, the Vestal Virgins, to tend the fires of Vesta. Interpretation of the sacred law was delegated to a college of five *pontifices* and of the omens to the board of three *augures,* already mentioned. The king was responsible for foreign relations, the making of treaties, and the waging of war: as war leader he took the field as *imperator.* He was little concerned with civil law, which rested with the *paterfamilias,* but the penal law was within his province and he appointed special judges for the purpose. The system of public administration did not yet call for heavy finances and most of the expenses were met out of the king's personal estate, from customs dues, from licences for the salt monopoly, and from fines. Any surplus funds were kept in the strong room, or *aerarium,* of the Temple of Saturn, the keys of which were held by *quaestores paricidii.* This strong kingship steadily lost popularity, fell for a time into the hands of a line of Etruscan rulers, and was eventually superseded by a republican system, according to Roman tradition, in 509 B.C.

The changes were modest enough, for it was always the Roman way to retain old institutions wherever possible. The royal powers were transferred to two magistrates, or *praetors,* who were later to be known as *consuls.* They held joint office for one year and each had unlimited power to veto the other. The Senate continued as an advisory body, but the constant changing of the chief magistrates meant that the main power rested in its hands. The powers of the *Comitia Curiata* remained as before, but its approval was sought more frequently, for the ultimate sovereignty of the people was accepted in theory, if it as yet meant little in practice. The consuls were entitled to regal ceremonial and were accompanied by twelve *lictors,* who bore the *fasces* (i.e. bundles of rods and axes representing authority and unity), which had already been used by the Etruscans as a sign of the king's *imperium*. The religious powers of the king were now exercised by the *Pontifex Maximus*.

The exclusion of the plebs from office and the worsening economic conditions under the early Republic were the basic causes of the struggle between the orders which led to the separate organization of the plebs, who set up *Tribuni Plebis* to act as spokesman and represent their grievances to the consuls or Senate. Their corporate power to withhold their labour or obstruct military enrolment often proved sufficient to obtain redress.

In 451 B.C. the law was codified on the Twelve Tables, as a result of pressure from the plebs who saw in a written code a safeguard against the arbitrary penalties of patrician magistrates who had hitherto based their interpretations on the customary, or common, law. To undertake the revision the patricians had appointed a Commission of Ten, who had sent missions abroad to obtain information and guidance from Greek cities in Southern Italy and in Greece. The new code, which was not intended to make additions to the existing law and was scanty enough, was destined to remain in operation to the end of Roman history. It certainly guaranteed the plebs against arbitrary judicial sentences and secured for them a final appeal to the popular assembly, but the plebs were not satisfied. They reacted by seceding to the Aventine Hill where they set up a sort of state-within-the-state, under a new assembly, based upon the tribes, known as *Concilium Plebis Tributum*. As executives they appointed two *aediles* and ten *tribunes* whose duty it was to convene the new assembly whenever they considered it necessary. The plebeian body placed their own magistrates under the protection of Ceres, thus pledging themselves to resist, by force if necessary, their arrest or intimidation by patrician magistrates. The *aediles* had a general disciplinary jurisdiction over the plebs and were responsible for the custody of the archives in the temple of Ceres. Fines imposed by them could be used for an occasional distribution of grain or towards public works in the plebeian quarter of the Aventine. The tribunes represented the plebs before the consuls and the Senate, and protected individuals against the harsh exercise of magisterial power. The patricians neither acquiesced nor opposed the new institutions, but by their sheer will and the creation of precedent in the usual Roman manner these institutions gradually established themselves and exercised a general power of veto on behalf of the people. The mere possibility of such a separate system of administration functioning within the city state affords conspicuous evidence of the flexibility of Roman institutions, and of the peculiar distribution of power to separate foci with overlapping spheres within the wider fabric, by which they were characterized.

At about the same time the patricians carried out an extensive reorganization of the army, which led to the setting up of still another general assembly. The basis of the new organization was the company of one hundred men, or *centura*. Preparation of the new register was given to a college of *Censors* which came to be renewed about every five years. The inspection parade on the Campus Martius, in which the citizens were mustered by centuries, came to be known as *Comitia Centuriata*. It developed into a third political assembly and, subject of course to the approval of the Senate, received the duty of appointing its censors, as well as the consuls, who led its members in battle. After a time membership of *Comitia Centuriata* ceased to be confined to those on the censors' roll, for *seniores* who had passed the customary military age became entitled to form separate centuries and to continue in membership.

During the fourth century, when Roman expansion in Italy was well under way, further important developments in their republican constitution took place. The *Comitia Curiata* had declined in importance and was now overshadowed by the other popular assemblies. The *Comitia Centuriata* acquired legislatory and important judicial functions, and was reorganized to represent all citizens. The *Concilium Plebis,* appointed by the plebs, was to all intents and purposes duplicated by a *Comitia Tributa,* constituted in 366 B.C. by the patricians on a similar tribal basis with the task of electing the quaestors and two newly introduced magistrates, known as the *curule aediles.* This new council also acquired legislatory powers. Gradually the *Concilium Plebis* received recognition and its legislatory powers were accepted as binding upon the whole community. Although these two tribal assemblies continued to exist as separate legal entities their membership and powers were so similar that they virtually constituted one democratic body which effectively represented plebeian interests. Despite these democratic advances patrician ascendency was maintained in the Senate, which retained important powers of initiation and extended its administrative capacity. One important new responsibility, which it assumed during this period, was the *prorogatio,* or power to extend the office of a serving magistrate, where there was some good reason to do so: for example, of a commander engaged upon a campaign.

Important administrative developments had already been taking place. As we have seen, under the impact of the struggle of the orders and the expanding needs of the state, republican Rome's unique system of magistrates had emerged. The two Consuls, as joint heads of state, stood at the top, with power to overrule any other magistrate except a Tribune. At an early stage two *Quaestors* had been appointed to assist them in their day-to-day administration. Gradually the number of *Quaestors* increased but they remained the least important of the magistrates. They specialized in financial administration. Two *Censors* were introduced to assess the citizens' tax, on the basis of the census, which it was their job to hold: they also chose new members of the Senate. Next came the *Praetors* who had the important office of relieving the Consuls of their legal business and of presiding over the law courts. The *Censors* and *Praetors* shared power with the Consuls and in some ways were almost as important. Less important were the *Aediles* whose job was to supervise the affairs of the city and to arrange public festivals and shows. At the outset all magistracies were held by patricians, but gradually plebeians became eligible and one of the impulses to create new offices was the Senate's desire at each stage to maintain privileged positions for the patricians. The two special patrician *cerule aediles,* already mentioned, were an example of this, but it soon became the practice to assign one to each class. Nevertheless, the patricians continued to dominate if not to monopolize the magistracies. A regular *cursus honorum* developed, by which an aspiring politician gradually rose rank by rank from quaestorship upwards, though the censorship was usually reserved for one of consular rank.

The plebs certainly had their preserve in the Tribunate. These ten Tribunes of the people were not strictly magistrates, and they have sometimes been called 'counter-magistrates' because of their power, in order to protect the rights of citizens, to exercise a veto on the executive and to hold up almost any public business. A Tribune could even veto the acts of one of his colleagues! The Tribunes were so distributed throughout the city that any citizen should have easy access to one of them in case of trouble.

The work of these magistrates was partly political and partly administrative. Tenure of office was normally for a year, although re-election was possible and a gradual acquisition of administrative experience was facilitated both by such extensions and by the successive holding of different offices. As at the outset public administration was not a very complicated business, little expert assistance was needed. The magistrates would normally be aided by members of their own household and by craftsmen

from among the plebs. But gradually a permanent lower service
was built up although there is little information on it during the
republican period. It is known that there was a professional
scribal class attached to the several offices, whose members
through long service could attain a high level of competence,
and were undoubtedly able to exercise considerable influence
upon some of their short-term masters.

Looking at this strange conglomeration of dispersed powers,
with numerous divisions and overlaps, checks and balances, one
cannot help wondering how it could have worked. But in the
empirical spirit in which it was built it did indeed work, as
history shows. Despite their internal controversies, the Romans,
unlike the Greeks, were able to evolve harmonious government
and, when necessary, to close their ranks against the enemy from
without. The atomized system of administration and the primitive
methods available, especially in matters of finance, were still
adequate for the comparatively simple needs of the city state.
Here the Senate certainly made an important contribution by
supplying a measure of administrative co-ordination lacking in
the general structure of magistracies. By arranging the spheres
of competence of particular magistracies, or by prescribing their
duties at the beginning of their term of office, or even by supporting one magistrate against another in case of deadlock, the
Senate were competent and indeed usually willing to act as
general co-ordinator of the public services. The practice of
nominating magistrates to vacancies in the Senate undoubtedly
provided that august assembly with a reservoir of political and
administrative talent, while the procedure whereby discussions
were conducted in strict order, according to rank, ensured that
the more conservative views should normally prevail, for usually
the general opinion of the chamber had been made clear and the
question had been put before the turn of the more junior grades
had been reached!

ROME EXPANDS

During all this time the military sway of Rome had been
expanding: by 338 B.C. she was supreme in Latium, by 272 B.C.
her power extended throughout Italy and her first struggle with
Carthage was imminent. This expansion of the territories of the
city state to nation-wide extent was unique in this area. It
depended partly upon Rome's favourable geographical situation
in the very centre of the Italian peninsula, partly upon her
military prowess and efficient organization, but neither of these

essential factors would have taken her far without the statecraft that enabled her to obtain and retain the support of other Italian cities and to devise political links with more distant communities. The armies, technically competent in battle and continuously ready to accept new ideas, were commanded by generals who carried the *imperium* of Rome which enabled them to exact obedience in the field through the operation of an accepted code of military law. Moreover they had access to administrative means that assisted them in the consolidation of their gains. Communications were assured by the construction of a system of trunk roads continually extending outwards from the city: army camps were constructed at suitable points on a well-conceived defensive pattern; and *coloniae* of Roman and Italian settlers were planted at strategic points with a dual military and economic purpose. Prestige, fair-dealing, and the offer of economic gain through land settlement combined to ensure the allegiance of their neighbours.

The new territories were linked to the parent city in various ways. Everything depended upon their particular situation and stage of development. Some were annexed, particularly those with an affinity in language and culture whose lands were nearer the capital, and they were given the full franchise which meant the right of representation in the assemblies and to hold magistracies, and the obligation to serve in the army and to pay taxes. The more distant Latins were given only a limited franchise, while the non-Italian communities, as *socii,* were bound to Rome by separate treaties drawn up for each specific case.

To ensure enforcement of the state's financial requirements in the annexed territories *quaestors Italici* were appointed and stationed in the district. The praetor appointed *praefecti,* or deputy-judges, to go on circuit. In other words the metropolitan constitution was merely expanded to cover the widening realm, but the existing local government or locally appointed magistrates continued to function and the Roman agents were concerned mainly with supervision. The *socii* had to supply military aid when required and to meet other obligations as specified in their treaty, but they were not subjected to taxation or the supervision of Roman officials. In other words they were closely bound dependent allies who gained from falling under the umbrella of Rome's military might and shared the fruits of her victories, but could be made to suffer grievously through the exercise of that power in case of disloyalty. For the time being extension of the franchise was limited by the material facts of the age and there was no thought of extending the range of the central government by introducing confederal institutions. Rome's empirical approach to the changing world around her ensured a highly flexible attitude in moulding existing institutions to new political and social needs and it was clear to the ruling destinies, if not to contemporary mortals, that a wonderful new age of government and administration was already in its chrysalis stage.

PUBLIC ADMINISTRATION IN THE CITY STATE

The political and administrative activities of government are not easily differentiated in the city state. The kings had their servants: there were tribal officials and officials who had sacred duties, but the characteristic official who later replaced the king was the magistrate, whose powers were a mixture of the executive, administrative and judicial. However important his post the magistrate was a short-term official, essentially an amateur. Public administration was a duty of citizenship which circulated among the citizenry, although there could be restrictions on this where there were definite class barriers as in Republican Rome.

The techniques of administration were uncomplicated, although the introduction of alphabets and writing and the widespread use of papyrus which characterized this period, considerably facilitated the making of records and the transmission of messages. Apart from the massive administrative centre at Knossos the office of the magistrate, or board of magistrates, was usually elementary, although the number of subordinates tended to increase. In the Greek city, for example, the several boards had their meeting place where the magistrates deliberated and dined, to which might be attached officials under a sort of secretary or *grammaticus* who also might have magisterial rank.

Not only did the public service depend upon the devotion to duty of the citizen, who was supposed to know all about the business of the state, but also the system of finance, still in a very primitive state, depended largely upon personal contributions by the wealthy.

Yet below the magistrates there were numerous minor posts and menial offices which often had a more permanent status — policeman, town-criers, clerks and workmen of various types. Many of these offices were held by private or public slaves. At these lower levels the beginnings of a professional service can be more clearly discerned. Latterly, with the advent of the specialist notably in the Hellenistic states, the amateur status of the higher officials came to be modified.

The functions of public administration were simple enough,

being concerned with the security and good conduct of the city, and the normal housekeeping activities necessary to ensure good government. Here too the trends were in the direction of greater complexity: constructional works at an early stage became important, calling upon considerable architectural and engineering skills and of course generous finances, while in the Hellenistic phase social services were beginning to reach quite an advanced stage of development: education, food centres, baths, and health services.

Of the lives of officials and the way they conducted their offices little has been placed on record. In view of the fact that every citizen at one time or another was expected to participate it would be justifiable to select almost any historical character of the period and present him as the normal administrator. Pericles and Alexander have thus been mentioned in the text. Among Pericles's colleagues not the least notable was the poet Sophocles who acted as Treasurer of the League during 443-442 B.C. Significantly, an another occasion Sophocles, as elected General, sailed with Pericles to suppress a revolt of a member of the League.

Among the early Greeks there is a reference, on a tablet found at Pylos, to a certain Axotas, who was inspecting crops in five areas and was probably a palace official.[22] Among the scribal class in early Rome we know only of Gnaeus Flavius, scibe of the Aediles, who wrote about the civil law and the calendar and who himself graduated to the Aedileship in 304 B.C.[23]

From the Hellenistic period more records have survived of distinguished officials. There was, for example, late in the fourth century, Apellis, clerk of the City of Priene, a post to which he was re-elected for twenty years, during fourteen of which he held concurrently clerkships to the generals and the guardians of the law. The city clerkship was still of modest stature, but as time went on growing dependence of the magistrates on their clerk was bound to increase his importance. It would be interesting to know what manner of man was this Apellis! Does his constant re-election indicate that he was a sort of Samuel Pepys of his age? Another official of the same city has left his name on record for a different reason. This was Zozimus, a wealthy citizen, who, among other offices, took his turn as clerk of the city. To show his mettle he decided to keep all his records in duplicate, the ordinary copy being on papyrus and the second on the much more expensive parchment!

The public administrator of the age had his problems. His tasks may have been mundane and usually uncomplicated, but he was required to watch his step. Under most of the systems mentioned there was some form of censorate to keep a check upon the activities of the magistrate, who thus had every inducement to play safe. Nor could he always tie his decision to logic or common sense, for the conduct of public business, both in Greece and in Rome, was subject to divination and there were days on which the most urgent administrative steps could not be taken.

REFERENCES

1 G. & C. Charles-Picard, *Daily Life in Carthage,* (Allen and Unwin, 1961), and B. H. Warmington, *Carthage,* (Robert Hale, 1960).
2 Warmington, *op. cit.,* (Penguin edn.), pp. 144-5.
3 John Chadwick, articles on 'The Earliest Greeks' in *Manchester Guardian,* June, 1954.
4 Michael Ventris and John Chadwick, *Documents in Mycenaean Greek,* (Cambridge, 1965), p. 117.
5 J. B. Bury, *A History of Greece,* (Macmillan, 2nd edn., 1913), p. 19.
6 M. Pallottino, *The Etruscans,* (Penguin, 1955) and Raymond Bloch, *The Etruscans,* (Thames & Hudson, 1958).
7 See, for example, G. Glotz, *La Cité Grecque* in 'L'Evolution de l'Humanite' series, (La Renaissance du Livre, Paris, 1928), pp. 7-8 and 39-69.
8 Bury, *op. cit.,* p. 122.
9 Thucydides, *Peloponnesian War,* (Dent's Everyman Edn.).
10 Thucydides, *op. cit.,* Book VII, Chapter XXII.
11 J. A. Spender, *The Government of Mankind,* (Cassell, 1938), p. 91.
12 Ernest Barker's translation of *The Politics of Aristotle,* (Oxford, 1946), pp. 386 and 377-84.
13 Aristotle, *op. cit.,* Chapter XV.
14 *Report of the Machinery of Government Committee,* Cd. 9230, (H. M. Stationery Office, 1918), p. 7.
15 Aristotle, *op. cit.,* Book VI, Chapter VIII.
16 The argument of Fustel de Coulanges in his *La Cité Antique,* (Paris, 1876), that the appointment of magistrates by *sortition* (lot) was religious in origin is now discounted: see Hignett, *A History of the Athenian Constitution to the end of the Fifth Century, B.C.,* (Oxford, 1952), p. 228.
17 See, for example, R. J. Bonner, *Aspects of Athenian Democracy,* Berkeley, 1933).
18 Thucydides, *op. cit.,* Book VII, Chapter XXI.
19 E. A. Freeman, *History of Federal Government in Greece and Italy,* (Macmillan, 1893), p. 221.
20 A. H. H. Jones, *The Greek City,* (Oxford, 1940), pp. 211-12.
21 Jones, *op. cit.,* p. 222.
22 T. B. L. Webster, *From Mycenae to Homer,* (Methuen, 1958).
23 A. H. M. Jones, *Studies in Roman Government,* (Blackwell, 1960), p. 153.

CHAPTER 4

IMPERIAL ROME : 146 B.C. to A.D. 330

There was no room for both Rome and Carthage in the Mediterranean, and the first settlement of accounts had taken place in the middle of the third century B.C., much to Rome's advantage. With the defeat of Carthage in the Second Punic War at the end of the century, after the inspired military genius of Hannibal had all but succeeded in subduing the lion in his own den, Republican Rome can be said to have reached its most effective period. The extended constitution, unwritten and flexible, was still providing efficient government for an ever-expanding realm. The Senate, at the apex of power and staffed with the state's elite, was still capable of ensuring good administration. But movements were in process that would shortly make radical changes necessary in the management of the city state, if the decline that had overtaken previous imperialist experiments was not also to be Rome's fate.

The order of knights, or *Equites,* who figured below the Senatorial order, had grown out of a military class whose wealth entitled them to bring a horse to the wars. Unlike the members of the Senatorial class to whom business was anathema, the new middle-class Equestrian order throve with the increasing wealth derived from wartime trading and a new power was thus being created which was to prove no friend of the democracy. In the countryside the smaller holdings of the peasants were being absorbed into large-scale farms and orchards, or *latifundia,* run mainly by slave labour. There was increasing unrest. Rome's relations with the provinces began to decline, while in Rome itself mob-rule began to shake the integrity of the magistrates. Already the ancient Etruscan custom of staging gladiatorial combats between condemned criminals or slaves had been reintroduced and the people of the city were taking great delight in these bloody and degrading spectacles. The leaders, by embarking on a policy of providing *panem at circensem* were discovering a new way of obtaining the political support they required. Free issues of grain to the mob paved the way to political power, while the appetite for grand shows led to the construction, not only in Rome but throughout the provinces, of massive amphitheatres and extensive circuses whose ruined splendour even today stands witness to both the might and depravity of Rome's historical contribution.

Despite these stresses and strains, the state had been so well founded and Rome's military prowess was still so outstanding that during the second century a new phase of expansion ensued. Rome was drawn into conflict with the Greek states, still at loggerheads among themselves, and by 146 B.C., with the barbarous sacking of Corinth, she emerged victorious. Yet such was the magic of Greece's name that the Romans left the Greeks with a high measure of autonomy, even refraining from appointing a Roman governor and from reducing the country to provincial status. Instead, the proconsul of the neighbouring province of Macedonia was given responsibility for supervision and peace-keeping, while some of the cities, including Athens, continued as 'allies of the Roman people' and retained their city institutions.[1] At about the same time, worried by the commercial success of Carthage, which continued to flourish despite the great burdens imposed by her previous defeats, and urged forward by the ceaseless propaganda of Cato, the Censor and great advocate of public service reform, who relentlessly punctuated his public speeches with the phrase *Carthago delenda est,* Rome at last decided to administer the *coup de grace* to her age-old enemy. The Carthaginian capital was razed to the ground, but such was the importance of its situation that it was later replaced by a Roman prototype. During this highly successful military phase Roman domination of the Mediterranean was almost complete.

END OF THE REPUBLIC

Despite the continuing success of her armies Rome seemed to be losing her administrative grip. At home there was widespread distress which culminated in slave risings. The diffusion of power among numerous magistrates and several assemblies rendered such comprehensive solutions as were needed to meet the situation difficult to achieve. Indeed the concentration of power required to cope with the new political, economic and social problems was so incompatible with current governmental philosophies as to inhibit any clear-cut solution from commending itself. New political and administrative means had to be worked out by a process of trial and error, and it speaks well for the Roman genius that practical solutions were to emerge before a total breakdown intervened to undo centuries of effort and to deprive the world of such an experience of unity as mankind was not again to enjoy even to the present day.

As we have already seen, the Roman system permitted the concentration of *imperium* for limited periods and, reflecting to some extent the age of the tyrants in Greece, a line of Roman dictators emerged. First the Gracchi brothers, Tiberius Sempronius Gracchus (163-133 B.C.) and Gaius Sempronius Gracchus (153-121 B.C.), acting successively as tribune, tried to introduce modest home reforms and were eliminated for their pains. Then Gaius Marius (157-86 B.C.), raised to ruthless power through success in war, was equally unsuccessful on the civil side. He too was replaced, by Lucius Cornelius Sulla (138-78 B.C.), even more ruthless with his enemies. Sulla seized the power, curbed the tribunate and restored the ascendency of the Senate, but despite an undoubted flair for dealing with immediate practical difficulties he seems to have lacked the imagination required to introduce such safeguards as would save the state from future adventurers. He took steps in the direction of royalty by introducing a personal bodyguard and having his name and effigy inscribed upon the coinage, a break from tradition. But disappointed at the outcome of his efforts, in 97 B.C., he took the extraordinary step of relinquishing his dictatorship and retiring to his estates, where he died naturally the following year.

During a period of wars conducted under the leadership of Lucullus, Pompey and Crassus, [Lucius Licinius Lucullus (110-57 B.C.), Gnaeus Pompeius (106-48 B.C.) and Marcus Licinius Crassus (115-53 B.C.)], Pompey rose to the highest fame and popularity. With the aid of his army and the support of Crassus he compelled the Senate to concede the consulship, for which he was not personally eligible, and both he and Crassus were elected by the Assembly in 70 B.C. Pompey was now in a position to pursue his policy of weakening the power of the Senate and of reviving the Tribunate. Undoubtedly he could have grasped the supreme power had he been so minded.

Amidst subsequent plots and counterplots a certain Gaius Julius Caesar (102-44 B.C.) was achieving military glory in the provinces. So far, apart from thus demonstrating outstanding military ability, Caesar had been profligate and burdened himself with debt. But with his election in 63 B.C. successively to the posts of Pontifex Maximus and praetor all this was to be changed. Four years later he achieved his first consulship, sharing the office with Pompey and Crassus, and thus the First Triumvirate came into being. He soon showed his hand by using military power to compel the Senate to legislate upon essential reforms at home and in the provinces. While Caesar was building up his military reputation abroad, including his successful campaigns in

Gaul and Britain, Pompey, left to deal with anarchy in Rome, found himself in a favourable position to grasp power. Crassus had already been overwhelmed by a Parthian force at Carrhae in 53 B.C., and the struggle between Pompey and Caesar, which had been going on behind the scenes, now came out into the open. Despite the support of the Senate, which declared Caesar a public enemy and gave Pompey command of the Republic's troops, Caesar, who stood poised upon the banks of the Rubicon, the small stream dividing his province from Republican territory, decided to invade the homeland. His success in the far-flung military campaigns that followed ensured his supremacy. Unlike his dictatorial predecessors Caesar showed great clemency to his defeated enemies, a policy which certainly paid off, at least in the short term.

Despite numerous upheavals and the recent attempts at reform, the structure of Roman government had not changed much during the last two centuries. The popular assemblies remained to exercise the sovereign powers of the citizenry: the elected magistrates continued very much as before to manage the essential business of the state, while at the same time checking and counter-checking one another's activities: and the Senate, although nominally an advisory body, continued, in virtue of its powerful membership, to exercise the greatest influence, except during temporary periods of dictatorship. Its powers still depended largely upon the prestige of its experienced ex-magistrate members and the nature of the business it had to transact, aided and abetted by the comparative lack of ability and initiative on the side of the people.

To grapple with deep-seated evils in public administration certain specialist tribunals had been established to cope with specific official crimes and misdemeanours. As early as 149 B.C. a tribunal *quaestio de repetandis* had been introduced to deal with excessive exactions by governors of provinces: while, during the course of the next fifty or sixty years, a tribunal *quaestio de ambitu* to consider cases of illegal canvassing for office and bribery, and another *quaestio de peculatu* to adjudicate on cases involving the misapplication and embezzlement of public funds, were also introduced.[2] The use of such tribunals does not seem an effective way of purifying the administration but possibly there was little alternative so long as political and administrative powers were broken up and dispersed among a group of individualistic magistrates. A new sort of public service might have been germinating in the groups of professional scribes, already mentioned in the preceding chapter as associated with the several magistracies, but as yet no real attempt had been made to plan forward to the sort of administrative machine that Rome's expanding realm required. So long as old forms could be bent and modified to new uses there was no limit to what the unwritten constitution could be made to do, but Rome now found herself in the midst of a crisis, for the solution of which a continuing application of gradualist doses was no longer enough.

Julius Caesar was faced with the task of resuming the unfinished reconstruction undertaken by Sulla. He put in hand a thorough overhaul of the administration, set about introducing better public order, planned the rebuilding of the city, and, while cutting down the free issue, improved the corn supply by inaugurating the construction of a new harbour at Ostia, through which imports could more freely move. Public works, franchise extension, administrative reform and tax reduction were extended vigorously to the rest of Italy. Steps were taken to strengthen the defence of the Empire. Caesar improved the coinage and reformed the calendar, and among other interesting projects was a scheme for an impressive public library under the charge of Rome's outstanding scholar, M. Terrentius Varro (116-28 B.C.). Caesar's popularity was greatly enhanced by his lavish expenditures on public entertainments and generous payments to the troops.

Caesar's constitutional position as dictator was confirmed when in 46 B.C. he was elected for a third term as *dictator rei publicae constitudenae causa* for ten years. It was still understood that this was a temporary expedient, to be dispensed with as soon as the crisis had passed, the aim being to preserve not to abolish the republican constitution. Yet, despite the comprehensive nature of his dictatorial powers, Caesar continued to occupy numerous other magistracies. True, he increased the number of *aediles* from four to six, of *praetors* from eight to sixteen, and of *quaestors* from twenty to forty. Such a policy might have indicated his intention to widen the scope of the executive had he not at the same time shown scant respect towards the magistracy by failing for whole periods to make the necessary arrangements for their election. During such periods their executive functions were gathered into Caesar's own hands and those of his Master of the Horse, looming as a sort of Roman Grand Vizier. Caesar certainly kept the Senate in the picture, but left them with little initiative. In his public manner a growing imperiousness was manifested and some of the usages of royalty were adopted. He took steps to suppress public criticism, a long established Roman freedom.

When, on 14th February 44 B.C., Caesar assumed perpetual

dictatorship it was clear that conversion to monarchy was at hand, although such aspirations continued to be denied. Undoubtedly there was widespread support for such a change, as the only known way of providing an effective government for an imperial realm, but certain senators, still imbued with a conservative republican patriotism, found little difficulty in convincing themselves that Caesar's death was necessary to the health of the Republic. The leaders of the conspiracy, (Gaius Cassius Longinus (died 42 B.C.) and Marcus Junius Brutus (85-42 B.C.)), both pardoned Pompeians, planned his mass assassination in the Senate on 15th March, a day which Shakespeare has so dramatically immortalized. On that notorious Ides of March a great leader died and a new era in Roman government and administration was inaugurated.

EMINENT REPUBLICAN ADMINISTRATORS: CATO AND CICERO

While the conduct of public business in Rome was reaching its lowest ebb there were individuals who did what they could to alter things, but their scope was necessarily limited. As in the case of Athens almost any public figure in Rome could be taken as the typical public official, for all combined administration with their other, usually more prominent, activities. An example of such an official at his best was Marcus Porcius Cato (95-46 B.C.), whom Plutarch included in his *Lives*.[3] He was a great grandson of Cato, the Censor, whose severe morality and strict integrity he sought to emulate. As a capable soldier he had served with distinction during the slave rising led by Spartacus.

Whenever the occasion arose for him to accept magisterial office it was his habit to ensure that he knew all about his new duties and the relative law before allowing his name to be offered. Once in office he strove continuously to keep in touch with the actual conduct of business and to devise improvements. His first problem was to deal with experienced clerks and under-officials who had been in the habit of practically ignoring their annually-elected and usually ill-informed masters and of carrying on the business of office much to their own liking and advantage. Even in those administratively simpler times the ponderous public records kept by the scribes and the complicated laws by which they were conditioned, accumulating precedent upon precedent, were not easily understood except by the expert. But Cato meant these lower officials to be his servants and not his masters, and he set himself to root out the corruption which he found at every turn. Plutarch remarks 'Being bold, impudent fellows, they flattered the other quaestors, his colleagues, and by their means endeavoured to maintain an opposition against him'. Cato reacted by bringing them before the specialist tribunals and, even where he failed to overcome the chicanery by which the proceedings were sometimes beset in the interests of influential clients, he refused to employ the clerk in question or to pay his salary. In this way he managed to purify the immediate reaches of his own administration and gained a great reputation for his integrity. We can hardly improve upon Plutarch's praise of the admirable activities of this old conservative, who fell inevitably among those who failed to recognise that more radical remedies were needed to restore the Republic to health:

'Cato's assiduity also, and indefatigable diligence, won very much upon the people. He always came first of any of his colleagues to the treasury, and went away last. He never missed any assembly of the people, or sitting of the senate; being always anxious and on the watch for those who lightly, or as a matter of interest, passed votes in favour of this or that person, for remitting debts or granting away customs that were owing to the state. And at length, having kept the exchequer pure and clear from base informers, and yet having filled it with treasure, he made it appear that the state might be rich without oppressing the people. At first he excited feelings of dislike and irritation in some of his colleagues, but after a while they were very well contented with him, since he was perfectly willing that they should cast all the odium on him when they declined to gratify their friends with the public money, or to give dishonest judgment in passing the accounts; and when hard-pressed by suitors, they could readily answer it was impossible to do anything unless Cato would consent' . . . 'Cato, after he had laid down his office, yet did not cease to keep a watch upon the treasury. He had his servants who continually wrote out the details of the expenditure, and he himself kept always by him certain books, which contained the accounts of the revenue from Sulla's time to his own quaestorship, which he had bought for five talents.'

It seems fitting that Cato, having attached himself to the party of Pompey, should, after the final defeat in Africa, take his own life rather than submit to Julius Caesar, whose generous admiration he nevertheless still retained.

As an example of the statesman-administrator we may briefly cite Cicero, famed orator and philosopher, with whom Cato had been closely associated. Born in 106 B.C. Cicero lived through the last troubled days of the Republic. His works included *De Republica*, which was concerned with the ideal constitution and much influenced by Plato, and *De Legibus,* from which we learn a good deal about the constitutional history of Rome. Cicero was an essentially aristocratic and intensely patriotic member of the senatorial class who considered devoted service to the state to be the only proper object of life. His chief political aim was to discover ways of uniting Senate, knights and people and to ensure the leadership of the best and soundest elements of the whole community, a *concordia ordinum,* as he called it. His was a conseravtive plea to preserve the Republic, but amidst the pervading gloom of civil strife he was quite incapable of visualizing the type of leadership that would really bring about an effective solution. In his last philosophical work *De Officis* he endorsed the conspiracy against Julius Caesar.

Although, in accordance with the traditions of the time, Cicero was both man of action and of ideas, we should distinguish him as politician and statesman rather than administrator. He served successfully as consul in 63 B.C., at the time of the conspiracy of Catiline, and was indeed then successful in ranging the sound elements behind the state. He also served a short term as governor of Cilicia, an experience which provided the basis of his criticism of the evils of provincial administration in his *Verrines.* Cicero was put to death by Marc Antony in 43 B.C.

THE IMPERIUM AND THE NEW PUBLIC ADMINISTRATION

Following Caesar's assassination, control of the administration fell into the hands of his close assistants Marcus Aemilius Lepidus (died 13 B.C.) and Marcus Antonius (83-30 B.C.) of whom the former soon took second place. At first Antony adopted a conciliatory attitude towards the conspirators, but trouble with them soon arose. The position was complicated by the early arrival on the scene of Caesar's adoptive son, Gaius Octavius (63 B.C.-14 A.D.). The choice of Octavius as his heir appears to have been the one insurance against the future that Caesar had made, although the wisdom of his choice could hardly have been apparent at the time, for at the age of eighteen Octavius was not a promising candidate for a position of such overwhelming responsibility. On the face of things the future appeared to rest in the hands of the clever and experienced Antony, whom Caesar had appointed trustee in his will.

Caesar's heir immediately adopted the name of *C. Julius Caesar Octavianus.* He soon quarrelled with Antony over his share of Caesar's private fortune which the latter, following his normal proclivities, had lost no time in dissipating. The struggle, complicated by the campaign against the conspirators, gave the advantage to Octavian without eclipsing the power of Antony and, the former having compelled the Senate by a show of force to permit his election as consul in 43 B.C., the two rivals joined with Lepidus to form the Second Triumvirate. For long, and expensively for Rome, the issue remained in doubt. With his military ability far outshining his rival's and a faculty for winning the support of his soldiers Antony's major mistake was to take responsibility for the Eastern provinces, leaving the astute Octavian in Rome to obtain every advantage from his prestige as Caesar's heir. Antony became involved with the beautiful and masterful Cleopatra, who schemed to restore the power of the Ptolomies in Egypt, and by this ill-conceived policy destroyed the loyalty of his troops who, in the winter of 31-30 B.C., surrendered to Octavian without a fight. Antony and Cleopatra committed suicide and the way was at last cleared for Octavian's supremacy. How far he merited the opportunity is open to question and the debate has gone on endlessly. An extreme view is taken by Ronald Syme in a recent work: 'Yet the new dispensation, or *novus status,* was the work of fraud and bloodshed, based upon the seizure of power and redistribution of property by a revolutionary leader.'[4] Certainly there were unattractive traits in Octavian's character and he would hardly have succeeded in his struggle for power without a deal of good fortune, but in the initial phases he undoubtedly displayed qualities of patience and pertinacity, and subsequently showed consummate ability in consolidating his position. He profited from the lessons of Caesar's fate by introducing essential changes without destroying the facade of the Republic. In fact, by the time Octavian returned to Rome in the summer of 29 B.C. with a personal popularity that transcended anything Sulla or Caesar had commanded at their zenith and the secure support of the army which he was to retain throughout his reign, a scheming autocrat appears to have become a balanced statesman overnight.

With the military *imperium* securely in his hands Octavian could surely have assumed the mantle of absolute monarch, but his indifferent health and genuine republican leanings induced him to delegate certain functions. Preferring to be accepted as Princeps, or first citizen, he rejected the title of *Imperator,* but exercised the semi-dictatorial power of consul for the time being. In conjunction with his son-in-law, Marcus Vipsanius Agrippa, (63-12 B.C.), with whom he was to share much of his power as his potential successor, he obtained a special grant of censorial powers and set out to purge the Senate in order to restore its old effectiveness, and to build up both the Senatorial and Equestrian orders, whose status was henceforth to depend upon personal integrity, military service and the possession of property of a set minimum value. In 27 B.C. Octavian offered to resign his offices but the Senate, with apparent sincerity, rejected his offer, and his indispensibility was thus finally recognized. The Senate now conferred upon him the new cognomen 'Augustus' and he renounced his previous name. Henceforth the several provinces were to be shared between Augustus and the Senate.

As a consequence of a serious illness in 23 B.C. Augustus decided further to lighten his burdens. He relinquished the consulship and thus divested himself of certain onerous duties which influential members of the Senate were only too pleased to shoulder. In its place he brought into more frequent use the *tribunicia potestas,* which had been conferred upon him for life by a grateful people in 30 B.C. This power entitled him to convene the Senate, to present legislation to the *Comitia Tributa,* and to exercise criminal jurisdiction. He received the right to submit motions to the Senate by written message and to wield a supervisory control of the senatorial provinces.

Augustus's position was now clearly distinguished from that of the ordinary magistrates. He claimed that he had handed the power back to the Republic, but he continued to stand firmly in the wings, exercising his influence all the time and ready to act if matters began to go badly on the stage. He consistently refused additional powers and maintained a style of life appropriate to a wealthy nobleman, wearing the purple-edged toga of a *curule* officer and carrying only the insignia of a consul. But every Roman soldier continued to swear personal allegiance to him and as permanent master of the legions he maintained control over foreign policy and a decisive influence in matters of finance. Finally, in 12 B.C., he accepted the dignity of *Pontifex Maximus,* an office that had fallen vacant through the death of Lepidus. In fact, while retaining and indeed revivifying the old Republican forms in a manner dear to the heart of traditional Roman constitutionalism, Augustus, by consummate statesmanship, succeeded in concentrating in his own hands ultimate control of a realm such as the world had not hitherto seen. Unlike his great predecessors he had rejected the shadow in order to retain the substance of power.

While the old republican institutions had been maintained—magistracies, Senate and popular assemblies—they were now being fitted into an extended governmental system designed to meet the needs of a world community. The great new institution of the Principate not only effectively concentrated the governing power but enabled its occupant to carry out the co-ordinative function essential to the administration of the wider realm. Two arrangements were being developed which were to exercise a decisive influence in the future: on the one hand the concentration of military power essential to the maintenance of Augustus's leadership but susceptible to a misuse which would eventually contribute decisively to the downfall of the Empire, on the other hand the new public service which would ensure the Empire's survival long after its saving virtues had faded away. Our particular concern is with the new officialdom.

Augustus found a need for an administrative council but his solution fell short of a full cabinet system. He continued the established custom whereby magistrates appointed *consilia* of assessors in judicial cases, but his main aid came from a committee of the Senate, appointed for six-monthly periods, whose chief task was to prepare and expedite the business of that body. When this committee was first constituted in 27 B.C. its membership consisted of the two consuls, one representative from each of the other colleges of magistrates, and fifteen private members. In A.D. 13 members from the Imperial family and nominated members of the Equestrian order were added. By this time Augustus had adopted the practice of implementing its recommendations without further reference to the Senate. In this way a privy council had been carved out of the larger body.

With the close assistance of Agrippa, Augustus took a personal interest in the administration and reconstruction of the city of Rome which, despite Julius Caesar's earlier building plans, had, through structural decay and social anarchy, continued to deteriorate and become a ramshackle place. Extensive building and replanning were now undertaken and a permanent Board of Works (*curatores operum publicorum*) was appointed to enforce building regulations and take care of repairs. Agrippa concerned himself particularly with improvement of the water supply, construction of aqueducts and the building of baths. After his death in 12 B.C. his technical staff of trained slaves were taken into employment under a *Curator Aquarum,* and a house-to-house water supply was gradually laid on throughout the city. Overall control was placed in the hands of a magisterial board. Its first chairman, M. Velerius Messalla, had been a great courtier of his day. To improve communications a Highway Board and a Tiber Conservancy were introduced, and the problems of safety and police protection were also taken in hand. Fire risks in particular had been high in the matchwood tenements of the city, with its narrow streets across which the flames could leap without hindrance. Spurred by the initiative of an enterprising *aedile,* named M. Egnatius Rufus, who had established a private fire brigade, Augustus took this grave problem in hand. In 22 B.C. he placed a force of six hundred public slaves at the disposal of the *aediles,* but it was another fifteen years before the other magistrates were called to their assistance. The city was now mapped into fourteen districts, each with its own corps of fire-fighters. Then, in A.D. 6 the fire service was professionalized by the appointment of a *Praefectus Vigilum,* who was given control of a brigade of 3500 firemen organized in seven cohorts.[5] To repress petty crime and public disorder special police were introduced. For the former function seven cohorts of *vigiles* were appointed under a prefect who took over the summary jurisdiction of the *triumviri capitales,* minor magistrates who had performed this function from as early as the fourth century B.C. Three *cohortes urbanae,* each one hundred strong and organized on military lines, under a high officer of senatorial rank, the *Praefectus Urbi,* were introduced to maintain the public peace. In case of need these could be reinforced by the nine military *cohortes praetoriae* and henceforth sufficient power seems to have existed to keep the mob sternly under control. An endemic weakness of the later republican times was thus effectively eliminated.

One of the more significant of the public departments was the Board for the Distribution of the Corn Doles. This organization had already appeared under the Republic and Augustus toyed with the idea of its abandonment by abolishing free distributions, but the service had become indispensable to the public welfare and the *Princeps* confined himself to pruning the list of recipients, under a much improved system of control and distribution. Distribution was becoming increasingly difficult through cumulative population congestion and strains on the available transport. The shadow of famine compelled the government to give this problem constant attention. Towards the end of his reign Augustus appointed a *Praefectus Annonae,* or Commissioner, with very wide powers to charter necessary shipping, to look after the storage of imported food, and to punish private dealers who attempted to corner supplies. This magistrate's mixture of organizing, executive and punitive functions and powers are typical of the system. The first holder of the office was C. Turranius, formerly governor of Egypt, who so decisively demonstrated his organizing ability that he continued to hold the post over a period of thirty years and several reigns.

In wider fields the rationalization and expansion of the administrative structure proceeded steadily. Increasing permanency and professionalization gradually produced an administrative tool capable of meeting the needs of an expanding realm. Augustus was discovering how to assess the actual and potential resources of the empire and to construct an effective system of finance to sustain its development. The census had been adopted in 27 B.C. in the Western provinces as a necessary preliminary to improving the system of taxation. By the end of his reign Augustus was able to leave his successor an 'abstract of the whole empire'[6] which provided a survey of the armies, the sums held in the Treasury and separate *fisci,* or chests, and an analysis of outstanding payments due on indirect taxes, with the names of the responsible officials.

The structure and development of the Augustan system of finance is of considerable interest. There existed at the time four separate funds: namely (i) the *Aerarium Saturni,* (ii) the *Patrimonium Caesaris,* (iii) the *Aerarium Militare,* and (iv) the *Fiscus,* or Imperial Treasury.[7]

(i) The *Aerarium Saturni* had been the single Treasury under the Republic, but with the division of the provinces between *Princeps* and Senate, it came to serve only the latter. Nevertheless, the *Princeps* appointed its officials and virtually obtained control. With the gradual centralization of state finances the *Aerarium Saturni* eventually became the treasury of the municipality of Rome.

(ii) The *Patrimonium Caesaris* looked after the *Princeps's* private funds, including the revenues of Egypt which belonged to the *Patrimonium.* This fund was administered by numerous officials, both in Rome and in the provinces.

(iii) The *Aerarium Militare* was responsible for the payment of pensions to veterans. It was mainly fed from the proceeds of two taxes—*vicesima hereditatium* and *centesima rerum venalium* —which were specially earmarked for this purpose. The fund was controlled by three men of praetorian rank, chosen by lot and serving for three years, although later the task of selection was taken over by the *Princeps,* and the officials were then known as *praefecti aerarii militaris.*

(iv) The *Fiscus* was solely the concern of the *Princeps.* Its main purposes were the support and supply of the armed forces, the payment of officials, the cost of the corn supplies and of the military roads, posts and public buildings. Its main revenues came from the imperial provinces, where responsibility for collection and transmission was in the hands of imperial *procuratores.* The general trend was for both imperial and senatorial funds to flow into the *Fiscus* in Rome, which thus developed into a centralized treasury. There were also separate *fisci* in the provinces.

An important consequence of improvement in financial control was the reduced influence of the much hated *publicani* who, under the Republic, had been responsible for the collection of taxes. These *publicani* were companies of rich men, usually of the Equestrian order, to whom the taxes were farmed for periods of five years on payment of a lump sum. This easy alternative to the organization of a proper state administrative machine placed incredible burdens upon the people. The *publicani* were concerned to make as much profit as possible from their farm and extortion was resorted to. Nominally subject to the supervision of the provincial governor they exercised so much influence that they were able to do much harm to the career of a magistrate were they so minded. Consequently governors were more likely to share in their exploitations than to attempt to curb them. Total replacement of these influential farmers was bound to be a slow business. In the meantime, therefore, two imperial taxes on land (*tributum soli*) and on personal property (*tributum capitis*) were introduced and officially collected, while the activities of the *publicani* were placed under the close supervision of imperial agents.

THE PUBLIC SERVICES OF THE EARLY EMPIRE

The more rationalized and professional public services needed to cope with the administrative burdens of an expanding state was gradually shaped by a process of trial and error rather than consciously invented. In seeking for structural improvement Augustus never lost sight of the importance of the personal link for ensuring the effective transmission of authority. The personal relationship between the noble citizen and his household was reflected in the relationship between magistrate and his staff, or between *Princeps* and his household. There was as yet no idea of a separately organized public service, no impersonal state. The intimate administrative arrangements of the compact city state were not to be superseded overnight. On the other hand the new organizational complexity about to appear within the administration was not entirely new, since the Romans were already used to the large estate, with its experts, clients and slaves, and need for expert management.

Augustus had a large pool of administrative experience within the broad bounds of the Empire to call upon, and the developing institutions — apart from their derivation from existing Republican forms — incorporated ideas from far and wide. The Greek communities and Egypt were liberal contributors. The professionalized service from its very beginning was a complex organization. This was largely because it was not conceived as a simple structure but as a complex of separate careers at both upper and lower levels.

In the first place Augustus was careful to ensure that the Senatorial order should participate fully in administering as they had done hitherto. Thus, the Senatorial career maintained its predominance in the new system. On the other hand, partly because Augustus shrewdly decided to avoid complete dependence on the nobility and partly because the expanding administration offered more leadership posts than the narrow Senatorial class could adequately fill, the Equestrian order was given important administrative responsibilities, especially in the provinces. It would be no exaggeration to claim that this was Augustus's great administrative contribution.

Each order depended upon the possession of a minimum of wealth and each career in consequence came to be divided into stages with a fixed order of importance. With the introduction of payment to these career-men the several stages became distinguished by differing salary levels. The Senatorial career included the most important posts and combined civil, military and judicial powers, and its members were also eligible for the highest religious offices. The career had six distinct stages, in which the posts were graded according to responsibility and experience. The relative salary figures are not known, but they probably ranged above the highest career rate for the Equestrian order, namely 300,000 sesterces a year, up to at least one million sesterces, the salary for the Governorship of Africa.[8]

The lists of the Equestrian career were drawn up under the *Princeps's* direct supervision. It included both knights by birth and newcomers appointed by special favour. Members were eligible for certain posts in the Imperial Council as well as for selected executive offices. The career was of a mixed character and came to be divided into four stages to which specific salaries were assigned: namely, 60,000; 100,000; 200,000 and 300,000 sesterces respectively. From these amounts the titles of the grades were derived. They were known as the *Sexagenarii,* the *Centenarii,* the *Ducenarii* and the *Trecenarii.* A good idea of the activities and relative importance of these middle-grade officials can be derived from an examination of a selection of the posts to which they were assigned.

The *Sexagenarii* occupied higher positions in the central administration, such as Clerk in Charge of Greek Correspondence, Assessor of the Prefects of the Praetorium and the City, and Directors of Public Libraries: in Italy, they held such posts as Official in Charge of the Corn Supply in Ostia, and Sub-prefect of the Italian Fleets; while in the provinces their main charge was the important financial offices, such as Epistrategi of Egypt, Census Officials, Procurators of the Troop of Gladiators, and Advocates of the Fiscus.

The *Centenarii* held such Roman posts as the Clerk-in-Charge of Italian Correspondence and the Sub-prefects of the Corn Supply and the Watch; in Italy the post of Prefect of Vehicles; in the provinces the posts of Financial Procurator of the Imperial Provinces and the Imperial Mines, as well as Prefects of the Fleets of Britain, Germany and the Euphrates.

The *Ducenarii* held such Roman posts as Procurators at the head of certain Departments, including Inheritances, Patrimony, etc., the Postmaster General and the *Magister Rei Privatae;* in Italy the posts of Prefects of the Praetorian Fleets of Misenum and Ravenna, of the Financial Procurators of the Consuls, the Procurators of indirect taxation, and of certain high officials in Egypt.

The *Trecenarii* held important chief posts in the central administration, such as Prefect of the Praetorium, heads of Offices of the Secretariat, the Director of Finance, the Prefects of the Corn Supply and the Watch, while in the provinces they held the two highest Prefect-Governor posts which were located in Egypt and Mesopotamia.

Here can clearly be discerned an emergent class of professional officials who were acquiring the sort of administrative expertise that would entitle them to participate in the policy-moulding functions of the magistrates above them. The position of the Equestrians was not static; their scope and importance gradually extended. For the time being they were assistants of the *Princeps,* but they would later acquire the potentials of a bureaucratic order.

Below the magistrates and the officials of the Senatorial and Equestrian orders there were separate civil and military careers of subordinate rank. The civilians officiated as cashiers, record-clerks, despatch clerks, employees of the mint and other technical departments, watchmen, ushers, lictors, heralds and the numerous menial workers needed for running even the most primitive office organization. The military career included members from the ranks, various non-commissioned officers and junior officers. These lower careers were normally self-contained, although exceptionally the *Princeps* might advance deserving officials to higher posts.

It is not easy to picture the organization of these lower services either from surviving records (mainly Imperial inscriptions) or by analogy from later institutions. Officers of each grade were grouped in panels or *decuriae,* as had become the practice under the Republic, although the higher magistrates often had their own officials of various grades.[9] The *decuriae* apparently operated as pools from which magistrates drew their staffs as required. Assignment seems to have been by lot, although the evidence that some *scribae* served the same magistrate throughout his tenure of a succession of offices suggests that there were ways of getting round this obstacle. According to Cicero a place on the *decuriae* could be obtained by purchase. This may indicate that the office was originally held as a freehold, thus enabling subsequent transfer to be arranged by purchase, a custom that has been prevalent in public services throughout the ages. Salaries do not appear to have been high and one may wonder why such posts were saleable. In fact the performance of many public services—even the doubtful privilege of having a tax collected—entitled the official to a fee, and such fees could mount up considerably. Posts could be highly remunerative even when the official was completely honest. Unfortunately there were plenty of opportunities to obtain a rake off by less warranted practices.

The public services of the Principate also recruited officials from two new sources, which shows how the expanding demands of officialdom were reaching out for suitably educated or skilled personnel among other ranks of the community: these were the freedmen and slaves who assisted the secretaries and the procurators, and the army clerks who formed the *officia* of the provincial governors.

Imperial slaves who entered the public service were usually manumitted later but children born to them before this occurred remained in servitude and were available for the service. In this way recruitment was automatic from this source and the system was not expensive to the *Princeps,* who had an expanding slave household to assist him. Such slaves could acquire considerable personal property and even maintain a household of their own. There is the much quoted inscription of Musicus, slave of Tiberius, who occupied the quite modest position of *dispensator* in the *fiscus Gallicus provinciae Lugdunensis.* His domestic staff consisted of a business manager, two accountants, two cooks, two footmen, a valet, two chamberlains, a doctor, and a lady whose duties are not made clear! As Musicus died while still a slave all these servants, together with his silver plate and wardrobe, were transferred to the Emperor. The Imperial household and its relationships continued to be important in the development of the new administration.

The practice of seconding soldiers for staff duties in the provinces which had begun modestly under the late Republic, was considerably extended under the Principate. A soldier selected for staff work obtained a substantial advancement and usually continued to perform administrative duties, unless he was fortunate to obtain a commission as centurion. Some were assigned to such duties as soon as they enlisted, others were subsequently selected as suitable types. A series of gradings evolved, through which the soldier-clerk advanced by a system of promotions. Apart from their pay these officials received other perquisites, such as the *penniculariae* or personal effects of executed prisoners, a custom which certainly made reprieves very unwelcome to officialdom! Various less lugubrious sums were also collectable, and it was laid down later by Ulpian (died A.D. 228) in his *De Officio Proconsulis* that these should neither go to the individual official nor be pocketed by the governor: it was better for them to be paid into a fund to meet such expenses as the cost of paper used by the officials, rewards for bravery to the troops, and presents to barbarian envoys. These new officials were stationed in the provinces and did not travel out from Rome with the new governor as had been the previous practice. Thus military staff gradually became almost completely separated from the fighting forces.

DEVELOPMENT OF ADMINISTRATIVE MEANS AND SERVICES

Competent office organizations had existed, as we have already seen, before the time of the Romans, who also had the experience *inter alia* of contemporary Greeks and Egyptians to call upon. Plentiful supplies of papyrus were forthcoming from Egypt and there was no longer a shortage of suitable media for the conduct of correspondence on a scale needed by more advanced administrative arrangements. For some purposes the booklike codex, consisting of separate sheets linked or stitched together, was coming into use. The codex form proved more convenient than the continuous roll for reference and was more easily portable.

The use of parchment, made out of hides, in its formation considerably increased the codex's durability, for papyrus was extremely fragile. Tablets of parchment could also be waxed and written on with a stylus.

An early form of shorthand had been invented to bridge the gap between the oral and the written tradition. There was nothing original therefore in its use by administrators. It is recorded that Cicero dictated to Tiro, a freedman who used shorthand, and that stenographers were employed by the Senate as early as 63 B.C. Four years later Julius Caesar, as Consul, introduced an official gazette to record official events and the activities of the Senate. These new written processes are said to have had a powerful modifying influence on the older rhetorical attitudes.[10]

Numerous financial accounts have survived but they indicate that Roman accountancy remained in a primitive state, though it must have been adequate for the type of economy and business that had so far been developed.[11] There seems to be no evidence that the idea of a system of double-entry book-keeping had been thought of. The awkwardness of the systems of numerical notation employed by both the Greeks and the Romans would not certainly have facilitated the development of more advanced accountancy methods had they been needed. It remained for the Arabs to find the solution, but in the mean time existing techniques were sufficient to the tasks they were called upon to perform.

In comparing the administrative arrangements of those early ages with those of our own day it is well to remember that the tempo was much different. A precise sense of time had not yet emerged in the absence of the means of accurate measurement that are available today. The mechanical clock had not yet been invented to regulate men's lives.[12] Consequently the attitudes of the magistrates' staffs were similar to those of the field worker whose work rhythms were determined by the incidence of daylight and darkness, an the seasons. No doubt a special drive had sometimes to be made on constructional jobs, especially when ganged slave labour was being employed, but in the main there was little urgency in the conduct of current business and normal attitudes to work would not have been dissimilar to those usual among the dwellers in undeveloped tropical lands.

Specialization of administrative processes rapidly appeared with the continuing growth in the size of offices. Important changes of this type are associated with the reign of Claudius (A.D. 41-54) or more precisely with his freedmen Narcissus, Pallas, Callistus and Polybius, who figured among the directing staff. An effective Chancellery had now emerged. It comprised four important bureaux, two of which — *ab epistulis* and *a libellis* — already existed in a rudimentary form while the other two — *a cognitionibus* and *a studiis* — were new to the imperial administration. The bureau *ab epistulis* (correspondence) dealt with the receipt and expedition of all important imperial documents. It was organized in two sections to deal respectively with Latin and Greek, the two official languages of the Empire. The bureau *a libellis* (petitions) prepared replies to all petitions addressed to the Emperor. The bureau *a cognitionibus* (inquiries) was responsible for providing information required in the Emperor's court, while the bureau *a studiis* (preliminary examinations) was concerned with providing information needed in the conduct of administration and judicial business generally. Each of these bureaux had a head designated by the title of the bureau (*ab epistulis,* etc.) who was assisted by deputies (*adjutores, proximi,* etc.) and numerous other employees (*scrinarii, custodes,* etc.). It has to be emphasized, however, that this Chancellery remained a part of the Emperor's domestic service and its posts were not accessible to the ordinary citizen. The senior staff were freedmen, the others personal slaves.[13]

It was not until the reign of Hadrian (A.D. 117-138) that the Chancellery, or Secretariat as we should call it today, was completed by the addition of a fifth bureau, *a memoria,* to supply the Emperor personally with essential basic information, and the whole organization at last became a state institution open to recruitment from outside the household. Under the new regime posts were held by persons of the eminence of Suetonius (A.D. 70-140), the historian, who directed the bureau *ab epistulis* during the reign of Hadrian, and the eminent Syrian jurist Aemilius Papinianus (died A.D. 212), who headed the bureau *a libellis* under Septimus Severus.

Some typical Roman public services may now be mentioned. A service important among these and significant of a literate society was the provision of libraries. Julius Caesar's state library, which its constructor, Gaius Asinus Pollio (75 B.C.-A.D. 6) modelled upon the great library of Alexandria, was the forerunner of many similar institutions, introduced under public and municipal auspices, both in Rome and in the provinces. Libraries were even associated with the magnificent bathing establishments for the convenience of their clients! Public control, however, had its drawbacks, since the prefects and procurators who had charge of the libraries were authorized to exercise a censorship which could be most easily operated by the gradual elimination of distasteful texts.

The power of the state to mould public opinion is also illustrated in another direction: namely, through monopoly of the currency issue which had been assumed by the state as a matter of course. Under the Republic manufacture of coinage had been centralized in a board of three officials who, by the time the precious metals had been brought into use, were styled *tresviri aere argento auro flando feriundo* (IIIviri a.a.a.f.f.) which was often shortened to *IIIviri monetales*. These three magistrates, who were originally of junior rank, supervised the operation of the mint, comprising the preparation of the blanks of the required weight and quality, and their striking with an approved type. While the importance of the Roman mint increased both on account of technical advances and of the greater interest shown by the government, it did not supply all Italian needs. Other mints were established, but their relationship with the central mint is not clear. Under the Empire provincial mints were managed by magistrates appointed by the *Princeps,* who was thus able to ensure the implementation of a consistent policy throughout his realm. As a consequence similar standards and types were used. Coins were marked to indicate the name of the supervising moneyer, who could thus be brought to account for any discrepancy.

In the beginning all coins were stamped with religious motifs and later with legendary designs, and it was not unitl the final year of Julius Caesar's rule that his head appeared on the coins and broke the tradition that personal portraiture should be avoided, although Sulla had earlier introduced the practice of engraving his coins with his name and indications of his power and victories. The way was now clear for the establishment of an imperial coinage by the emperors and for its subtle use in propaganda supporting their rule. How the diminutive surface area of the coin was used for this purpose by a form of symbolism and the careful selection of captions is fascinatingly described by C. H. V. Sutherland in her *Coinage in Roman Imperial Policy 31* B.C.-A.D. *68* (Methuen, 1951). Thus by the inclusion of Aggrippa's portrait with his own Augustus established in the mind of the people his intentions with regard to the succession.

The importance of the road network in providing an everextending communications system for a growing empire has already been mentioned. It was one of the most characteristic and enduring factors in maintaining Roman power. Rome in this had taken a leaf out of the Achaemenians' book and indeed improved upon their original conception. The road net-work was so shaped as to facilitate the concentration of military power with the least possible delay at the point of immediate danger, but it had the other primary advantages of facilitating public administration and aiding the expansion of trade. Usually existing routes were followed, but the Roman contribution was to supply the road with solid foundations, which called for a minimum of subsequent upkeep, and to reorganize the routes into a unified system. Many of the roads out of Rome continued to bear the name of the censor responsible for their construction. Examples are the Appian and Flaminian Ways.

A rudimentary postal service had been evolved under the Republic but it remained for Augustus to introduce an efficient system. Couriers carried ordinary messages on foot, but more important correspondence was entrusted to messengers who carried the diploma of the *Princeps* or governor, which entitled them to requisition transport along the route. By this method it has been calculated that speeds of as much as fifty miles a day could be reached.[14] The system laid a considerable burden on the towns, but, as it was devised solely for official purposes, the general citizen was normally compelled to make private arrangements for carrying messages with travellers happening to be going in the right direction. No doubt the official post was frequently used surreptitiously by those who had influence but this was decidedly against the law.

Road construction, important as it was, represented only part of the building activities carried out by the public authorities in Rome and the provinces. Numerous architectural works were undertaken for both utilitarian and ceremonial purposes. Remains on Roman sites of extensive fora, vast amphitheatres, impressive temples and highly embellished triumphal arches are too well-known to need further emphasis, but there were other structures, such as the large housing tenements in commercial areas like the port of Ostia and the numerous hospitals whose remains are less widespread.

Among the great monuments of Rome that have survived to this day the massive commemorative marble Column of Trajan ranks high. Today it bears aloft a statue of St. Peter which replaced that of Trajan in 1588. Winding upwards on the outside of the column and formed like large scrolls, are a number of spiral panels sculptured in relief with representations of events in the Emperor's two Dacian campaigns. From the market that was situated at its base a high five-storied semicircular brick structure still rises to demonstrate the massive proportions of Roman constructional work. It is of special interest that the original building was used for both commercial and public purposes. The lower stories were devoted to the market, to storage places and merchants' warehouses, while on the fourth storey there was a public hall where official distributions of food and money were made. It was here that, from the second century, the offices of the public assistance organization *stationes arcariorum Casaerianorum* were located. On the top storey were situated the market fish-ponds, served by channels linking them to aqueducts which supplied both fresh and seawater.[15]

The hospitals began as an appendage of the military camp, but during the first century properly organized public *valetidinaria* began to appear in various parts of the Empire. These institutions were carefully planned as a system of wards and corridors. Beginning as purely military establishments, they were extended to serve imperial officials and their families in the provincial towns; and later, under Christian influence, to a much wider use. This important Roman contribution to public health administration undoubtedly had a direct influence on the religious foundations of the Middle Ages.[16]

The development of water-supply and drainage works was basic to the evolution of an urban civilization and the public administrators of Rome added appreciably to the experience of this sort of constructional work that had already been accumulating under previous civilizations. The characteristic remains of extensive aqueducts and massive baths that figure on Roman sites today stand witness to the importance of such services.

In Republican times, as early as 312 B.C. when the first aqueduct was constructed by Appius Claudius Calcus, this task was undertaken by censors or praetors. The maintenance of the waterways was let out by the magistrates to contractors, who employed a fixed staff of slaves whose names had to be entered in the public records of the region. The work was inspected by the censors, or the *aediles* on their behalf. Under the principate Agrippa had taken responsibility for this service and on his death his staff of two hundred skilled workmen were bequeathed to Augustus who handed them over to the state. These were maintained as the *familia publica* by the *Aerarium Saturni* and from the proceeds of a water rate on private concessionaries. The new arrangement dated from 11 B.C. when the administration was placed under a board of three *curatores,* the president of which stood high in senatorial rank. His two assistants acted as technical advisers. They were assisted by a staff of officials, which included both experts and clerks.

A good deal is recorded about the *curatores*,[17] who included some distinguished citizens in their membership. At the outset the office seems to have been assigned as an honour to distinguished magistrates, but eventually, with the growing importance of the job, the appointment became available in the normal senatorial *cursus*. The change took place with the advent, in A.D. 59, of Gnaeus Calpurnius Piso, who had been consul two years before. The *adiutores,* or technical advisers, are less well-known and only a few names are recorded, although to these may perhaps be added a number of names which have been found on lead pipes without further identification. From A.D. 52 the office of *procurator aquarum* was appointed by the Emperor to look after the *familia Caesaris,* a band of four hundred and fifty slaves added to the water staffs by Claudius. At first the holder was a freedman but members of the Equestrian order were later occasionally given the post. The *familia publica,* already mentioned above, is not known after the reign of Hadrian. The staffs of the *familia,* known collectively as *aquarii,* included overseers, reservoir-men, inspectors, paviors, plasterers and the like. There were also clerks, usually freedmen, who were probably responsible under the procurator, for the funds out of which the personnel and costs of repairs were paid. To these should be added a number of specialists, such as *castelarii* and *vilici,* who were respectively responsible for testing the *calices,* or delivery-necks, through which the water was conveyed into the lead pipes and to stamp them as correct, subject to the overall supervision of the procurator. The special contribution in this field of the notable administrator Frontinus calls for a separate section on the subject.

However, there is one interesting Roman institution connected with the water service, that first deserves to be mentioned, as an example of the limitless ubiquity of public services and their capacity to reflect the *mores* of the particular age. The public lavatory is one of the least publicized, though by no means the least useful, amenities provided by local government in modern Britain. Its contribution to the cleanliness of cities can hardly be overrated and its mere existence may well be a mark of advanced civilization. The Romans certainly had their solution. While satisfactorily advanced for the times their sewage system was still very primitive. The majority had recourse to the public latrine. If they could afford the small charge they would use the impressive establishments administered by the *conductores forica-rum.*[18] These *forica* were indeed public, the seats being arranged communally in rows as in the case of soldiers' latrines on active service. They were often decorated with a lavishness and attention to detail that we should consider misplaced today. But the

Roman *forica* was a place of social intercourse where people assembled without embarrassment to exchange personal back-chat, and perhaps to give or receive invitations to dinner! The existence of a stream of running water no doubt greatly increased the salubrity of this, to us, strange social amenity, but one cannot imagine that it was completely effective in removing the usual effluvia of an open sewer. *'Autres temps, autres moeurs.'* We must not forget that it is only recently that we have acquired a high fastidiousness and sensitivity to smells, and even now only in well-administered industrial communities. A walk through an authentic Tudor village, so pleasing to the modern eye, would no doubt quickly bring home to us one of the most easily over-looked blessings of our public administration.

EMINENT IMPERIAL ADMINISTRATOR: SEXTUS JULIUS FRONTINUS

In the work of Sextus Julius Frontinus, who distinguished himself as lawyer, military theorist, engineer and administrator, we are fortunate to have a more detailed account of the Roman water service than perhaps of any other branch of Roman administration.[19] Frontinus seems to have been born round about A.D. 35 and to have held the magisterial office of *praetor urbanus* in A.D. 70 and *consul suffectus* four years later. He is of particular interest to us as imperial legate in Britain about A.D. 74-7. Later he served as proconsul of Asia. During the time of Domitian he devoted his leisure to studies and writing, particularly on survey-ing and military organization and strategy, but he returned to public life under Nerva and Trajan. His responsibility for the water service dates from A.D. 97, when he was invested with the *cura aquarum* to root out the corruption that had beset that administration. He was also placed at the head of a Commission on Public Expenditure and twice held the authority of consul, in A.D. 98 and 100. Honoured with the life assignment of membership of the College of Augurs, Frontinus was succeeded by Pliny the Younger in A.D. 103-4, so that he can be presumed to have died just before this, in his late sixties.

It is clear that the Roman water supply service had been carefully organized to meet the growing burdens placed upon it, but the success of such a system of administration depends upon the calibre and integrity of its personnel. It was therefore fortunate that the services of such a man as Frontinus were available at the critical juncture when growing scandal was reducing the efficiency of the service. He had a high reputation, as we learn from Tacitus and Pliny, who speak of him in glowing terms as *vir magnus* and *princeps vir*.[20]

Frontinus's habit of setting down in writing the precepts of administration and of formulating administrative theories has been cited as proof that he was a dedicated supporter of the senatorial system of short-term public service, as opposed to the growing professionalized Imperial system. Certainly short-term officials needed such guidance by the very nature of their tenure, but this is not conclusive, for while the long-term professional can get by with a slow-moving process of trial and error, the formulation of basic principles is even more important in strengthening his professional expertise. In fact Frontinus had a sound practical reason for placing his experience on record. He had already devised this method for use in similar situations as the best way of informing himself about the service for which he had been given responsibility. He felt that he could not give the correct instructions unless he understood clearly what his subordinates were about, and they would not readily accept a leadership built on ignorance. He asserts that 'There is nothing so disgraceful for a decent man as to conduct an office delegated to him according to the instructions of assistants'.

As a result of his investigations Frontinus concluded that much more water was being delivered than was indicated by the official total of available supplies. Faulty technique had led to incorrect estimates, but experts have since shown that Frontinus's revisions were not a lot better and it was in fact the actual abuses which he brought to light that were significant.

Foremen were in the habit of allowing men to execute private work. Frontinus put a stop to this practice 'by writing down the day before what each gang was to do, and putting in the records what it had done each day'. But there were much more serious abuses than this, actual frauds perpetrated by tapping off supplies through unauthorized pipes and selling them secretly: pipes stamped for a specific flow were deliberately enlarged. Some of the frauds were the more serious because they called for collusion from the procurator. Apart from the frauds involving the connivance of the staff there were others in which landowners were involved. Frontinus, who was highly critical of these private malpractices, explained in detail how they were perpetrated.

Having strenuously applied himself to rectifying these faults Frontinus went on to improve the service. In this way he left behind him a great reputation as an administrator of vision and high integrity. An examination of the water service at that time is sufficient to indicate that the inherent dangers of administra-

tive inefficiency, which are not confined to the failings of officials
but also to the malpractices of scheming outsiders, have not
changed much throughout the ages. It also demonstrates that the
best way to counter them is to foster the employment of honest
and competent officials. Possibly Rome at that time was fortunate
to have such an administrator as Frontinus, and it would be
interesting to speculate how many additional officials of his calibre
at later stages of Rome's history could have been effectual in
providing an administrative service great enough to have rendered
an efficient system of government possible and thus to have
arrested Imperial decline.

HISTORICAL INTERLUDE: PRINCIPATE TO EMPIRE

Between the Augustun era and the late Empire of the fourth
century the administration of Rome was subject to a slow
process of development, for a full appreciation of which an
examination of the whole history of the Roman Empire during
the period would be essential. Only a few brief paragraphs on
certain important matters can be included here.

Frustrated in his arrangements for the succession by the death
in 12 B.C. of Agrippa, who had shared the *imperium* with him
since 23 B.C., Augustus had to make other arrangements. These
were to prove equally unfortunate. Agrippa's two sons, Gaius
and Lucius, being children, he turned to Tiberius and Drusus,
sons of his wife's first marriage. Tiberius, stern, reserved and a
fine general, soon fell into disfavour and was sent into exile in
6 B.C. The popular Drusus died three years later. By this time both
Gaius and Lucius having died, Augustus, in A.D. 13, felt impelled
to recall Tiberius and to adopt him. On Augustus's death the
following year, the Senate and the people — the latter partici-
pating in this process for the last time — elected Tiberius
(42 B.C.-A.D. 37).

Tiberius, already a disappointed and weary man, did his best,
but without hope or initiative. The one important happening
during his reign was the crucifixion of Jesus of Nazareth at
Jerusalem, a potential world shattering event that caused not the
least ripple in contemporary Roman society. Roman justice was
of course deeply implicated but if the Roman governor on the
spot, from A.D. 26-36, Pontius Pilate, chose to placate the local
Jewish Sanhedrin who co-operated closely with the authorities,
he was only acting expediently as he did in other cases brought
before him. Whether it was Roman or Jewish justice that was

being administered it is undeniable that the particularly cruel punishment of crucifixion was specifically a Roman penalty with definite administrative overtones. It was horribly designed to give the maximum of publicity to the penalties of wrongdoing. There was a strain of savagery in the Roman character that offset the manifest virtue of its political institutions.

Tiberius was followed by the promisingly virtuous Caligula (A.D. 12-41) who was so changed, following an early illness, as to become an uncontrollable tyrant and to imagine himself divine. He was assassinated by a Praetorian tribune in A.D. 41. The Praetorians now raised the unpromising Claudius (10 B.C.-A.D. 54) who, despite manifest personal defects, emerged as an effective ruler and came to be honoured in the provinces for his good government. He liberally extended citizenship and created an effective public service, divided into departments with freedmen at their head. He also provided plenty of shows and did not neglect the Empire's might. It was under him that Britain was conquered. In A.D. 54 Claudius was succeeded by Nero (A.D. 37-68). History again repeated itself for, after a quiet start, Nero came to surpass even Caligula in cruelty and self-indulgence. It was under him, partly with the object of distracting the populace from his own extravagances, partly from a real fear of underground opposition, that the Christians of Rome — at that time a humble, friendless sect — were unmercifully persecuted.

The high ideals of the Principate had already dwindled while members of Augustus's house were still in power. The diminished profligate emperors had come to depend upon the support of the Praetorian Guard. Yet, for a time, with the advent in A.D. 98 of Trajan (A.D. 53-117) the Augustan tradition was restored. Under him and his immediate successors — particularly Hadrian and Marcus Aurelius — the Empire throve and good government again characterized the Mediterranean world. Marcus Aurelius died in A.D. 180, leaving his son Commodus, (A.D. 161-192), an insignificant youth, to develop into a second Nero.

By the third century the Roman Empire was weakening. The old Roman stock had been swamped by new elements and lost its influence. The armies now had a firm hold on the political machine. The cities had begun to decay and in some cases the holding of urban offices had to be made compulsory.

In A.D. 285 the Illyrian Diocletian (reg. A.D. 284-305) fought his way to the top, where he was to reign for twenty years. He abolished the Augustan Principate and made the Empire an autocracy under a dual-emperor. Eastern ideas were gaining ascendency. The creation of a permanent mobile field force was put in hand and the public service further strengthened.

Gaius Arelius Valerius Diocletianus (A.D. 245-313) shared the Empire between two Augusti, each with a Caesar designed to succeed him. This meant in practice that the Empire was now divided into four distinct administrative realms or prefectures. Within these prefectures the provinces, increased in number and placed under civilian governors, were grouped into larger units called *dioceses,* each under a *vicarius.* There were twelve *dioceses* with varying numbers of provinces, whose governors were given different ranks, ranging from *proconsuls* down to *consulares, correctores and praesides.* The vicarii carried the important rank of *spectabiles* and were only equalled by the few *proconsuls.* All the other governors were their subordinates. The Emperor usually issued orders direct to the *vicarii* and *proconsuls,* but he could also deal with any of the governors direct and an important effect of the new system was the strengthening of the central administration and the consolidation of absolutist control at the top. It was Diocletian who first regularly received the title *dominus.*

The most serious attempt was now made to destroy Christianity, but in this Diocletian failed. It remained for Constantine I or 'the Great' (A.D. 288-337) to become Augustus in the West in A.D. 306 and subsequently to adopt Christianity. The East remained under separate augusti until A.D. 323 when Constantine finally defeated Licinius (*reg.* A.D. 307-324) who had previously gained the leadership of the eastern provinces. For a brief spell the Roman realm was united under one leader, who reaffirmed his belief in Christianity. In A.D. 330 Constantine transferred his capital to the wonderfully sited town of Byzantium on the Bosphorus, the waters that both divided and linked Europe and Asia, to which he gave the name Constantinople. His policies upheld the supremacy of Christianity as the religion of the Roman world and settled the decline of paganism. The 'New Rome' of the East began its long career as a great Christian capital and administrative centre.

ADMINISTRATION OF THE LATER EMPIRE

While Diocletian and Constantine can justly share the honour of finally combining the several civil careers into one consolidated Imperial public service, earlier emperors had undoubtedly made an important contribution to this work of administrative reconstruction. Among them Aurelian (A.D. 270-75) may be mentioned as having created a number of new offices and as having been responsible for the separation of the civil and military functions, a reform often attributed to later rulers.[21]

An absolute monarchy, now openly accepted, needed a powerfully knit administrative service if its rule was to be effective. Such an instrument had now been forged. The Emperor's central administration, or *comitatus,* had developed into a large and complex organization which continued to travel about with him, although naturally it lost much of its mobility after A.D. 395 when the Eastern emperors settled permanently in Constantinople.[22] The three original avenues of recruitment were maintained, namely the Senatorial order, or *clarissimi,* the Equestrian order, or *perfectissimi,* and the lower posts. There were in fact two concurrent orders of rank, one of classes and one of titles, which were strictly co-ordinated.

At the top were the heads of the administration, some of whom held ministerial rank. These included the Prefect of the Praetorium, the Counts of the Treasuries, the Master of the Offices and the Quaestor of the Palace. In addition there were the great officials in the districts, such as vicars, governors of provinces, the prefects of the two capitals, dukes, counts and financial agents, and below these the great mass of lower posts. Each high official of the central and local administrations had his staff of *officiales* who worked in the separate *scrinia.* Their numbers varied according to the importance of the particular service and indeed the leaders exercised powers and enjoyed privileges of office in proportion to the number of their employees, a vicar having three hundred, the Proconsul of Africa four hundred and so on, up to the thousand despatch clerks assigned to the Prefect of the East.[23] Heads of department were usually assisted by subdirectors or assistant directors, bearing such titles as *proximus, secunderius, melloproximus, cornicularius* or *adjutor.* Although the military careers were now specialized the army organization had left its impress on the civil side, which continued to be organized strictly on the military pattern. Similar titles were assigned and civil officials wore the *cingulum,* or belt, as if they were soldiers. Retired civil officials were classified with retired soldiers as *veterani.*

Imperial officials had an exact administrative status whereby their privileges were granted in return for the undertaking of definite professional duties. Detailed rules for (i) recruitment, (ii) training, (iii) promotion, (iv) remuneration, (v) judicial privileges and (vi) honours, foreshadowed the codes or statutes that have been promulgated for modern civil services.

(i) *Recruitment:* Appointment was made by a decree, or *probatoria,* of the Emperor, on the recommendation of the head of a department, but actual recruitment depends upon two processes which both restricted the head's power of selection, namely hereditary succession strictly according to caste, and sale of office, neither very satisfactory ways of achieving merit appointments. Upon the issue of the Emperor's decree the applicant's name was entered upon a register which constituted the official authority for his position in the service.

(ii) *Training:* Preparation of the new official for his work, or to improve his knowledge of it, was undertaken by *scholae* attached to the separate offices. This staff training was divided into two distinct levels, organized according to the standard of knowledge required by the nature of the work to be performed. These were the *ministeria litterata,* which provided a general literary education, and the *ministeria illitterata,* designed to meet the needs of lower office personnel such as ushers, messengers, etc.

(iii) *Promotion:* The official's status was strictly defined and promotion was made by seniority. The rule was enunciated by Constantine in A.D. 315, when he decreed that 'The order of promotion must be observed in such a way that the highest rank of the *officium* shall go to him whose Imperial warrant of appointment is older'. This order, however, did not put an end to the evils of favouritism and the normal abuses of personal recommendation.

(iv) *Remuneration:* A regular salary was paid in accordance with the principles already introduced during the early Empire. The official was exempted from certain taxes and services and was entitled to retirement pay at the end of a fixed term of office, which varied from fifteen to twenty years according to the importance of the office.

(v) *Judicial privileges:* Government employees were not subject to the ordinary courts. The head of their department was their judge in both civil and criminal cases and there was no appeal from his sentence. This appears to have been a reflection of the powers of the *paterfamilias* rather than a system of *droit administratif.*

(vi) *Honours:* There was a scale of honours which went according to function, but while some attached to the function itself others were conferred on retirement as the crown of a man's career. To the existing titles of *clarissimes* and *perfectissimes* there were added, during the fourth century, the titles of *illuster* and *spectabilis* replacing all the more important *clarissimes* at the top, while the *perfectissimes* had been rapidly absorbed upwards into the ranks of the *clarissimes*.

Leon Homo's criticism of this system is worth considering. Despite the great advances, he considers the administrative structure still to be defective. Certain ministerial divisions did not exist at all. For example, foreign affairs were still a matter for the head of state and no separate diplomatic service had yet been developed. There were no ministers for such matters as agriculture, public works, education and labour, and trade was cared for by a number of local departments spread throughout the Empire. In paying attention only to higher education — and that not to any great extent — Roman public administration was undoubtedly neglecting a service vital to any general development of the community. There was as yet no separate system of justice nor any definite separation of powers. Both civil and military officials exercised judicial power in addition to their executive functions. However, on the financial side the principle of judicial specialization had to some extent been adopted by the appointment of the Advocate of the Fiscus to defend the interest of the Treasury. It is difficult to assess the administrative needs of one age in terms of arrangements developed to meet the needs of a later age and, while we may be inclined to agree with Leon Homo that the Roman administration could have profited by a more vigorous development of departmentalism, it is not easy to be confident that our modern ministerial pattern would have been suitable to the Roman situation of the fourth century onwards.

Such a public service as we have sketched here could indeed have been powerful, a veritable state-within-the-state with bureaucratic tendencies, over which only the strongest and most competent emperor could hope to exercise effective control. The existence of one modern symptom certainly tended to moderate this power, namely the constant criticism of the service by contemporary writers. These popular accusations covered favouritism, caste-spirit, arbitrariness, extortion, greed, slackness, slavery to routine, and many others. No doubt these were often exaggerated but, despite the real advances made towards the shaping of a properly regulated public personnel system, some of the rules and customs which have been mentioned above would inevitably at any time and place lead to faults so grave as to threaten the efficiency of the whole system. One need only mention the constantly recurring practices of hereditary appointment, sale of office, 'empire building' as represented by the numerical allocation of subordinates according to the chief's rank rather than the needs of the work, dilatoriness and red tape, and promotion by seniority. The overall effectiveness of the Roman Imperial administration throughout a long period suggest that there must have been strong counteracting factors that ensured a high efficiency. Despite these serious defects, there must have been a high leadership talent among the heads and a widespread sense of loyalty and devotion to duty among the lesser ranks to have achieved such notable results as undoubtedly were achieved.

REFERENCES

1   A. W. Gomme on 'The Roman Republic' in *European Civilization,* (Oxford, 1935), Vol. II, p. 101.

2   Leon Homo, *Les Institutions Politiques Romaines,* in 'L'Evolution de l'Humanite' series, (La Renaissance du Livre, Paris, 1933), p. 108.

3   Plutarch, *Lives,* essay on 'Cato the Younger', (translated by A. H. Clough, Dent's Everyman edn.).

4   R. Syme, *The Roman Revolution,* (Oxford, 1960), p. 2.

5   M. Cary, *A History of Rome,* (Macmillan, 1935), p. 485.

6   H. Stuart Jones on 'Administration' in *The Legacy of Rome,* (Oxford, 1930), p. 117.

7   W. T. Arnold, *The Roman System of Provincial Administration,* Blackwell, 2nd edn. 1906), pp. 215-19.

8   Leon Homo, *op. cit.,* pp. 422 *et seq.*

9   A. H. M. Jones, *Studies in Roman Government,* (Blackwell, 1960), p. 155.

10 H. A. Innes, *Empire and Communications,* (Oxford, 1950), p. 120.

11 G. E. M. de Ste. Croix on 'Greek and Roman Accounting' in *Studies in the History of Accounting,* (Sweet & Maxwell, 1956), pp. 14-74.

12 Jerome Carcopino, *Daily Life in Ancient Rome,* (Penguin, 1956), pp. 150-4.

13 Leon Homo, *op. cit.,* pp. 373-4.

14 G. H. Stevenson on 'Communications and Commerce' in *The Legacy of Rome,* (Oxford, 1936), p. 160.

15 Carcopino, *op. cit.,* pp. 15-17.

16 Charles Singer on 'Science' in *The Legacy of Rome,* pp. 293-96.

17 Thomas Ashby, *Aqueducts of Ancient Rome,* (Oxford, 1935).

18 Carcopino, *op. cit.,* pp. 49-50.

19 Frontinus, *De Aquis Urbis Romae,* (Loeb Classics).

20 Ashby, *op. cit.,* pp. 26-7.

21 Arnold, *op. cit.,* pp. 171-2.

22 A. H. M. Jones, *The Later Roman Empire, 284-602,* (Blackwell, 1964), Vol. II, p. 366; an important work which includes valuable chapters on 'The Administration' and 'Finance'.

23 Leon Homo, *op. cit.,* p. 430 *et seq.*

CHAPTER 5

INDIA AND CHINA : 5000 B.C. to A.D. 1125

Western horizons had extended beyond Persia into India only during the meteoric conquests of Alexander: distant China remained a mysterious land far beyond Rome's everyday world. Yet the discovery of artifacts of the two worlds within the areas of each other — as when Roman coins have been unearthed in India — affords startling evidence of the existence of important trade routes stretching far across the frontiers. The *Periplus of the Erythraean Sea,* written by a Graeco-Egyptian merchant somewhere about A.D. 70, tells how trade between India and Rome, via Egypt, had operated in a number of stages. To India from China, both by sea and across the central Asian plateau, silk was transported which eventually found its way to the markets of the Roman west. Sometimes more direct contacts were achieved. The arrival at the Chinese court of a personal embassy from Marcus Aurelius (A.D. 121-180) is reported in the *Han Annals.*[1]

GOVERNMENT AND ADMINISTRATION IN EARLY INDIAN CIVILISATIONS

Remains of extensive civilizations in the river valleys of the Indus and the Ganges have come to light during the present century and the picture is ever emerging in increasing detail. The most important Indus sites are at Mohenjo-daro in Sind and Harappa in Punjab, which appear to have flourished from a little before 2500 B.C. for a thousand years. Connections with the contemporary civilizations of Mesopotamia are not clear: intercommunication was almost certain and there are close parallels between the two societies. On the other hand the organization of the Indian communities had its own characteristics.[2]

Extensive built-up areas in the two Indus centres included a citadel, or acropolis, with ritual buildings and places of assembly. In Mohenjo-daro the public buildings included a state granary, while in Harappa the remains of subsidiary granaries have been unearthed. The construction is mainly of baked brick, sometimes reinforced with timbers and thus differing from the ordinary mud structures of Mesopotamia. There are extensive traders' and workmen's quarters and evidence of comprehensive drainage and sanitation systems. As the two main sites are four hundred miles apart and other sites have been discovered over a wide area there is a strong possibility of the existence at one time of an important imperial organization.[3]

The rulers probably had priestly attributes, but there was a flourishing civic life, suggesting a more liberal type of civilization than usually accompanied such regimes. Information about the basic agriculture and irrigation systems has not yet come to light, but the granaries suggest a form of state socialism which probably extended to other spheres of activity. Numerous workmen's dwellings suggest the use of coolie labour in the absence of time-saving mechanical means. On the other hand there is little evidence of a progressive attitude to life. Repetitive rebuilding suggests that we have to do here with a somewhat stagnant society.

Obviously there was an efficient public service, or a series of municipal services, but so far there is no surviving information about its form or the personalities and activities of its members. There was a script, which was peculiar and is still undeciphered. Writing materials have not survived the Indian climate, and writings survive only on hard objects: seals indicating ownership, signs stamped on pots and small copper tablets. None of these inscriptions exceeds twenty words.[4]

The Indus civilization appears to have ended in a slow stagnation and decline, possibly due to the denudation of the surrounding forests or the neglect of the irrigation and sanitary systems. At Mohenjo-daro at least the end came with bloodshed: the posture of disinterred bodies suggest a warlike raid by outsiders who found no further use for the decayed metropolis.

There is much more to be said about the Indian contribution to public administration than this, but space does not permit us to dig deeply in the later annals, except to refer to a notable historical phase which, Piggott suggests,[5] may provide a reflecting light on the sort of organization that existed at Harappa before its decay. This was the period of the celebrated Mauryan Dynasty (322 to 184 B.C.) founded by Chandragupta, who drove out the Macedonian garrisons within a few years of Alexander's conquest.[6]

With the close support of his wise but crafty adviser, Kautilya Chanakya, who became his vizir, Chandragupta rapidly built a kingdom in Afghanistan and Hindustan which was probably as powerful and well-ordered as any in the world at the time. Among the numerous cities of northern India included in the new realm Pataliputra (modern Patna), the capital, was laid out on a plan reminiscent of ancient Harappa, while Taxila was a flourishing military and university town whose fame drew students from far and wide.

Founded upon force and sustained by great military power, Chandragupta's government was essentially despotic, though not without its benevolent aspects. The ruler himself was a virtual prisoner of his own system, numerous statagems being devised to evade the assassin. He was indeed fortunate to have a chief executive who, despite his unscrupulousness and ruthlessness, remained faithful to the end. The king wielded unlimited power, but had a council of notables who were empowered to legislate, regulate the finances and foreign affairs, and to appoint all the more important officers of state. The cities were ruled by large commissions, the villages by the headman or a *panchayat,* or council, of five. There was a complete system of law courts to administer an extremely severe system of justice, with the royal Council at the top and the king as final court of appeal. Mauryan society had its graces in a flourishing art and literature, and its public administration provided amenities for the people not widely available in Asia at the time. There was no slave class, but as an alternative the existing caste system was long to continue as a special and somewhat limiting characteristic of Indian society. We have a contemporary account by the Greek Megasthenes, who came to Chandragupta's court as ambassador from the King of Syria, to corroborate the satisfactory state of contemporary society and the efficiency of the administration.

The management of the realm was conducted through a departmental system staffed by a carefully graded hierarchy of officials. The main departments, each under a Superintendent, dealt with agriculture, forests, mines, cattle, commerce, warehouses, mint, communications, navigation, frontiers, passports, revenue, customs, excise, public games, prostitution, and intoxicating drinks. Of these departments those dealing with navigation and communications are of particular interest. The former regulated water transport, maintained bridges and harbours, provided government ferries and protected travellers on rivers and seas; the latter provided and kept in repair a widespread road network covering the empire, over which a variety of transport circulated which was without rival at the time — chariots, palanquins, bullock-carts, horses, camels, elephants, asses and men. The road was marked at about mile intervals with pillars indicating both distances and directions, and the route was amply provided with wells, shade-trees, police-stations, and hotels at regular distances. The administration of public games included the actual provision and management of gambling halls and the collection of the percentage due to the government. The Superintendent of Prostitution was responsible for regulating the charges made by public women and for the collection of two days' earnings per month for the state exchequer. Two of the more honoured members of the profession were assigned to the services of the royal palace, for entertainment and intelligence service!

Taxation was heavy, falling on all professions, occupations and industries, while rich men were expected from time to time to offer 'benevolences' to the king. The state regulated prices, ran certain factories and maintained monopolies in mines, salt, timber, fine fabrics, horses and elephants.

The welfare of the people was not overlooked. Care was taken of public sanitation and public health. There were hospitals and poor relief stations, and supplies were kept in state granaries for distribution in periods of famine. The rich were also compelled to contribute to the assistance of the destitute, while great public works were organized for the unemployed in times of depression. Here certainly was an administrative effort fit to be compared with those of modern times.

The departmental system was also applied to the management of the cities. The city Commission of Thirty which controlled Pataliputra was divided into six sections, each with its own sphere of responsibility, namely (i) regulation of industry, (ii) supervision of strangers, (iii) recording births and deaths, (iv) licensing merchants, checking weights and measures, and controlling sales of produce, (v) controlling sales of manufactured articles, and (vi) collection of a ten per cent tax on all sales. The result of their care was a well-ordered city that again would have provided a worthy example to later ages.

Little can be said about the individual administrators, though the evidence is that they employed efficient methods and can be accepted as worthy members of their profession. At the top were both ruler Chandragupta and vizir Kautilya, whose constant concern with power politics could not free them from extensive administrative participation. A great burden must have fallen upon the shoulders of the vizir, who was obviously competent to bear it. His influence was felt in every field, his eyes could rarely have been closed. Yet in the best traditions of his kind he found time to set down in writing his formulas for warfare and diplomacy.

It is said that he was author of the *Arthasastra,* a treatise on statecraft and the oldest surviving Sanskrit work.[7] Worthy to be compared in so many ways with Machiavelli, Kautilya's vastly greater success as a practical politican and administrator would have filled the Italian with unquenchable envy. Chandragupta himself lived in accordance with an administrative routine which, even if it existed more as an aspiration than a daily reality, is still worth quoting as astonishing evidence of the unchanging nature of the administrative art.[8]

'Except when he rode out to the hunt, or otherwise amused himself, he found his time crowded with the business of his growing realm. His days were divided into sixteen periods of ninety minutes each. In the first he arose and prepared himself by meditation; in the second he studied the reports of his agents, and issued secret instructions; the third he spent with his councillors in the Hall of Private Audience; in the fourth he attended to state finances and national defense; in the fifth he heard the petitions and suits of his subjects; in the sixth he bathed and dined, and read religious literature; in the seventh he received taxes and tribute and made official appointments; in the eighth he again met his Council, and heard the reports of his spies, including cortesans whom he used for this purpose; the ninth was devoted to relaxation and prayer, the tenth and eleventh to military matters, the twelfth again to secret reports, the thirteenth to evening bath and repast, the fourteenth, fifteenth and sixteenth to sleep.'

CHINESE PREHISTORY

The experience of China is of dual importance here, in virtue of its continuous development right up to the present age almost uninfluenced by the experience of the West, and of its long-standing administrative institutions which enjoyed an extended life for the best part of two thousand years until the beginning of the twentieth century. Geographical factors, supported by her own self-sufficiency, virtually isolated China from the other continents, although there was always plenty of interaction with immediate Asiatic neighbours and a good deal of assimilation of different nationalities in the process of political integration. Chinese leaders were always imbued with the idea of achieving world government, which was not contradicted by their knowledge that there did exist another, albeit barbarian, world beyond the distant frontiers. The dominant barbarians of Europe long appeared to the Chinese as the Germanic, Slavonic and Negro tribes did to the Greeks and Romans.

Historical records abound, for the Chinese, also from very early ages, have regarded the production of national annals as one of the important tasks of public administration, sure evidence of her long-standing culture. Until quite recently scholars had accepted as authentic a history-span for China going back to 5000 B.C., in parallel with contemporary civilizations of Mesopotamia and Egypt, but in fact China does not emerge from the mists of prehistory before 1500 B.C., existing accounts of earlier epochs being legendary and written down only in later texts. By that time, however, advanced political and social institutions had already evolved and there is good reason to expect that, with advances in archaeology to which the Chinese are giving increasing attention, the confines of actual knowledge will be pressed back much further. There is plenty of scope for this, since widespread evidence has come to light of a Stone Age culture reaching way back to 50,000 B.C., while skeletons have been unearthed near Peking of an early human type known to anthropologists as *Sinanthropus*.[9]

Writing appeared in early times though not, on existing evidence, as early as the systems of Mesopotamia and Egypt. It was first associated with augury and the script-magician appears to have been one of the first of the numerous band of Chinese public officials. He officiated as historian, astrologer and knowledge-holder whose function was to give advice whenever called upon to do so. The first communication or 'writing' appears to have been effected by means of knotted cords similar to the *quipu* or knot-writing of pre-Spanish Mexico (see Volume II, page 115). A system of written pictographs was in use by the time of Shang — before 1600 B.C. — and a completely ideographic form was developed which, even to this day, has not been superseded by an alphabetic system. From this cumbrous method of writing the Chinese have derived the great advantage that ideographs, being representational, can be widely understood despite differences of dialect. This has contributed to the unification of China. Early records were made on perishable materials such as the ubiquitous bamboo and this accounts for the non-survival of voluminous records that undoubtedly existed in the earlier centuries.

A remarkable discovery was made by Chinese scholars in A.D. 1899 when they came to the conclusion that the marks on so called 'dragon-bones' which had been widely unearthed during farming and sold to drug-stores for medicine, were an early form of writing and that these oracle-bones, as they are now called, had been used in connection with divination. The bones bore the questions which had to be answered and covered such subjects as (i) to what spirits should certain sacrifices be made? (ii) travel directions, where to stop and how long, (iii) hunting and fishing, (iv) the harvest, (v) the weather, and (vi) illness and recovery.[10] From these details alone it would be possible to reconstruct a simple picture of the sort of society and administrative organization that already existed, but later writings, though dealing with legend, will take us much further.

A dynastic system appears already to have been established by about 2000 B.C. The early rulers were probably priest-kings with no fixed seat of government, the court being continually on the move. Thus, early public administration comprised the regular inspection tours of the king and the journeys of homage of the princes. Since the oases of these communities were the river valleys of the continent, especially of the Yellow and Yangtze rivers, there can be little doubt that from an early date irrigation works were the primary concern of the king's deputies. To one of these legendary rulers, Shun, many important administrative developments have been attributed, even the use of examinations to test competence for promotion, but much of this may be little more than conjecture on the part of later writers.

However, even if looked at with due reserve, the suggested list of Shun's nine ministers is well worth considering. They were (1) *Si K'ung,* the Chancellor (held by Yu), (2) *Hou Tsi,* Lord of the Millet (held by K'i), (3) *Si T'u,* Master of Schools (held by Sie), (4) *Shi,* Supreme Judge (held by Kao Yao), (5) *Kung Kung,* Director of Works (held by Chu), (6) *Yu,* Master of Forest (held by I), (7) *Ch'i Tsung,* Master of Rites (held by Po I), (8) *Tien Yo,* (Master of Music (held by Kuei, and (9) *Na Yen,* Master of Communications (held by Ling). That such a wide conception of the scope of public administration, as is suggested by these ministerial offices, may well have been held is not at all unreasonable in the context of the times, for it is not incompatible with subsequent developments which are more definitely authenticated.

The religious and philosophical attitude to government assumed by Chinese thinkers of the time is characterized by 'The Great Plan' which is contained in an early work *The Book of History*. The Plan had nine divisions, which may be summarized as follows: (1) the five elements, (2) practice of the five businesses, (3) earnest devotion to the eight objects of government, (4) harmonious use of the five time arrangements, (5) establishment and use of sovereignty; (6) correct use of the three virtues, (7) intelligent use of the examination of doubts, (8) thoughtful use of the various verifications, and (9) hortatory use of the five happinesses and deterrent use of the six extremities. Here surely is a complete concept of paternal government which is characteristic of China's long-standing civilization. The eight objects of government under (3) are (i) food, (ii) commodities, (iii) sacrifices, (iv) provision of work, (v) provision of education, (vi) punishment of crime, (vii) guests and (viii) the army. There is no question here of the ruler adopting a *laissez faire* attitude to his people. The multiplicity of public tasks indicates the existence of an extensive administration, many of whose characteristics were no doubt handed down to their better-documented successors. The three virtues under (6) are defined as straight-forward government, strong government and mild government, being severally applicable according to the state of the realm at the particular time. Only the ruler could confer favours, strike terror and receive jade food. Whether jade food represented the ordinary public revenues or the royal viands at sacrifices and at entertainments for the princes is not clear. Concentration of power in the hands of the ruler was endorsed and its usurpation by his officials was strongly condemned.[11] Already a natural fear of bureaucracy was being manifested!

THE CHOU PERIOD AND CONFUCIUS

Chinese history is accepted as beginning with the feudal states of the Chou period, somewhere about 1030 B.C. The Chou conquered the Shang people, whose civilization was apparently more advanced than theirs and whose institutions therefore foreshadowed most of the elements of the later system, which developed into a benevolent paternalism with important communistic elements. The king, ruling by heavenly decrees, was known as the Son of Heaven and bore the title *Wang,* or ruler. He had the assistance of a chief minister and other ministers who attended to the several branches such as agriculture, public works, religious rites, military affairs, punishments, and the personal business and domains directly ruled by the *Wang.* Below these was a regular hierarchy of officials forming a considerable public service for the time, with bureaucratic tendencies growing more and more stereotyped as time went on. All lands outside the domains of the *Wang* were assigned as fiefs to a hierarchy of feudal princes and lords organized into a graded nobility. Each feudal lord had his own officials. Difficulties of travel over the long distances that often separated them from the centre tended to enhance their autonomy. Relationships were conducted in accordance with prescribed ritual, the princes paying allegiance and homage to the *Wang.* The clans were divided into families whose heads wielded considerable power and whose members were bound together by elaborate rituals which amounted to a system of ancestor worship. There was a strict division between the feudal nobility and the masses and, while special care was taken of the needs of the latter, their incomes never rose above subsistence levels. But care for widows and orphans, the sick and the aged was enjoined upon the feudal lords, and the system received widespread popular support in consequence. Originally the people's main functions were to care for the lands of the princes and to provide soldiers, who were settled in families in villages which formed the basic political unit. As time went on outsiders were admitted to the village groups and leaders came to be chosen by common consent rather than in accordance with kinship relations. This system was to continue throughout Chinese history.

The Chou period was an age of great cultural and educational activity. Books consisted of wood or bamboo strips inscribed either with ink or varnish.[12] Literature emerged in the form of religious texts and poetry and records of events were begun by official scribes who were also responsible for records and documents dealing with such matters as lawsuits and the granting of fiefs. Among the interesting texts that have survived the *Chou Li,* or 'Rites of Chou' is of particular interest to us. Its origins are obscure, for it has been ascribed to the famed Chou Kung, also known as the Duke of Chou, an early regent to whom is attributed an administrative organization which formed the pattern for future generations, but an anonymous author of the fourth or third century B.C seems to have been its more likely author, although a date as late as the first century A.D. has been suggested.[13] The *Chou Li,* which outlines an idealized version of the Chou system of administration, is of importance for the great influence it had upon later political and social reformers.

It was, however, the early philosophers who were destined to leave the greatest impress on China's administrative history, as upon much else. They were concerned with the creation of the ideal society. Influential schools were inaugurated by Confucius, Mencius and Lao Tzu; and the greatest of these was Confucius, who lived from about 551 to 479 B.C.[14]

Confucius himself was a teacher and not an administrator. Despite his personal ambition to hold office he appears to have occupied but one modest official post for only a short time. He considered good government to be impossible under the existing system of hereditary rule, which nevertheless he felt was not likely to be superseded. The dilemma, he thought, could be overcome by separating the administrative from the political functions and entrusting them to virtuous and well-trained ministers and assistants.[15] Preparation for official positions was to include long study of the principles of government and the discussion of situations that were likely to arise, so that the students would know what to do when they took over practical responsibility. The case study is not so modern as we may sometime imagine! This system of education was destined to be a success, largely because the rulers had sufficient perspicacity to realize that the young men so trained had the very skills they needed and that it was to their interest to employ them.

The new system was based upon the principle that government should be handled by men chosen according not to birth but to virtue and ability, and that its main aim was the happiness of the people. Thus poverty was no bar to studentship and eventual selection for office. Instruction was informal and individual, conducted mainly by question and discussion. The students studied prescribed texts, and selected passages were discussed. Character-building was the aim. To assist in this the traditionally aristocratic and peculiarly Chinese art of *Li* was taken over. *Li* has been translated as 'ceremonial', 'ritual', and 'the rules of propriety', while the idea of sacrifice is undoubtedly present: it amounted to a very special religious code and a mode of proper conduct, which was needed to counteract the degraded moral standards of the age.[16] Music was held to be important, a point that, a century later, would have interested Plato and Aristotle, of whom Confucius was surely an unconscious forerunner at the other side of the earth. Confucius's system advocated the middle way and emphasized the need to recognize mistakes in order that they might be rectified. It was humanitarian: for example, human sacrifices, which were common at the time, were condemned. Above all the importance of training for public administration was recognized at a time when privileged rule accepted as axiomatic the allocation of state offices by favour.

The sway of the Chou emperors does not appear to have been very stable, and in fact from the eighth century B.C. this was exemplified by the existence of several semi-independent states which at one time numbered as many as twenty-five. They contended for the hegemony which passed through a number of hands. It was during this phase that the custom arose of dividing the population into four classes, a system that was to persist into later history. These were (i) the *shih,* or lesser nobility, knights and scholars; (ii) the *nung,* or peasant farmers; (iii) the *kung,* or artisans; and (iv) the *shang,* or merchants.[17] As we have just seen the sixth century B.C. saw the rise of the philosophers who were to exercise such widespread influence upon society and government. Of particular interest is the Academy of the Gate of Chi in the capital of the State of Chhi, which welcomed scholars from all the other states, providing them with quarters and maintenance, thus forming a true university. It is interesting to note that this institution, founded by King Hsuan of Chhi about 318 B.C., was almost contemporary with Plato's Academy at Athens.[18]

The state of Chhin — not to be confused with Chhi already mentioned; the latter was situated on the coast, the former far inland — paid particular attention to the construction of irrigation works, an activity which encouraged centralization and the absorption of weaker feudal neighbours. The strengthening of bureaucratic at the expense of feudal institutions inevitably followed. This led to a struggle for power among the states, from which Chhin was destined to emerge victorious. Thus its ruler Cheng, with the defeat of the powerful Chhu in 222 B.C., found himself the head of a united China, with the title Chhin Shih Huang Ti.

The new ruler, ably assisted by his minister Li Ssu, showed great vigour in introducing the changes required to replace feudal institutions. The administration was further strengthened. Estates were broken up and placed under the control of officials. The country was reorganized into thirty-six, later forty-one, prefectures with military governors and civil administrators. Officials were constantly transferred to prevent the growth of personal relationships between them and their areas. Widespread measures of standardization and reconstruction were undertaken. Communications were vastly improved. Even the written language was standardized. It is said that the Emperor ordered the burning of books that favoured feudal influences, as well as the putting to death of a large number of the literati, but doubts have been thrown upon the authenticity of such reports.[19] Whatever truth there may have been in this there can be little doubt that Chhin Shih Huang Ti, who worked indefatigably on the numerous reports that flooded his in-tray and made tiring official journeys to ensure that his orders were being inmplemented, thoroughly earned the title of Great Unifier. He died in 210 B.C. leaving the traditional ineffective son who was to prove incapable of holding his realm together.

RISE OF THE HAN AND THE GREAT EXAMINATION
SYSTEM

After the death of Huang Ti the revolutionaries inscribed their banner 'Back to Feudalism', but in fact the tide was strongly against the success of traditionalism. The new centralism had come to stay. In 206 B.C. began the leadership of the Han dynasty which, with one brief interlude, was to endure for over four hundred years. Gradually an extensive Chinese empire was consolidated under these new rulers and their able assistants. The new realm was divided into provinces, but for a time provinces and feudal states existed side by side, with border territories constituted as *tao* or chief prefectures. Eventually, however, the whole empire came to be organized on a three-tier administrative pattern of thirteen provinces, each subdivided into chief prefectures, which were further divided into districts.[20]

The significant development was the rise of Confucianism to a position of overwhelming authority as the literary philosophy of the community. This was no doubt largely due to its capacity in providing an effective alternative to the Legalist school which had fallen into disfavour through its association with the autocratic methods of the preceding dynasty. In addition there was a special virtue in Confucianism which was to enable it, through its moulding influence on the form of government, to project and shape an officialdom which was to stabilize the Chinese system for two millennia, an outstanding performance to say the least.

The new rulers recognized the magnitude of the administrative task that increasing centralization was to place on their shoulders. Complex nationalized services, needed to consolidate the new system, could not be serviced by the old self-seeking type of official. A career open to the talents was called for and impartial examination tests would prove a more effective method of selection than the personal choice of provincial governors, each with his own interests to satisfy. Yet similar situations arose throughout history in all parts of the world without being solved in this way, at least until modern times. Obviously the circumstances in China must have been particularly favourable for such an unusual solution to be adopted.

Abundant evidence survives of the new officialdom's widespread activities, as Wilhelm writes:[21]

"From various objects, pictures, and manuscripts on paper, wood and bamboo we gain an insight into the life and doings of those Chinese officials who combined with the strict discipline of the Romans the serene calm of the Greeks. We get some idea of the precision and exactitude with which the wheels of administrative machinery revolved. We come across brief letters and notes containing invitations to a meal together and find literary exercises and calligraphic efforts in the latest style alongside clumsy arithmetic by children of tender years.'

According to Max Weber[22] examinations had still been unknown at the time of Confucius and it was not until the Han period 'that the bestowal of offices according to merit was raised to the level of a principle'. It seems unlikely that examinations were completely unknown in earlier times, but there can be little doubt that Confucian influences greatly facilitated the spread of the idea. It is not wrong therefore to attribute the establishment of examinations as a system to the Han period, when they had such an important impact in shaping Chinese public administration. To Tung Chung-Shu, a scholar who wrote the *Chhun Chhiu Fan Lu,* or 'String of Pearls on the Spring and Autumn Annals', which still survives, is given the distinction of founding the bureaucratic practices and procedures which came to be laid down in texts that provided precedents for later decisions. It became the practice for scholars to meet together to determine a kind of administrative law on the basis of the ancient writings. There are records of such important assemblies in the Shih-Chu Pavilion of the palace in 51 B.C. and in the White Tiger Lodge in A.D. 79. At another such meeting the question of nationalizing the salt and iron industries was discussed.[23]

With the long reign of Emperor Wu Ti (140 to 87 B.C.) the Han dynasty rose to its greatest glory. A vast empire was extended and consolidated, special attention was given to economic affairs and the centralized system of government was strengthened, especially through the increased power of the officialdom. There was perhaps little that was new in the system, but the best of past institutions and practices were selected and reinforced by the shrewd emperor, who placed himself at the head of the public service. His policy was to select both his civil and his military agents on the basis of ability irrespective of birth, a principle which strongly commended itself to the Confucian school of thought, whose supporters gained the emperor's favour. To render more effective the practice of imposing competitive tests for determining qualifications for office the educational system was remoulded to equip it for the preparation of suitable candidates. Thus, in 124 B.C., the Po Shih Kuan, or Imperial University, was set up with a chair for each of the classical books. This central training school was supplemented by similar schools in the provinces, which appear to have dated back even earlier, i.e. to 145 B.C., when Wen Ong, Governor of Szechuan, is said to have established his own Department of Education to provide studies for boys from outlying districts.[24] An important outcome of this new system was its effect of increasing general respect for scholarship, for even those who were unsuccessful in obtaining office might receive honorary titles and privileges and in this way others were encouraged to aspire to scholarship, sometimes as a life's vocation.

There was another side to the coin. In donning the mantle of 'Chief Bureaucrat' the emperor weakened an important check on misgovernment which had ensured that all members of the administration, however important, should be open to criticism. The tendency now was for centres of power to move further down the hierarchy. For example, the Chancellors became figureheads in favour of the Masters of Writing who screened all documents before they reached the emperor. Later the subordinate, but better placed, Palace Writers, by taking over this function came more prominently into the picture. As eunuchs, they enjoyed a great advantage over the ordinary officials in having access to the emperor inside the royal apartments. The influence of the eunuchs goes back to earlier times, the first reference to this institution, according to the *Tso Chuan* of Duke Chao,[25] dating to 535 B.C. As a result of a new office organization coupled with the cult of fair women which held sway, the eunuchs constituted a counter-power under the throne. The new system, supported by the family doctrines of the Confucians, also encouraged the growth of nepotism among members of the Empress's family and court favourites and a tendency among provincial governors, as viceroys, to make their offices hereditary. The struggle between the scholar-administrators and the eunuchs was never-ending, but in assessing the occasional virtues and much-advertised vices of the latter, it has to be remembered that it is to the former that most surviving evidence is to be attributed and one must take into account their loyalty to their own order.

For a short period, from 9 to 23 A.D., the Han period was broken by an interregnum under the usurper Wang Mang, who had risen to high favour on account of his scholarship, temperate living and considerable charity. Acting as regent for a weakly boy-emperor, Wang Mang, after a short period, took the throne as Emperor Hsin Huang Ti. During his brief reign he attempted widespread reforms which have often been instanced as an early attempt to build a socialist system but which in effect seem to have been astutely directed towards strengthening the bureaucratic institutions of the state.[26] A complete agrarian reorganization was attempted through land nationalization, and the control of state monopolies was consolidated under central departments.

Thus the supply of the main necessaries of salt, wine, iron, wood, water power and copper received special attention from the state. Currency reform was undertaken and steps were put in hand to reorganize the bureaucratic structure, mainly in the direction of reinstituting old titles and systems of office tenure. But Wang Mang made many enemies. Insurrections broke out. He was murdered in Ch'angan, his capital, in A.D. 23. Chinese historians, influenced possibly by his violation of the cardinal Confucian virtue of loyalty to his prince, have been highly critical of Wang Mang who nevertheless appears to have been an able statesman with the welfare of his people very much at heart.

The Han period was marked by a number of important techno-logical improvements and advances, not the least of which was the invention of paper by Tshai Lun in A.D. 114.[27] This was to be of outstanding importance in the history of administration. Need-ham remarks that at the time this was far from being an unmixed blessing, and adds:

'Karlgren goes so far as to say that the invention of paper in the second century was a great misfortune for China. Although the Chinese were ahead of the West in printing also, this did not begin till the eighth or ninth centuries, leaving a gap of 700 years during which all manuscripts were written on perishable material instead of the clumsy but durable parchment of the West. In Europe, on the other hand, the art of mass-production was obtained soon after the appearance of the fragile non-durable material.'[28]

Towards the end of this period in A.D. 220, corruption was spreading throughout the Han Empire and the bad practice of sale of offices was becoming widespread.[28] The following period up to A.D. 588 was a sort of Dark Age, characterized by the division of the Chinese realm into a number of states under several dynasties. A new era of cultural prosperity was ushered in with the Sui dynasty which rose rapidly to its brief heyday in A.D. 589.

This was a time of considerable public works activity. The Great Wall in the north, which had been begun before the Han to keep out the nomadic barbarians on the frontier and incidentally keep in the settled Chinese south of the wall, was extended; numerous canals were dug; palaces and administrative centres were constructed. Extension of waterworks was a notable con-tribution to the stability of the empire, calling forth a colossal engineering effort and representing a remarkable feat of organi-zation and administration. The *Khai Ho Chi,* or 'Record of the Opening of the Canal', published in Sui times[29] remains as evidence of the tremendous concentration of resources involved. Five million and a half workers are said to have been assembled and put to work under the supervision of fifty thousand police. The immemorial Chinese method of using human hand power in innumerable small doses is exemplified in this vast undertaking and the episode of the Egyptian pyramids may well have been eclipsed. According to the 'Record' over two million men were 'lost'—either died or ran away—in the process. These losses could only have been partially due to cruelty and punishment involved in the actual work operations and it seems probable that such occurrences as epidemics and food shortages, against which the administrators had failed to provide, were even more to blame.

To facilitate the accomplishment of such large-scale projects a radical revision of the administrative services was undertaken. Schools were supported and the Imperial Library was extended. The examination system was thoroughly overhauled and, in fact, placed upon the basis that was to persist for over a thousand years. The degree of *Chin Shih* to which the important examination led continued into the twentieth century. A new class of travelling inspectors were appointed to report on officials, with the object of improving their performance and preventing sedition. In A.D. 618 the Sui were replaced by the T'ang, whose rule was to continue till A.D. 907.

Under the T'ang all the institutions existing under the preceding dynasty—themselves going back mainly to the Han period—were continued and improved. The administration was now distributed over ten *tao* or provinces, each of which was divided into *chou,* or prefectures. In A.D. 639 there were 358 *chou.* The *chou* were further divided into *hsien,* or sub-prefectures. Thus the three-tier system continued very much as before.[30]

The officials assigned to these several territorial divisions were all appointed centrally and subject to frequent transfer, but there were also imperial commissioners who were sent out specially to handle particular emergencies, such as floods, drought and rebellions. The officials were charged with caring for the welfare and morals of the people. Apart from the extensive works programmes already briefly mentioned the state gave special attention to the fostering of agriculture; public granaries were maintained and grain stored for general issue in times of shortage.

State schools were improved and support for the Confucian cult continued. But the examinations were set in subjects besides the Confucian classics: for example, in calligraphy, history, law, mathematics, poetry and even Taoist philosophy.[31] Later emphasis came more and more to be concentrated on the classics and among these the works most highly esteemed were the *Li Ki,* or 'Record of Rites' and the *Tso Chuan,* or 'Tso's Commentary'.[32] The emperor exercised his right to appoint recommended candidates outside the examinations, but the growing esteem in which the examination system was held gradually led to its overwhelming predominance. Moreover the emperor learned that in this way he not only obtained competent officials but effectively checked the power of the hereditary nobility, replacing it by a sort of intellectual aristocracy. Nevertheless the hereditary nobility continued to share to some extent in official preferment: they were much too influential to be excluded by the examination requirements.

The examination system undoubtedly raised official standards of competence far above the levels usually attainable through nepotism and favouritism, but it had its drawbacks in encouraging a purely literary approach, tending to idealize the past at the expense of inventiveness and gradually to become stereotyped. Achieving an official post, via the State examinations, became a sort of national obsession and other activities, which were freely developed in the West, tended to be neglected. Yet they had the virtue of continually injecting new blood into the administration and of providing a generally accepted democratic element in the constitution which had important long-term effects in curbing unrest. The feeling that the élite did not constitute a closed-shop undoubtedly exerted an important influence on Chinese society.

An important advance during this period was the introduction of printing. This was due to a number of circumstances. The Confucian classics, which had been inscribed on stone as early as the Han period, were again cast in this form under the T'ang. It had been the practice to take copies of the inscribed stones on paper by means of inked squeegees. Wooden blocks were introduced for this purpose in A.D. 932 and by A.D. 953 all the Confucian classics had been printed. But the Buddhists, whose growing power had been clipped in A.D. 845 by the suppression of their establishments, also contributed to this development through their widespread use of religious texts in the form of charms. The earliest block-printing is said to have been used for the production of a Buddhist charm in A.D. 770 although it may have dated back to the reign of Ming Huang (712-56).[33] In addition to this there was the great potential demand for text-books for the examinations, and the long-standing availability of paper and ink. The strange thing is that it took so long to bridge the gap and thus to bring about an important revolution in administrative techniques. To gain a more intimate picture of the administration of the

T'ang period we shall shortly look at the remarkable career of Po Chu-i, one of China's outstanding men of this period.

HISTORIOGRAPHY AS A GOVERNMENT FUNCTION

Chinese official history is contained in the twenty-six Standard Histories (*Cheng-shih*), which cover the period from before 221 B.C. until 1911, the last being published in Taipai in 1961.[34] As Etienne Balazs, the Hungarian authority on Chinese civilization emphasized, these histories were written by bureaucrats for bureaucrats with the aim of providing information and precedents of value in educating and guiding officials in the art of government.[35]

The first of these, the *Shih-chi* or *Records of the Historian*, written by Ssu-ma T'an and completed by his son Ssu-ma Ch'ien, was based upon materials no longer in existence and made use *inter alia* of the annals of the pre-imperial State of Ch'in, in which there was reference to the appointment, in the thirteenth year of Duke Wen (circa 753 B.C.), of scribes to record events. Evidence exists that even before this date there were appointed in other states scribal officials whose functions included divination, the recording of court events and the keeping of archives. Such records included both annals (*chi*) and genealogies (*shih*). Entries were terse and very much to the point, as the following quotation indicates: 'In the twentieth year of his reign (678 B.C.) Duke Wu died. He was buried at P'ing-yang in the district of Yung. For the first time human victims were made to follow a dead person in the grave. Those who were sacrificed numbered 66 persons.'[36]

With their administrative use in view the Standard Histories deal with the several spheres of official activity and they demonstrate progressively how the officials' preoccupations tended to change throughout the ages. Thus their interest in ritual, cosmology and omens, which was at its highest under the Han, gives way in time to concern with the day-to-day conduct of government business, such as the practical administration of justice, taxation, currency and the like, and particularly of staff management and the personal conduct of officials.[37]

An office of historiographers was maintained under each dynasty to record the deeds and doings of the emperor and acts of government, to keep daily notes of public events, to collect and preserve reports and documents and to build up archives.[38] On the basis of such materials the Standard History was completed under the next or a later dynasty. The overall importance attached to these annals is attested by the fact that the process went on irrespective of whether the preceding regime was Chinese or alien, although it is true that usurping regimes could always cite the activities of their predecessors to justify their own rule. These Standard Histories continued to make use of the earlier annal-genealogy form in contrast to the more straightforward chronological form favoured by other historians.

Of particular interest to our period is the outstanding work of Ssu-ma Kung who lived during the eleventh century and who dealt comprehensively with the period 403 B.C. to A.D. 959, in his *Comprehensive Mirror for Aid in Government* (Tzu-chih T'ung-chien), which comprised a history of China in annalistic form. This was a personal achievement on different lines from the Standard Histories and, as a mere chronicle, would have been rather less effective had it not been for Ssu-ma Kung's advanced methods and high critical standards.[39] It is interesting to note that Ssu-ma Kung was a fierce opponent of the notorious reformer of the Sung period, Wang Anshih, to whom reference is made in Volume II of the present work.

Chinese history, which developed in a pattern that was maintained over long periods, was unavoidably stereotyped because of (i) the long-established habit of cutting history into dynastic slices, (ii) the historians' official status, saving certain notable exceptions, (iii) the lavish use of quoted passages, (iv) handicaps imposed by the nature of the language, and (v) the constant copying which stifled intellectual initiative. As a consequence its stereotypes became impressed upon the minds and practices of the Chinese bureaucracy.[40]

EMINENT T'ANG ADMINISTRATOR: PO CHU-I

The celebrated Chinese poet Po Chu-i was born in the small town of Hsin-cheng in Honan in A.D. 772.[41] He began to build up his reputation as a poet at an early age, but as the son of a poor and comparatively unsuccessful provincial official lacked the influence that was normally required even to obtain permission to sit the examinations. It was fortunate therefore that when poverty compelled Po Chu-i to seek official preferment, his application had been delayed some eight years later than usual and that by this time the Chief Examiner was Kao Ying, who was determined to abolish the numerous practices whereby well-placed candidates had hitherto obtained preference. Po Chu-i satisfied his examiners in the provincial examination of A.D. 799, which entitled him to compete in the Metropolitan examinations at Ch'ang-an the following spring.

In order to curry favour with Ch'en Ching, the Supervising Censor, as was the usual practice in such cases, Po Chu-i sent him a fawning and servile letter.[42] He enclosed twenty pieces of prose and a hundred poems and asked for an opinion on their quality, as justification for his proceeding with his candidature. The reply, if there was one, is not known, but, according to Waley, there is evidence that Po Chu-i did not receive much encouragement: not that this was to deter him from going ahead.

Several examinations were conducted by the Board of Rites at that time, but Po Chu-i's choice lay between the *Ming-ching,* or Classical, and the *Chin-shih,* or Literary examinations.[43] The former comprised tests in five classics; the latter was concerned with only one, but included the composition of *fu,* a peculiar literary form, and ordinary poems. Both examinations called for essays on general moral principles and on current administrative problems. As opposed to the Classical examination, which had become largely a memory test and was no longer accepted as admitting successful candidates to the highest positions, the Literary examination was regarded as a test of talent and originality. Po Chu-i's poetic gift obviously led him to sit the latter. His actual test called for a *fu* of 350 words on a theme from Confucius's *Analects XVII* which ran 'By nature near together; by practice far apart'. The theme of the poem from a well-known anthology was a quotation from a work by Yen Yen-chih which may be interpreted as 'Jade-bearing waters may be recognized by their rectilinear ripples'. Five essays had to be submitted. Four dealt with general principles which were stated in such an allusive way that, despite the narrowed scope of the examination, to tackle them satisfactorily the candidate's knowledge needed to range over the *Book of Changes,* the *Book of History,* Confucian works like the *Analects,* as well as the Taoist Classics. The final question was more concerned with practical affairs. In this case the candidates were asked whether they were in favour of reviving an abandoned practice of harmonizing purchase whereby, in order to stabilize supplies, grain was purchased by the government at above market prices in good years and sold below market prices in bad. Po Chu-i argued in favour of the system, but later as a practical official was to learn that the policy could degenerate into a form of unauthorized taxation. He obtained a First Class in the success lists and, as his was to be a typical career ending in honoured retirement, it is worth following stage by stage.

Successful candidates in the Metropolitan examinations were often offered posts as assistants to higher provincial officials, and with this end in view Po Chu-i addressed a long poem to Ts'ui Yen, the Inspector General, praising his administration, but to no avail. Successful candidates often had to wait years before an official appointment came along. However, there was the alternative of sitting the Placing examination held by the Board of Civil Office. Po Chu-i, having decided to do this, set out for the capital in the autumn of A.D. 801. Apart from fulfilling certain conditions[44] candidates had the choice of certain tests. Po Chu-i chose the composition of *p'an,* or judgments, which had to be composed in a special style known as *p'an-t'i,* or judgment form. One of his three judgments—which could range over legal, moral or ritual issues, or even be concerned with matters of minor social etiquette—consisted of the following problem: 'A professor at the university for the sons of grandees teaches the young men to adapt themselves to mixed society. The Director of Studies contends that this is contrary to the principles of education and disapproves. What do you think?' We have it on Arthur Waley's authority that 'Po, in a rigmarole of archaicisms and allusions which utterly defies translation, came down on the side of the professor'.[45]

The eight successful candidates included, besides Po Chu-i, Yuan Chen with whom he was to strike up a life-long friendship famous in Chinese history. They both received the modest post of Collator of Texts in the Palace Library, a poorly paid almost sinecure office which entailed only two attendances a month at the library and really constituted a pool of gifted young men retained for future use.

At the end of A.D. 803 it happened that both Kao Ying, who had passed Po Chu-i in the Literary examination, and Cheng Yü-ch'ing, who had been in charge of the Placing examination, were made Chief Ministers. Po-Chu-i set himself to write a *fu* of congratulation to them under the title 'Afloat on the Wei River', in which he managed to include some flattery of the Emperor Tê Tung, whose long reign of twenty-five years was nearing its end. In fact the Emperor died in A.D. 805, having seen through a modernized system of taxation and witnessed the rise to military power and political domination of the eunuchs.

By the following year both Yuan and Po had withdrawn from the Collatorships to prepare long essays for the Palace examination, in which they were destined to take the first and second places respectively. On the assumption that official attitudes at the moment would, contrary to usual practice, be favourable to critical dissertations, both scholars acted accordingly. One question referred to current difficulties and asked how the Empire could be restored to its former prosperity. Yuan Chen's answer was both the more comprehensive and the more original. He attributed the decline to unpractical methods in selecting official personnel and advocated a new system of examinations whereby the Board of Rites would conduct the tests which should be based on up-to-date materials, and the Board of Civil Office, instead of holding a second examination of its own, should make appointments strictly according to the examinations and promotions or demotions on the basis of actual records and achievements. This revolutionary proposal testifies to Yuan's outstanding vision. Had it been adopted, as of course it was not, China could have been governed by men whose minds were firmly focussed upon present institutions and problems rather than upon the sometimes fabulous past, and the whole stream of Chinese history could surely have been different. Chinese officialdom knew how to deal with such distressing suggestions, for office pigeon-holes are not a modern invention.

As a result of the examination, Po Chu-i in the autumn of A.D. 806 took up a small post at Chou-chih fifty miles out of Ch'ang-an. Yuan Chen, on the other hand, received the much better appointment of Commissioner in the *Men-hsia,* or State Chancellery. It is not common to officialdom for outspokenness to be rewarded in this manner, and probably there were other reasons for Yuan's appointment. His interesting office was concerned with 'picking up things dropped', or in other words with sending up criticisms of policy, though whether the office made him merely the channel for such action or actually authorized him to initiate criticism himself is not clear. In any case Yuan, characteristically, showed unusual initiative by submitting a ten-point plan for rehabilitating the dynasty.[46] Despite support from several prominent statesmen and an audience with the Emperor, he incurred the wrath of Cheng Yu-ch'ing, the Chief Minister, who had him arrested. However, other influences prevailed and Yuan was shortly at large again, though reduced to a modest post in the Eastern capital Lo-yang, from which he later withdrew for a time in order to fulfil the normal period of mourning for his mother.

In the meantime Po Chu-i found his routine duties little to his taste and it was perhaps fortunate that in A.D. 807 he was called to act as Collator and Arranger in *Chi-hsien Tien,* or the Hall of Assembled Worthies, which had just been reorganized in accordance with proposals made by Ch'en Ching. The function of this characteristically Chinese department was to supply historical information required by the Emperor which was not otherwise available. At about the same time Po was successful in the examination for doctor in the Han-lin Academy. The main task of the Academy was the composition of documents, such as letters of appointment, letters to foreign potentates, addresses to the souls of the dead, and the like, which were put out in the Emperor's name. In other words Po Chu-i had now become an administrative official vested with the task of drafting in high flown language various important state documents for the Emperor's signature. The practical nature of the test to which he had been subjected in the doctorate examination is clearly demonstrated by the topics of the five compositions that he had been required to submit. They were (1) a decree conferring fresh rank on a frontier commander, (2) a letter to officers and troops victorious in the recent campaigns in eastern China, (3) a letter to Kao Ch'ung-wen, hero of the Szechwan campaign the year before, (4) a short memorial to accompany a picture of a peculiarly shaped ear of grain, supposed to be a good omen; and (5) a hymn of victory over rebels, to be chanted at the Great Shrine.[47] Po Chu-i must have revelled in propounding his solutions! During A.D. 808 he was appointed Ommissioner and was thus at last truly launched on his official career.

With the encouragement of P'ei Chi, the Chief Minister, Po Chu-i achieved considerable success during the next three years in the multifarious tasks that fell to him as Ommissioner. Surviving records of his activities throw an interesting light on the wide scope of Chinese public administration at the time.[48] He was prominent in challenging the maleficient activities of the eunuchs who formed a special class in court society. They were mainly recruited as castrated boys from among the aboriginals of the south and were trained specially for such duties as attendants in the Imperial harem by older eunuchs who were known as their 'fathers'. Their duties as a matter of course gave them access to intimate confidential information and placed them in the way of receiving valuable perquisites or of rising to important posts. Thus their activities extended to the provision of stores for the palace community; the staffing of secret palace police; attachment as superintendents to provincial armies to report on the efficiency and reliability of commanders; providing a confidential messenger service; acting as palace spies; taking charge of the religious life of foreign monks and others, and thus becoming protectors of Buddhism. Most of these functions are found in other administrative systems but certainly not in this particular form. The political struggles in China, instead of being between different economic and social interests, raged between the palace and the administration or, as the Chinese put it in their picturesque style, between the 'within and the without'. Among other matters Po Chu-i pursued the cases of a number of prisoners who had been sent to local gaols years before and forgotten, and he went on to suggest measures of prison reform.

Towards the end of A.D. 810 the Chief Minister had a stroke and was obliged to resign. He was replaced by Li Chi-fu whom Po had offended by his defence of the year 808 examiners.[49] During the same year Po Chu-i had made a plea on compassionate grounds for promotion to a post with a higher salary and he was appointed Intendent of City Finances, although he does not appear to have actually taken up duty at the city headquarters. The following year he was compelled to relinquish all official positions in order to fulfil his obligations of mourning for his mother. In view of the disfavour of the new Chief Minister, who was a comparatively young man, it seemed now as though Po's official career had ended. He turned to literary pursuits.

In fact there was much more to follow. Po Chu-i was to continue in public service until his retirement after reaching, in A.D. 841, the official retiring age of 69. During this long spell he held a number of posts of varying importance, some in the capital others away in the provinces, as was the custom. Some carried heavy official burdens, some were little more than sinecures, as fortune and changing policy decreed. His career was inevitably moulded by changes at the court, as the result of which Po suffered alternating periods of favour and disfavour, the latter often being deepened by his own critical attitudes, which were often not as one would have expected from an official. In this connection he was no doubt helped by his great prestige as a poet. His interests were wide and he wrote on such matters as music, in which, for example, he supported the traditional styles, attributing their decline to the Board responsible for the music of the Court Ancestral Sacrifices. Further consideration of these and many similar public service matters must be left to the reader's own exploration of Mr. Waley's masterly text.

In A.D. 842, Po Chu-i, at the conclusion of one hundred days sick leave on full pay to which he was entitled, went on to half-pay with the rank of President of the Board of Punishments, and, although most of the literary work of his last few years has been lost, it appears that his poetic output continued until his death in A.D. 846.

This account of an interesting career brings out a number of points that characterize the public service of the age. The more important may be summarized as (i) the primary importance given to literary skill in the selection of officials, (ii) the preference for the all-rounder rather than the specialist, as illustrated by the wide range of posts successively held by Po Chu-i, (iii) the peculiar mixture of impartial test and personal influence in the actual making of appointments, (iv) the encouragement of highly critical attitudes by officials to the conduct of affairs, although there was no guarantee that such criticisms would be accepted without prejudice, (v) the willingness of the authorities to grant well-paid sinecures to officials in difficulty or likely to cause difficulties, and lastly (vi) the sense of a carefully regulated code by which the official's entire career was orchestrated. Despite the difference in the setting one often has the impression that the situations and reactions in which Po Chu-i was involved have a universal validity. Whatever the differences between the Chinese and European ways of life it seems probable that the human official of one civilization would not have felt greatly out of his element if transferred to the other.

THE LIAO INTERLUDE

One of the persisting features of Chinese history has been the trend for large areas from time to time to fall under the sway of conquering or infiltrating outsiders, who have usually adopted Chinese methods of government and administration. An instance of this had occurred after the fall of the Han Empire, when northern barbarians had set up the Wei dynasty which maintained its sway in the north from A.D. 386 to 556. With the fall of the T'ang in A.D. 907 the Ch'i-tan nomads conquered the northern provinces and established the Liao Empire, which was to endure until A.D. 1125. The Liao realm covered parts of modern Mongolia and Manchuria, extending north to the Amur River, south to the Yellow River and the Great Wall, and—excluding the north-eastern coast—westwards across the Gobi Desert as far as the Altai Mountains. While not an outstandingly interesting period of Chinese history the Liao regime is important in showing how Chinese and alien institutions were made to work side by side, and in demonstrating the pervasiveness of Chinese administrative methods. It also happens that this period is very well documented.[50]. From A.D. 960 onwards the Liao had, as their southern neighbours and opponents, the important Chinese Sung Empire which flourished up to A.D. 1279.

The Ch'i-tan appear to have achieved only a partial victory

over the Chinese, and while they adopted many of the latter's well-tried methods—as indeed any nomadic community coming fresh to the institutions of a settled society is compelled to do in face of a total lack of the necessary means in their own system—it was the policy of their controlling groups to maintain their own tribal, military and religious institutions. Indeed the Ch'i-tan continued to exercise power from their old tribal territories outside the settled realm.[51] All this accounts for the peculiar duality of the government and administrative machinery.

According to the *Liao Shih,* the standard history on which Wittfogel and Chia-Sheng's comprehensive work is based, the administration of the Liao Empire was distributed among five capitals,[52] each with its own administrative circuit. This unusual system of plural capitals, which was copied from the conquered semi-agricultural kingdom of Po-hai, proved particularly suitable to the semi-nomadic situation of Liao.

For administrative purposes each of the five administrative circuits was sub-divided into *fu,* or administrations, each *fu* into *chou,* or prefectures, and each *chou* into *hsien,* or counties. Thus we see the normal Chinese pattern of local administration in operation. Besides these three tiers there were special divisions known as *chun,* or commanderies, *ch'eng,* or fortified cities, and *pao,* or fortresses, all of which owed their peculiar status to political and strategic causes. Separate organizations were also maintained for the fifty-two tribes,[53] and these had certain military, administrative and fiscal duties. Their military functions were of particular importance since the conquering sway of the Ch'i-tan continued to depend upon efficient military organization, which was an integral part of their system of government. Its outstanding arm was the mobile horseman and its basic unit was the *ordos,* or horde, a name since widely used by European countries to designate the Tartars or Huns by whom they were invaded. Under the Liao there were twelve *ordos,* which were literally camps consisting of numerous households whose male members provided the personnel of a highly mobile cavalry. They were recruited from many sources and included Chinese, particularly those who had been transplanted by the conquerors. While their members were not free they enjoyed special privileges. They acted as the Imperial Bodyguard and also came to acquire the status of elite troops in foreign campaigns. The military machine was complex, including also tribal armies, militia and certain special forces, as well as frontier garrisons. This efficient instrument of power, weaving throughout Liao society, must be kept prominently in mind when the system of administration is under consideration.

The division of the country, from both historical and ethnical causes, into two regions, each with its own government, emphasizes the division of the empire between the nomadic and the settled, between the Ch'i-tan and Chinese, though in practice there could be no hard and fast line between the two. The governments of both the Northern and the Southern Regions were centred in the Supreme Capital, where the royal court focussed the absolutist power of the Emperor and his entourage. Here the bureaus of both government were sited. Each had its own institutions and peculiar responsibilities, about which a good deal of information has survived.[54] It is proposed to look at each separately.

Northern Region: Within the central government of the Northern Region itself the basic dichotomy of the Empire was further emphasized by the existence of separate Northern and Southern Chancelleries, each controlling its own division, with its own Prime Ministers and Great Kings. The Northern Chancellery had control of the Ch'i-tan armies and horses while the Southern Chancellery had control of the Ch'i-tan people, which included the selection of civil officials and the taxation of the tribes and leading families. Each division had both a Left and a Right Prime Minister (making four in all) who assisted in managing important military and state affairs. The two Departments of the Northern and Southern Great Kings — each with its Director of Affairs, Grand Preceptor, Grand Guardian, Minister over the Masses, and Minister of Works — were concerned with the military and civil affairs of the tribes. Separate Masters of Court Etiquette were appointed in each division to take charge of the personal services to the Emperor. Under these high administrative offices were the following major departments:

(i) The Administration of the Grand *Yu-yueh,* originally a sort of major-domo whose post had become purely honorific, awarded for outstanding political services.

(ii) The Office of the Grand *T'i-yin,* mainly concerned with the administrative and educational affairs of the Imperial family.

(iii) The Department of the *I-li-pi* in charge of punishments, a high court for tribal litigants.

official writings of all kinds.

(iv) The Department of the Grand Scribe which supervised —

(v) The Office of the *Ti-lieh-ma-tu,* in charge of ceremonies.

(vi)   The Office of the Secretariat, concerned with routine correspondence and copying.

(vii)   The Office of *A-cha-ko-chi,* previously 'holder of the key' or treasurer, who had become a mere historical survival, superseded by more advanced financial organization.

In addition to these offices there were many other organizations (including minor court bureaux, such as the Bureau of Stationery, the Bureau of Tablets and Seals, the Bureau of Lamps and Candles, the Bureau of Carriages) various household officials, family appointments, tribal supervisors, offices to administer subordinate states, and workshop officials who supervised such matters as the government herd, iron smelting, arsenals, mints and the like.

Southern Region: The Central Government of the Southern Region was essentially Chinese in structure and working. Following the T'ang precedent the Liao Emperor had the advice of six elder statesmen, who were classified under the Administration of the Three Teachers (Grand Tutor, Grand Preceptor and Grand Guardian) and the Administration of the Three Dukes (Grand Commandant, Minister over the Masses, and Minister of Works). However, while enjoying great social prestige these high officials retained little political influence.

At the beginning of the regime the key institution appears to have been the Political Council, which had its Chief, Prime Ministers and other high officials. Then it was superseded by a newly established Chinese Chancellery and a Presidential Council, and finally the Political Council was converted into the Secretarial Council. The Chinese Chancellery appears at first to have acted mainly as a Ministry of War and to have been closely associated with the Presidential Council, which supervised the Six Ministries. Later these came under a much expanded Southern Chancellery. To complete the pattern of three councils of the T'ang system there was a Court Council which was mainly concerned with court and tribal ceremonies.

Only four of the traditional Six Ministries are actually mentioned in the records, and in any case such references are few, on the assumption, it has been suggested,[55] that the structure was too well known to call for discussion. Those mentioned are the Ministries of Civil Appointments, of War, of Works, and of Rites, which in themselves afford a striking epitome of Chinese government. Each ministry had a President, a Palace Chamberlain, a Palace Gentleman and a Superannuary Gentleman.

To these organizations must be added (i) the *Tu Ch'a Yuan,* or Censorate, that peculiar Chinese institution set up to criticize the government which, however, was given little scope under foreign-controlled Liao; (ii) the Han-lin Academy in charge of the literary affairs of the Emperor, (iii) the Department of Historiography, (iv) the Department of the Master of Court Etiquette, and (v) the Guest Council.

The main administration was carried out by a number of Halls and Boards, whose responsibility were allocated on a functional basis. The eight Halls, each with a Chief and a Junior Executive, dealt with Sacrificial Worship, Banqueting, Imperial Equipment, the Imperial Clan, the Imperial Stud, Judicature and Revision, State Ceremonial, and Granaries. The seven Boards, each with a Grand and a Junior Supervisor, dealt with Imperial Archives, Astronomy, the Government Treasury, Imperial Construction, Waterworks and included the Imperial Academy. At the centre there were also numerous other household and literary offices.

Even now the administrative picture is not complete, for there were special offices for the five capitals, already mentioned, for the regional and local government areas, as well as for a series of regional financial offices.

LIAO OFFICIALDOM

For complementing such an intricate system of administrative offices numerous officials were required. Liao officials were recruited in three ways: namely, (i) hereditarily, (ii) by examination, and (iii) through the *yin* system.

There hereditary officials were selected from the noble Ch'i-tan families designated for this purpose and assigned to specific offices. The aim of this system was to maintain political power within the ruling group. Thus the Northern Prime Ministership, about which sufficient information survives, was reserved for members of the distinguished lineages of the Hsaio clan. All members of the clan had an equal right to office and outsiders were not eligible, although in fact this rule could be broken in default of satisfactory candidates. Even the basic rule was often modified by restricting office to a few selected families within the clan. Furthermore, as time went on Chinese came more and more to be selected for such appointments. 'The strength of the restricted prerogative seems, therefore to have depended on a number of factors — status, personality, the favour of the court, or the exigencies of the moment.[56] The general policy seems to have been to reserve key posts throughout the administration to Ch'i-tan nobles.

The Chinese were the most numerous and important of the non-tribal officials, particularly in the government of the Southern Region, the T'ang system of examinations being employed in their selection. Examinations were held regularly from their inauguration in A.D. 988 and were available at local, regional and central levels. The Metropolitan examinations, organized under the auspices of the Ministry of Rites, a subdivision of the Secretarial Council, provided an entry to the highest careers. Their actual content is controversial as, according to contemporary authority, the papers were originally confined to poetry and classics but later changed to poetry and law. A subsequent Chin authority states that the subjects were the classics, their commentaries, the philosophies of the different schools, and history. However, passing the prescribed test was not enough. As under other Chinese dynasties successful examinees had to have other influences on their side. It is recorded, on Chin authority, that only two or three out of every ten successful candidates found government employment, and there is reliable evidence that a number of Chinese appointments were made from candidates who did not hold the official degree.

It is known that various methods of appointment operated at different times: such as purchase of office, which was actually legalized in A.D. 1088, or selection of persons with literary attainments as a result of official recommendation or of simple qualifying tests outside the normal examinations system. These methods however could not account for the large number of apparently non-qualified Chinese officials and it is clear that the concept of a self-perpetuating bureaucracy entered into the scheme of things.[57] The Chinese custom of allowing direct descendants of office-holders to offer themselves without examination was operative. This had existed as early as the Han under the institution of *jen-tzu* (i.e. sponsoring sons). In view of the existence of the examination system the new system was now known as the *yin* prerogative, which meant that such entrants were 'protected against the hardships and pitfalls of the regular examinations'.[58] (*Yin* means shade, shelter, to protect.) In this case the father's rank was significant and sons of senior officials might apply for posts in the Seventh Rank, whereas the holder of the top degree with honours could aspire only to a post in the Ninth Rank, second class, upper grade.[59]

The *yin* system which was copied by the Liao from the contemporary Sung did not guarantee further advancement of those selected nor was it sufficiently widespread to fulfil the desires of all aspiring sons and grandsons of officials, who were consequently antagonistic to the examinations. The argument in favour of *yin* offered by the T'ang statesman Li Te-yu deserves quotation:

'The outstanding officials of the court ought to be the sons of the highest officials. Why? because from childhood on they are accustomed to this kind of position; their eyes are familiar with court affairs; even if they have not been trained in the ceremonial of the palace, they automatically achieve perfection. Scholars of poor families, even if they have an extraordinary talent, are certainly unable to accustom themselves to it.'[60]

The system was to be pressed with even greater vigour during the Sung period: then the *yin* privileges were to be bestowed on special occasions — such as the great triennial *chiao,* or sacrifice, the Emperor's birthday, or the death of a distinguished official. The privilege of making the choice might fall to the same official on a number of occasions and it has been estimated that an official serving for twenty years might start some twenty of his relatives on an official career during that period. Although under the Liao the *yin* system gained additional weight because the Ch'i-tan rulers were less keen on the examinations for the discovery of ability, nevertheless the hereditary, examination and *yin* methods all continued to form part of the system of recruitment throughout the period.

It is clear that, whatever the method of selection, the Liao public officials were not expected to have any special knowledge of public administration before they took up office. Their professional requirements were essentially literary but, of course, the basic technique of calligraphy was important. The techniques of government were still comparatively simple, such that a basic knowledge of reading, writing and calculation was all that was needed. Skill in administration would be acquired by the young official as he went along, aided no doubt by the guidance of his elders.

Despite the abundance of records these are mainly concerned with offices and rankings and tell little of what their holders actually did or how they did it. The broad functional scope of the administration is clearly shown by the great variety of services and offices listed in this present section. As in all oriental government, service of the Emperor and his court was a primary responsibility and the conduct of ceremonials ranked high. Military and financial administration were necessarily important. Hydraulic engineering, essential to the basic productive activity of agriculture, and water transport were a vital concern of public administration. Communications called for the organization of a system of Imperial posts. There was also the *corvée,* or communal labour gangs to be organized and directed — although this was largely a local matter — and several state enterprises to be managed. Among the significant offices not yet mentioned were the Office of the Salt and Iron Commissioner of the Supreme Capital and the Office of the Transport Commissioner of the Southern Capital, and there were many others of this type.

The control of agriculture and the timing of public works rendered it imperative for the government to interest itself in astronomical calculations and calendar-making. These arts the Liao acquired from the Chinese who had for long specialized in them. The Ch'i-tan also copied the Chinese habit of producing an official history. It is significant that their Department of Historiography included members of both races on its staff. Despite their understandable pride in their practical outlook as ruling class, their superior horsemanship and shooting skill, and a natural distaste for literary pursuits, the need for a literate public service to ensure the effective administration of their numerous settled subjects impelled the Liao rulers to encourage literary activities. This included the provision of education and publication of books. Public Libraries were formed under government direction.

Thus the Ch'i-tan conquerors of Liao, while clinging to their tribal traditions and nomadic institutions, in order to ensure the effective administration of such a vast alien realm were literally compelled by circumstances to copy systematically the administrative practices of the conquered Chinese, who had such a long experience of efficient public administration behind them.

SUNG ADMINISTRATION

Despite the presence in the north of powerful though backward Liao for part of the time and the pressures of other barbarian neighbours elsewhere, under the Sung dynasty, which came to power in A.D. 960 and was to endure in one form or another until the advent of the Mongols in 1280, China was to achieve a pinnacle of culture and science that developed logically out of its long past.[61] Its system of government[62] followed logically upon the arrangements adopted and developed under the Han and T'ang regimes, but was geared to new conditions and requirements.

The Emperor, ruling under the mandate of Heaven, was advised by the Council of State, which had from five to nine members, whose job was to run the administration and the judiciary, and to draft decisions for the Emperor's approval. These decisions were influenced by the advice of the Han-lin Academy, a sort of Ministry of Culture, and by criticism proffered by the Censorate.

Below the Council of State the Administration consisted of three main organs: namely (1) the Secretariat-Chancellery (*Chung-shu Men-hsia*); (2) the Finance Commission (*San-ssu*); and (3) the Bureau of Military Affairs (*She-mi-yuan*). The senior executive posts in (1) and (3) were held by individual members of the Secretariat-Chancellery. This authority was concerned with general administration, operating through the numerous offices and agencies which had come into existence under previous regimes and covering all the functions involved in protocol and ceremonial, adjudication, personnel management, foreign relations and scholastic matters. The Bureau of Military Affairs was responsible for the defence of the Empire. The Finance Commission looked after economic administration, which was to receive special attention during this period and was involved *inter alia* with the departments specifically concerned with salt and iron, revenue, and the census of population. Irrigation and transport projects and the care of public buildings also came under its control.

In addition there was the Censorate (Yu-shih-t'ai), that interesting institution developed under the T'ang, which operated under a presiding official and two assistants and consisted of a number of Censors divided among three functional divisions. The first of these was concerned with general affairs, attended imperial audiences, and was responsible for impeachment of officials for unjust and irregular actions; the second was concerned with the affairs of the palace and in ensuring that the proper procedures were followed; while the third, in the form of an inspectorate, was concerned with the work, efficiency and integrity of officials. In A.D. 1045 an additional section was added whose task was to criticize the policy of the most senior state officials. Thus, more than a thousand years ahead of the West, the Chinese had introduced a body that combined the functions of Ombudsman, O & M expert and professional conscience into the conduct of public affairs. Whether the Censorate itself was sufficiently immune or protected from the evils it sought to eliminate is open to challenge. Certainly it operated in an age of considerable bureaucratic activity and achievement when the safeguards it aimed to supply were very necessary.

The eleventh century A.D., the somewhat arbitrary dividing line between the 'Ancient' and 'Modern' volumes of this present work, is not at all applicable to the Chinese experience. The Sung regime in particular spanned both eras. It is nevertheless considered desirable to leave its further discussion to Volume II.

REFERENCES

1 Mortimer Wheeler, *Rome Beyond the Imperial Frontiers,* (Penguin, 1955), p. 205.
2 Stuart Piggott, *Prehistoric India,* (Penguin, 1950) and Mortimer Wheeler, *India and Pakistan,* (Thames & Hudson, 1959).
3 Wheeler, *India and Pakistan,* p. 98.
4 Piggott, *op. cit.,* pp. 178-181.
5 Piggott, *op. cit.,* pp. 287-88.
6 Will Durant, *The Story of Civilization*: *Our Oriental Heritage,* (Simon & Schuster, 1935), pp. 441-45.
7 T. N. Ramaswamy, *Essentials of Indian Statecraft,* (Asia Publishing House, 1962), subtitled 'Kautilya's Arthasastra for Contemporary Readers'.
8 Durant, *op. cit.,* pp. 442-3.
9 General works: R. Wilhelm, *A Short History of Chinese Civilization,* (Harrap, 1929), J. Needham, *Science and Civilization in China,* Vol. I, Introductory Orientations, (Cambridge, 1954) and K. S. Latourette, *The Chinese*: *Their History and Culture,* (Macmillan, N.Y., 1934).
10 Wilhelm, *op. cit.,* p. 71.
11 Wilhelm, *op. cit.,* pp. 85-8.
12 Latourette, *op. cit.,* p. 64.
13 Latourette, *op. cit.,* p. 67.
14 H. G. Creel, *Confucius: the Man and the Myth,* (Routledge, 1951).
15 Creel, *op. cit.,* p. 4.
16 Creel, *op. cit.,* p. 93.
17 Needham, *op. cit.,* p. 93.
18 Needham, *op. cit.,* pp. 95-6.
19 Needham, *op. cit.,* p. 101; but for the opposing view see F. R. Hoare, *Eight Decisive Books of Antiquity,* (Sheed & Ward, 1952), p. 169.
20 Wilhelm, *op. cit.,* p. 168.
21 Wilhelm, *op. cit.,* pp. 182-3. See also an account of the remarkable find of administrative writings on strips of wood discovered at Chii-yen in Michael Loewe, *Records of Han Administration* (Cambridge University, 1967).
22 H. H. Gerth and C. W. Mills (editors), *From Max Weber,* (Kegan Paul, 1947), p. 423.
23 Needham, *op. cit.,* p. 105.
24 Needham, *op. cit.,* pp. 106-7.
25 Needham, *op. cit.,* p. 105.
26 Needham, *op. cit.,* p. 109.
27 Needham, *op. cit.,* p. 45 and B. Karlgren, *Philology and Ancient China,* (Oslo, 1926), p. 92.
28 Wilhelm, *op. cit.,* p. 194.
29 Needham, *op. cit.,* p. 123.

30 Latourette, *op. cit.*, p. 191.
31 Latourette, *op. cit.*, p. 191-2.
32 Wilhelm, *op. cit.*, p. 219.
33 T. F. Carter, *The Invention of Printing in China and Its Spread Westward*, (Ronald Press, N.Y., 1925-55), p. 41.
34 Michael Loewe, *Imperial China* (Allen & Unwin, 1966), p. 281.
35 Etienne Balazs, *Chinese Civilization and Bureaucracy*, (Yale University, 1964), pp. 129-149.
36 F. van der Loon on 'The Ancient Chinese Chronicles and Growth of Historical Ideals' in *Historians of China and Japan*, (Ed. by W. G. Beasley & E. G. Pulleyblank, Oxford, 1961), p. 25.
37 Balazs, *op. cit.*, p. 131.
38 Lien-Sheng Yang on 'The Organization of Chinese Official Historiography' in *Historians of China and Japan'* (*op. cit.*), p. 44.
39 E. G. Pulleyblank on 'Chinese Historical Criticism' in *Historians of China and Japan, (op. cit.)*, p. 152.
40 Balazs, *op. cit.*, pp. 129 *et seq.*
41 Arthur Waley, *The Life and Times of Po-Chu-i*, (Allen & Unwin, 1949), p. 18.
42 Waley, *op. cit.*, p. 19.
43 Waley, *op. cit.*, p. 20.
44 Waley, *op. cit.*, pp. 27-8.
45 Waley, *op. cit.*, p. 28.
46 Waley, *op. cit.*, p. 42.
47 Waley, *op. cit.*, p. 47.
48 Waley, *op. cit.*, pp. 50-63.
49 Waley, *op. cit.*, p. 65.
50 Karl A. Wittfogel and Feng Chia-Sheng, *History of Chinese Society: Liao*, Macmillan, N.Y., 1949).
51 Wittfogel and Chia-Sheng, *op. cit.*, p. 5.
52 Wittfogel and Chia-Sheng, *op. cit.*, p. 44.
53 Wittfogel and Chia-Sheng, *op. cit.*, p. 46.
54 Wittfogel and Chia-Sheng, *op. cit.*, pp. 428-504.
55 Wittfogel and Chia-Sheng, *op. cit.*, p. 447.
56 Wittfogel and Chia-Sheng, *op. cit.*, p. 453.
57 Wittfogel and Chia-Sheng, *op. cit.*, p. 457.
58 Wittfogel and Chia-Sheng, *op. cit.*, p. 457.
59 Wittfogel and Chia-Sheng, *op. cit.*, p. 458.
60 Wittfogel and Chia-Sheng, *op. cit.*, p. 459.
61 Needham, *op. cit.*, p. 132.
62 Loewe, *op. cit.*, pp. 158-9.

CHAPTER 6

BYZANTIUM to A.D. 1025

With the transfer by Emperor Constantine in A.D. 330 of Rome's capital to Byzantium, henceforth to be known as Constantinople, a remarkable span of a thousand years of administrative endeavour began. For a time the western and eastern wings of the great Roman Empire hung uneasily together, but their separation was rapidly becoming inevitable. As the traditions of Rome were to continue most consistently in the eastern realm it is proposed to deal first with the administration of Byzantium.

SHORT HISTORICAL SURVEY[1]

Theodosius the Great (A.D. 379-95) was the last ruler of the Roman Empire in its fullest extent. On his death the Empire, still considered one and indivisible, was allocated to his two sons: Arcadius taking the west and Honorius the east. Under the impact of the barbarian tribes from the north, particularly the Franks and the Goths, the western provinces began to disintegrate into independent barbaric kingdoms, and the unity of east and west was never fully restored. However, unity of the east was maintained into the sixth century, when a Macedonian peasant who had risen meteorically to the command of the palace guard, mounted the imperial throne as Justin I. His nephew and successor, Justinian the Great (A.D. 527-65) must be accounted the last purely Roman-minded emperor. His policy, in which he achieved a high measure of success, was to reconquer the West from the barbarians and to ensure the victory of the orthodox faith under his own absolute control. Africa, Italy and South Spain were recovered, a vast system of frontier fortification and garrisoning was undertaken; provincial administration was reorganized; and extensive schemes of public works development put in hand. The latter included the construction of the Cathedral of St. Sophia in Constantinople. With the object of improving the efficiency of his government Justinian undertook his celebrated codification of Roman Law, and special attention was given to the Empire's economic and financial organization. All the major activities of the Roman Empire were centralized in the eastern capital.

But the effort was too much for the West, which found it difficult to meet the costs of defence and efficient administration and was quickly alienated by the demands of the Byzantine official. Pressures by the Slavs from the north threatened the lines of communication between west and east, and after Justinian's death his successors had to devote all their attention to their northern and eastern frontiers, which were crumbling under pressures from many directions. At the beginning of the seventh century the Empire had virtually fallen into anarchy and it seemed as though the end was in sight. The might of Persia rose again and rolled in from the east, capturing Palestine, Syria and Egypt, thus cutting Byzantium off from its main food supplies, while European invaders ravaged the western provinces, flowing right up to the walls of Constantinople.

Not for the last time Byzantium was destined to demonstrate its marvellous capacity for recovery. The new leader came from Africa in the person of Heraclius, son of the Governor of Carthage, who sailed for Constantinople in A.D. 610 and replaced Phocus, a brutal centurion who had been elected Emperor at the time of an army revolt in A.D. 602. The new emperor had to bide his time, while the Persians and Avars drove into the Empire towards the capital. Factions had to be ruthlessly suppressed, the armies refashioned, the finances restored. It was not before A.D. 622 that Heraclius was ready to take countermeasures, but within a further seven years he had re-established the Empire in Asia and Egypt and returned to his capital in triumph.

But a new menace was already on the horizon. Mohammed had died in A.D. 632 and within a few years his hitherto obscure religious movement had given birth to a Muslim power whose sway stretched from the Middle East across northern Africa to the Atlantic and had even penetrated Southern Spain. The Library of Alexandria, storehouse of innumerable literary treasures, was destroyed by Amron, lieutenant of the Caliph Oman in A.D. 651. Byzantium was again on the defensive. The west fell away and the Latin element dwindled, the Bulgars became a constant menace in the north and the heart of the Empire moved to Asia Minor. The administration was reorganized for defence, the territories occupied by the armies being divided up into provinces, known as *themes,* under commanders who exercised both military and civil functions.

During the eighth century Byzantium came under the Isaurian Emperors whose Asiatic origin is attested by certain characteristics of their policy. Their military prowess again saved Byzantium. Leo III's yictory in A.D. 717, the first year of his reign, over the Arab armies at the very walls of the capital was even more decisive to the survival of the west than the celebrated victory of Charles Martel over the Moors at Tours in A.D. 732. During this reign the Iconoclastic movement was launched against images, specifically against the icons displayed in Greek churches. Later the attack was concentrated against the growing power and influence of the monasteries and the result was the maintenance of the union of civil and religious government which the monks were challenging. The new austerity was not, however, popular and by A.D. 843 the images were finally restored. In the middle of the eighth century Ravenna, which had become the centre of Byzantine power in Italy, fell to the Lombards and was shortly taken by Charlemagne who handed it over to the Pope. On Christmas day, A.D. 800 Charlemagne was proclaimed Emperor of the west in the Basilica of St. Peter, Rome. Little now remained of the Byzantine power in Italy.

Following another period of internal revolt and palace assassinations, Byzantium, under the Macedonian dynasty, which began with Basil I in A.D. 867, entered upon one of its greatest periods. This phase was characterized by successful military consolidation against the surrounding states, who for the time being had exhausted their offensive power, and a gradual recovery internally. The Emperor, embodying the absolutism of state and church, was now treated as almost divine. He wisely set out to curb the power of the aristocracy. A series of far-sighted legislation acts encouraged art and learning and resulted in a great cultural revival in which many great works of art and literature were produced.

THE RULING INSTITUTIONS OF BYZANTIUM

It is obviously impossible in a few paragraphs to epitomize institutions that developed over a thousand years, and historians have not found it easy to explain the reasons for such a long survival, particularly in face of the several factors that might well have led to Byzantium's early demise, as indeed did nearly occur on numerous occasions. The unifying force of nationalism never evolved, for the Empire remained a loose and varying co-operation of peoples differing little in this respect from its Imperial predecessor. Industrialism did not develop far enough to support a sound economy. There were periods when intrigue and corruption were rampant not only in the provinces but at the Royal Court, where changes were often engineered through terror and bloodshed. But Byzantium had the traditions of Rome, particularly in organizational and legal efficiency, and of Greece, in art and letters, to support it, as well as the new Christian religion, which attributed the need for imperial survival to the will of God. It was a cultured community with a well-founded system of education and was serviced by a series of efficient institutions. The widespread monastic system, providing centres of piety and inspiration to the people, had a stabilizing influence: the well-equipped army, carrying on directly the traditions of Rome of which both officers and men were proud, provided adequate defence; and the highly effective administration, also following the pattern and precedents of Rome, gave efficient support to the state. These three institutions are together sufficient to account for the Empire's long survival. Added to all this was the fact that the rivals of Byzantium were in the main less cultured and much less efficient communities on the barbarian fringe. Even when they boasted of culture and institutions capable of competing with Byzantium there were weaknesses that prevented them from making a sustained effort against the Imperial power. Byzantium seems to have survived so long and recovered so frequently from apparently inevitable disaster because it formed a largely positive power-focus amidst a cluster of somewhat negative communities. It was not until both the West and Islam had advanced sufficiently to offer a serious challenge to its power that Byzantium finally fell.

Although many of the Roman institutions and traditions were maintained the rulership of Byzantium was to all intents and purposes an absolutism, and once enthroned the Emperor was removable only by revolution or death. At the Royal Court oriental ceremonial, owing much to the customs of Sassanid Persia, deliberately emphasized the unapproachable character of the Emperor. It is true that his selection still rested with the Senate and the Army, but as time went on these actual powers devolved upon a small band of high officials in the one case and of a small body of army leaders in the other. The introduction of coronation by the Patriarch of the Church added to the prestige of appointment, while the fiction of approval by the people was maintained when the Emperor appeared before the townsfolk of Constantinople, assembled specifically to acclaim him. The Emperor retained the long-established right of choosing his successor during his lifetime and this was done by nominating one or more Co-Emperors, whose coronation the Emperor carried out himself. Usurpation, which frequently occurred in times of trouble, was justified by success, but one rule the incoming ruler had to fulfil: he had to be a Christian and member of the Orthodox Church. His office was subject to legal restrictions, but his was the supreme power to rule, to legislate, to direct the administration, to order the finances and to interpret the laws. It is from the continued success of such an institution, and not from the theories of eminent political thinkers, that we derive the evidence of its suitability to cope with conditions of the times. Nevertheless effective performance in serving such a large and socially varied realm cannot possibly be attributed to one individual, however powerful: such results point unmistakeably to the existence over a long period of an efficient administrative system, whose structure and methods we must now examine.

PUBLIC ADMINISTRATION IN BYZANTIUM

The governmental administration of the Byzantine Empire was a natural development of the Roman system and, while it was obviously subject to considerable changes during its long history, the pattern established in the sixth century under Justinian substantially continued to reflect its main characteristics.[2] The allocation of military and civil offices to different hierarchies was calculated to strengthen the control of the Emperor. Similarly the division of the civil administration in the provinces into prefectures, the prefectures into dioceses, the dioceses into provinces and the provinces into small administrative districts with both hierarchic and direct responsibilities and subject to central inspection, ensured that no single official should accumulate inordinate power and become a rival to the central administration.

The most important provincial official was the Praetorian Prefect whose functions were both administrative and judicial. He had direct control of the police and administered the important *annona,* or land tax, from which the salaries of both the officials and the army, including the cost of rations for the latter, were paid. An interesting and indeed unusual safeguard was achieved by placing joint responsibility for results on the subordinate staffs of the high official who were liable with their superior for any error on his part. This is a significant recognition that administering is a co-operative activity in which it is not always easy to assign responsibility either for success or for failure, although even then the Byzantine solution may not commend itself as entirely just.

Associated with the Royal Court in Constantinople were the high officials who constituted the executive under the Emperor and came to perform the functions which are today usually carried out by an executive council (ministry or cabinet). They functioned as individual heads of the several administrative branches. The most important of these high officers of state was the *Magister Officiorum,* or Master of the Offices, who supervised the imperial secretariat, the arms factories, and the postal system. He also had command of the bodyguard and, as master of ceremonies, introduced embassies from abroad. Working through his *agentes in rebu,* who operated both as couriers and secret police, the Master of the Offices occupied a key-position and was the most powerful instrument of imperial control, who may be compared in some respects with the Vizir of the oriental court. He was able to widen his control within the administration by placing senior members of his staff as *principes,* or chiefs of staff, in other branches.

Also of considerable importance was the *Quaestor Sacri Palatii,* chairman of the *Consistorium,* or State Council, who was responsible for the adjudication machinery, law making, and replying to petitions. He had the assistance of the staff of the *scrinia* and a number of *magistri scrinorum,* or secretaries of state, assisted him in dealing with other branches of the imperial correspondence.

High among financial officials was the *Comes Sacrarum Largitionum,* whose office had begun with the periodical distribution of largesses to the army which the Emperor had initiated. He acquired the headship of the Treasury, which had superseded the Fiscus. His department received the main tributes and taxes and controlled the mines and the mint. Other financial business, covering the management of the extensive domains belonging to the state and also the imperial privy purse, came under the *Comes Rerum Privatarum.* There was in fact no strict division between court and state, for the *Praepositus Sacri Cubiculi,* or Lord Chamberlain, was not only the highest court official but also ranked equally with the high state officers. One of his jobs was the administration of the domains earmarked for the upkeep of the court. A new official, known as the *Scellarius,* or Steward of the Privy Purse, was eventually appointed to manage the privy purse. Time and time again he had to be called in to meet deficits in the Treasury, with the result that eventually the *Scellarius* came to replace the *Comes Sacrarum Largitionum* as head of the Treasury.

The struggle against Persia brought changes in the organization of the provinces, which were replaced by a system of themes, each under a *strategoi,* or general, and the combination of civil

and military offices was restored. Changes in the boundaries of
the Empire were inevitably reflected in the internal administrative pattern. As the Empire contracted the trend towards
centralization increased. Under the Isuarian Emperors (A.D. 717-
797) the Praetorian Prefecture disappeared and the functions of
the Master of the Offices and the Lord Chamberlain were divided
up among a number of separate officials. Only the titles remained
as stages in the fourteen ranks, each with its own insignia, which
were granted in the tenth century A.D. Thus a higher official had
both an official designation and a title of rank. Appointments,
promotions and dismissals were controlled by the Emperor, but
offices were authorized by order of the Imperial Cabinet. The
Emperor himself usually conferred the title of rank in a ceremonial audience. Promotion meant a rise both in salary and rank
and was so ordered as to encourage the ambition of officials. An
interesting custom by which the Emperor emphasized his close
relations with his officials was the annual pay parade which he
carried out personally during the week preceding Palm Sunday
in one of the audience chambers of the palace.

The purely Court, or household, offices were usually held by
eunuchs who, on account of their influence, often constituted a
separate power in the realm. Each palace was under the control
of a *Papias,* or Warden of the Gate, with whom was linked a
Protovestiarius, who was head of the wardrobe and its associated
treasury. There were also a *Praepositus,* who was Master of
Ceremonies, and the influential *Parakoimomenos,* or 'one who
slept next to the imperial bedchamber'. These eunuchs often
acquired considerable fortunes, but they were favoured as being
ineligible for the throne and, being without descendents, did not
constitute potential usurpers as other influential officials might.

The central administration in Constantinople continued to be
confined to civil offices, but a partial division between *Kritai,* or
judicial offices, and *Sekretikoi,* or chiefly financial offices, was
mentioned by Philotheus, writing as Court Marshal at the end of
the ninth century. The highest official of the *Kritai* was the
Eparchos, or City Prefect, who was the senior ranking civil
official and head of the city after the Emperor. His office could
not be held by an eunuch. He had a numerous staff to look after
the affairs of the city, which was headed on the judicial side by
the *Logothete* of the Praetorium and on the administrative side
by the *Symponos.* As officer in charge of the guilds the Prefect
supervised trade and commerce, and controlled the police and
fire-brigade. Foreigners engaged in trade fell within his province
but the supervision of aliens in the wider sense was assigned to

the *Quaestor*, whose original functions had been joined with those of the *Quaesitor*, an office which had been introduced by Justinian. There were several finance offices, which had developed out of the finance department of the Praetorian Prefecture, and were under the *Sekretikoi*, whose senior rankings were usually known as *Logothetes*, or accountants, and *Chartularii*, or actuaries, the title being completed in each case by adding the name of the department: for example, *Logothetes tou Stratiotikou*, who controlled the pay and commissariat of the army, and *Logothetes tou Genikou*, who was responsible for the important land tax.

Two other officials deserve special mention: namely the Postmaster General and the *Syncellus*. Although not strictly speaking a financial official the Postmaster General ranked among the *Sekretikoi* and, in virtue of his influence, was able to extend the scope and importance of his office. He came to act as a sort of Minister for Foreign Affairs, having control of a staff of interpreters, and was received daily in audience by the Emperor, finally becoming a kind of Chancellor with the title of Great Logothete. The *Syncellus* was a high cleric, whose post placed him in a stategic position to succeed to the patriarchate. His appointment, which had to be agreed by the Patriarch, gave him precedence over all ordinary officials and his main function was to act as liaison between Emperor and Patriarch.

The *strategoi* of the themes were directly responsible to the Emperor who thus maintained direct control of the entire administration. Apart from their military establishments they had their own civilian staffs. Their chief financial officials had a dual responsibility to the central administration and in addition overseers and inspectors were sent out from the centre. This system of checks and balances was further developed by empowering the bishops to supervise the administrative arrangements in their dioceses, and even encouraging citizens to seek legal redress against official oppression.

Assisted by the Prefect of the City and the *Quaestor*, the Emperor was head of the judiciary. He remained the supreme court of appeal and retained direct jurisdiction over the highest officials. Some Emperors actually encouraged personal complaints, both as a check upon officialdom and as a means of assessing public opinion.

CERTAIN PUBLIC FUNCTIONS

From the records we obtain a reasonably clear picture of

Byzantine public administration as a series of rankings or graded posts, or as a patchwork of geographical authorities, but it is much less easy to picture the functional pattern in the absence of a developed system of departments. Certainly, Byzantine officials do not appear to have done much to remedy the defects of the Roman administration in this connection. It is proposed here to glance briefly at the ways in which four important public functions were ordered: namely, (i) Diplomacy, (ii) Social Services, (iii) Education and (iv) Finance.

(i) *Diplomacy:* The Byzantines placed great store on diplomacy as a more economical means than war for pursuing their foreign policies and went to considerable expense to make it effective. Nevertheless, despite the contribution of the Great Logothete, already mentioned, there appears to have been no foreign office or formal diplomatic service. Embassies were undertaken by specially appointed commissioners or plenipotentiaries. Such embassies were organized with a great ostentation, while the ceremonial reception of foreign envoys at the Royal Palace was staged with great pomp to impress the visitor with the might of the Empire. The Emperor himself remained silent during the interview, which was conducted in his presence by the Great Logothete. Everything was done to ensure that the foreign representative saw only what it was desirable for him to see, while all foreign envoys, whether on official missions or not, were before going abroad carefully briefed both on their own conduct and also on the sort of information they were expected to bring back with them. All the time-honoured methods were used to obtain the support of foreign powers: treaties of friendship, with reciprocal concessions; the payment of subsidies, even if such appeared as tribute to the recipient; political marriages; the incitement of other powers against a peaceful and friendly state, and so on.

(ii) *Social Services:* It would be misleading to suggest that the Byzantine Empire at any time had the makings of a Welfare State: there was too little democracy to make that plausible. Nevertheless, there was the practical example of the Hellenistic cities of providing modest social services and the Christian doctrine of universal charity to encourage the religious establishments to jump into the breach. The obligation of helping the needy was placed on all Christians and the monks particularly were exhorted to share what little they had with the poor. It was but a short step to the idea that the monastic bodies should establish hospital services and indeed Byzantium was well-endowed with such institutions. One of the most splendid of these was sponsored by John Commenus in the twelfth century. Attached to a monastery endowed with two churches was a hospital with fifty beds divided into five wards — one for surgical cases, one for medical cases, one for women and two for ordinary cases — with adequate staffing, including a woman doctor, a scheme that would have done credit to the modern age. It provided a well-balanced vegetarian diet and had out-patient departments for both ordinary and surgical cases. The settlement included homes for old men, epileptics, illegitimates, and orphans. It is true that this example takes us well beyond our present period but it was obviously the culmination of long experience. In practice the more advanced institutions were situated near the capital, but there is evidence of similar services further afield.[3]

Under Christian influences the Emperor competed with the Church and his wealthy subjects in endowing charitable institutions, which ranged over *xenodocheia,* or hostels for pilgrims, *ptochotropehia,* or refuges for the poor, *nosokomeia,* or hospitals for the sick, and *gerokomeia,* or homes for the aged, forming collectively an important public service.[4] Administration was usually left to the Church, even the *Orphanotrophos,* the official director of a large orphanage in Constantinople, was usually a priest. But the government exercised financial control through an office of the State domains, and the Emperor provided property out of his own estate.[5]

(iii) *Education:* Byzantium's long era of success undoubtedly owed much to its educational system, which included both private and public institutions. The young boy might be taught in his own home by his mother or a pedagogue slave, or attend a local school where he learned the essential orthography, i.e. reading and writing. Between the ages of ten and twelve secondary education would be undertaken. This concentrated on grammar, which aimed at a process of Hellenization of speech and mind. If education was to continue beyond this stage the youth might either enter a school for monks or go to a university to acquire higher learning. The education of females appears to have been restricted to instruction in the home.[6]

Specialized courses were available for certain professions, particularly for lawyers and public officials. Secretaries in the Imperial administration needed to practice speed-writing, monks had to become expert in fine calligraphy, and soldiers to specialize in military subjects. There was apparently no special training for teachers, who began teaching as soon as they had completed their school studies. Nevertheless, they were greatly helped by the general availability of literary texts. Copies of manuscripts were widely distributed, since reading was common, and private houses as well as public institutions had their own collections of 'books'. Text books were written on a multitude of subjects. In fact the value of learning was widely accepted even if in total the literary achievement of Byzantium never rose above modest levels. Three law schools were sanctioned under Justinian's constitution, two in the capitals of Rome and Constantinople and one in the provinces, the School of Law at Berytus (Beirut), which was the principal training institution for lawyers and public officials before the destruction of the city by earthquake in A.D. 551.

The University of Constantinople was a noted centre of legal study which depended upon Imperial initiative and state support. It is recorded that in A.D. 425 Theodosius II appointed thirty-one professors, who were paid by the state and freed from taxation. Under Constantine II (A.D. 913-59), an enthusiast for encyclopaedic knowledge, there were chairs of philosophy, geometry, astronomy and rhetoric, as well as teaching in numerous other subjects. All branches of Church and Government drew upon its professors and students to fill the highest posts. After a period of eclipse the University was reconstituted in A.D. 1045 by Constantine IX with the specific object of producing competent judges and public officials. The professors were subjected to a strict discipline, laid down by the State. There was a School of Law and a School of Philosophy, the latter being placed under the control of the celebrated Psellus, who was the great literary figure of the time.[7] We are told that he taught as many as eleven subjects, besides philosophy, and was 'the soul of the University'.[8] This was an arduous and sometimes dangerous post, and many of Psellus's successors fell into disgrace. Psellus himself, who also officiated as Imperial Chancellor, had to make a public profession of faith. By A.D. 1300 State-paid teachers came to be ranked as government officials, although private education continued to thrive. The School of Philosophy came to an end only with the Turkish conquest of A.D. 1453.

(iv) *Finance:* Something has already been said about the financial officials, but a country's financial arrangements are so vital that the contribution of public administration in this field calls for further consideration. As Andréadès points out, the Byzantine Empire 'was at once a bureaucratic state, a semi-oriental absolute monarchy, a Graeco-Christian community, and, lastly a nation in which the capital played a role almost as preponderant as in the states which, like Athens, Rome and Venice, were the creation of a city'.[9] Such a vast complicated organization called for very heavy expenditures and an effective system of financial administration. The Emperor was his own Minister of Finance, maintaining a personal interest in the entire system.

Defence constituted a heavy charge on the budget. The Treasury had to provide for the building and upkeep of a fleet of naval vessels of all types and of other arms and engines of war for the army. The officers were well paid, lands were distributed to citizens against an obligation to serve in the army and, to supplement these forces, mercenaries had to be enlisted at exhorbitant expense. In addition there was the item of tribute actually paid to neighbours, such as the Bulgars, as a surety against invasion. Obviously the cost of the impressive and lavish embassies, already mentioned, was also heavy.

The civil administrative machine was essential to the existence of such a complex realm, but as a bureaucracy it was bound to be expensive and liable to become burdensome. Officials were mostly paid by the state and the practice, widespread elsewhere and at other times, of offsetting their cost by the sale of offices was not adopted in Byzantium, except for the disposal of a few court posts or empty titles. The official's salary was composed of three elements: the *sixteresion,* or provisions, the *roga,* or cash payment, and clothing. The *roga* and clothing were distributed annually by the Emperor to higher officials, as mentioned above, while provisions were issued from time to time by the *parakoimemenos.*

The income of officials, however, was supplemented by the levying of *sportulae,* or fees, for almost any transaction carried out in the normal course of public administration. The tax collector even made a charge for his service, which of course really did constitute a service if it saved the citizen the trouble and expense of travelling personally to the administrative centre, as he was often bound to do, such as in the case of the census. But this sort of system could lead to serious oppression and corruption and was often one of the root causes of the widespread unpopularity of officials. Originally, under Roman administration, these *sportulae* were illicit tips and as such are still far from uncommon in some non-European communities. Constantine regarded them as a major administrative evil and did his utmost to stamp them out by imposing the severest penalties, even death, to induce 'the grasping hands of the officials (to) refrain forthwith'. In the long run, however, it was realized that this sort of thing was inherent in officialdom and that it was better to recognize and regulate it than to force it to operate 'under the counter'.

As early as the reign of Julian (A.D. 360-63) this had been done and the detailed schedule for the province of Numidia, applying to different grades of official and their respective functions, still survives, payments being calculated on the basis of so many bushels of wheat.[10]

For the maintenance of the magnificent Court, the construction of vast palaces, some of which were miniature cities on their own, and payment of a swarm of nobles, eunuchs and personnel of all sorts, a massive Civil List must have been involved: largesse to the troops, sumptuous banquets and the conventional presents added considerably to the total.

Although church foundations were financed by pious citizens the Treasury contributed in many directions to their upkeep and constructional works, while the Emperor contributed both to the Church and to the charitable institutions already mentioned. The city amenities of Constantinople also constituted a heavy charge, while the Roman tradition was followed of providing shows and free distributions of bread. These civic loaves were discontinued under Heraclius (A.D. 610-41) but came to be replaced on a smaller scale by occasional largesses in money and in kind.

There were three main sources of revenue: namely the property of the State, which was extensive, ordinary taxes often collected in kind, and extraordinary contributions. The State owned factories for the production of army equipment, and articles of luxury, especially fabrics. These were not normally for sale but were used at the Court or given to foreign potentates as gifts. The Emperor owned vast agricultural estates which, however, were reduced by distribution as military lands or donations to foundations, relatives and others. The State owned mines, quarries and other property. Of the direct taxes, the land tax, tax on grazing lands and animals, and the capitation tax upon each hearth were levied on the rural population; while the townsfolk paid a licence-tax, an inheritance tax and a tax, called the *aerikon,* whose nature is obscure. Indirect taxes were levied both as customs duties and excise. The burden of taxation was further increased by the immunities granted to certain monasteries, by the contributions in kind to the army and officials, and supplemented by the *corvée,* or forced labour, exacted for the construction of public works, such as fortifications, roads and bridges.

This system of public finance had many faults, but relatively it was an improvement upon existing systems. It had an almost insuperable task to perform and yet the Empire survived. Extortion was widespread, as in all earlier state systems, and sometimes the breaking point was barely avoided. Writing of the Iconoclast

Period (A.D. 717-842), Finlay points out how far precautionary measures against fiscal rapacity reduced society to a stationary condition, but at the same time admits that it still displayed a higher degree of prudence and honesty than that of any other absolute government.[11]

THE BYZANTINE OFFICIAL: SOME NOTABLE EXAMPLES

When it is realized what an important influence their activities had upon the Byzantine Empire, how much they contributed to its long survival and how many of them there were, a droning hive of back-room toilers whose achievements earned more blame than praise from their contemporaries, it is surprising how shadowy the Byzantine officials are as individuals and how little we know about their day-to-day operations: less certainly than we know of their Egyptian forerunners who engraved their biographies on the monuments of the dead. They seemed to be outstanding as stabilizers of society, which is perhaps an essential contribution of efficient administration everywhere, but they were certainly not inventive, as indeed the whole of Byzantine society was not inventive, even in their own business methods. Their techniques were derived from the Romans and the Greeks: certainly more attention was given to finance and the idea of an organized administrative service was developed, as opposed to the system of individual magistrates under preceding regimes. Papyrus continued to be used until Egypt was lost to the Arabs and in the monasteries parchment came into favour despite its cost. Paper, the great invention of the time, came from China via the Arabs, but this comparatively cheap medium which was destined to do so much to revolutionize the practices of administration was only beginning to spread in the West during the final phases of the Empire. Much of Byzantine history tells of the doings of the occupants of the seats of power and of their often internecine antics as masters of the administration, from the Emperor downwards, but it also discloses a great deal about the administrative policies of the age. Thus, to echo another dictum, it may be suggested that all history is administrative history.

Indeed there are a number of interesting original texts which are very much to our purpose, though they concentrate mainly upon the legal context and tend to exaggerate the ceremonial aspects of the subject. A state manual, the *Notitia Dignitatum,* dating from the fifth century sets down the grading of certain high officers and their staffs, while a list of court offices in the

Kletorologion of the Court Marshal, Philotheus, not only indicates what changes had taken place in the intervening centuries but provides a treatise on the regulations determining the precedence at a Court dinner in A.D. 899.[12] The real *magnum opus* on this topic was produced by Constantine VII (A.D. 913-59) in his *De Ceremoniis Aulae Byzantinae,* or Book of Ceremonies, which goes into detail on times, routines, dress, comportment and suchlike matters that were prescribed for the important object of upholding the dignity of Emperor and State. An important administrative text of the same period was the *Eparchikon Biblion,*[13] or Book of the Prefect, which shows the scope of the prefect's control over production and trade, and among other things, describes the duties of the guilds of Constantinople, whose prices for purchase and sale were controlled by that official.[14] Apart from the celebrated laws of such leaders as Constantine and Justinian, there were works like the *Ecloga* which, during the eighth century, set out a new legal code that aimed at humanizing the law, with obvious repercussions on the administration. There was a Book of Offices presenting the position as late as the fourteenth century, but in view of the situation at that time it is considered that, by citing earlier offices which retained only their titular appearance, this reflects the outward appearance rather than the sad reality.[15]

The exploits of a few successful administrators, who rose by a mixture of ability and chicanery to the heights of power, deserve a little attention here as representatives of a large class. Notorious among these was Nicephorus I (A.D. 802-11)[16] who, as holder of the financial office of Grand Logothete, by successful intrigue dethroned the demonic Empress Irene. He used his financial experience to reorganize the financial system, one of his first actions being to set up a court of review to revise the accounts of every public functionary. This was done in response to loud complaints against the extortion of the tax-gatherers, but the aggrieved citizens soon discovered that anything but an enlightened financial era was in prospect, for the new Emperor was soon being accused of applying the confiscated gains to his own uses instead of restoring them to the original taxpayers. Nicephorus showed his statesmanship in dealing with crisis and his power in maintaining the supremacy of State over Church, by appointing his own man, an historian who bore the same name as himself, as Patriarch. He continued to adopt a ruthless and oppressive financial policy to fill the State coffers, but could be lavish in expenditure on matters that he considered important. He extended the range of taxation and even imposed duties on church properties which had hitherto been exempt. Yet, despite his bad reputation in the annals, Nicephorus seems to have been humane in his punishments and to have refrained from imposing the death penalty on those who tried to overthrow or to assassinate him. He was killed during an invasion of Bulgar territories, largely through a failure on his part to take the most elementary military precautions.

Another outstanding administrator was Theoktistos, reputed to have been the ablest statesman of the Empire.[17] On the accession of Michael II (A.D. 842-67) while still a minor, his mother the Empress Theodora, became regent with the assistance of a Council of Administration consisting of Theoktistos and Bardas, the Empress's brother. Theoktistos, too, had held the post of Grand Logothete and had been appointed *Kanicleios,* or keeper of the purple ink with which the Emperor signed. Finlay remarks upon the especial efficiency of the educational system at this time in turning out experienced administrators. On the other hand it was a period in which oppressive administration led to resistance within the Empire, not that this could be attributed to Theoktistos, whose able financial administration was widely acknowledged. As a result of the intrigues of Bardas and of a revulsion on the part of the Emperor against the regency, Theoktistos was murdered in prison in A.D. 854. Subsequently, as witness to her successful administration under the inspiration of Theoktistos, the Empress Theodora rendered to the Senate a statement of the huge accumulation of wealth in the State Treasury. Finlay remarks 'The immense treasure thus accumulated would probably have given immortal strength to Byzantine society, had it been left in the possession of the people, by a wise reduction in the amount of taxation, accompanied by a judicious expenditure for defence of the frontiers, and for facilitating the conveyance of agricultural produce to distant markets'.[18]

The last of these political-administrators to be mentioned here is John the *Orphanatrophos,* or Minister of Charitable Institutions.[19] He was a eunuch and monk who had entered the household of Romanus, before he became Emperor as Romanus III (A.D. 1028-34) jointly with the much-married Empress Zoe (A.D. 1028-50), and who had subsequently risen to high office. John had a brother Michael of attractive figure, once a goldsmith and money-changer who had received an appointment in the Imperial household. Unfortunately he was subject to sudden and violent fits of epilepsy. But the Empress took a fancy to him, a situation of which John, who as a eunuch was ineligible for the throne, took full advantage. On the sudden death of the Emperor, John's brother became the Empress's next husband as Emperor Michael IV (A.D. 1034-42). John, acting as his brother's Chief Minister and President of the Cabinet, became a power in the land. He appears to have served his brother well, but his administration was rapacious and injurious to the Empire as a whole. Taxes were increased and extortions weighed upon the provinces. The murder of a tax collector at Antioch on the accession of the new Emperor was countered by ruthless penalties on the leading families of the city. Eventually these exactions caused insurrections which cost the Empire more than had been added to the Imperial Treasury. 'The collector of the revenues of the theme of Nicopolis was torn to pieces by the people, and the western parts of Greece welcomed the Bulgarian troops.'[20] John even aspired to the Patriarchate, but in this direction his ambitions were frustrated. During the reign of Empress Zoe's next and last husband, Constantine IX (A.D. 1042-55), John fell into disfavour and was exiled to Maryktos, where he was deprived of his sight. In this cruel deed Zoe's sister Theodora was probably implicated. She was certainly instrumental subsequently in having him murdered without the formality of a legal sentence. From such incidents it is clear that there were periods when the careers of successful Byzantine political-administrators could be prohibitively hazardous!

There are few portraits extant of the more typical Byzantine public official and to round off this account with a representative example we need to go back to the sixth century when the poet and antiquary, John the Lydian,[21] about whom a great deal is known, served in the central state offices.

John Lydus, as we may perhaps conveniently call him, achieved considerable literary eminence, although his purely literary works have not survived. In his book, *De Magistratibus,* which gives an illuminating inside account of the public service in the age of Justinian, and which was one of the works written by Lydus during his retirement, we are told how he entered the public service. This was under the consulship of Secundian (A.D. 511) when Lydus left his birthplace Philadelphia and came to the capital, where after much consideration he decided to 'join the *memoriales* of the Court and don the uniform with them'. These were the clerks in the office of *Magister Memoriae,* one of the Emperor's chief secretaries. It seemed indeed that Lydus's fortune was made when he was persuaded by Zoticus, a Lydian like himself, to take up a clerkship in the office of the Praetorian Prefect, where Ammianus, a cousin, also occupied an important position. In his early years Lydus not only found

his work most remunerative, but for a brief eulogy which he
composed for Zoticus he was both praised and paid at the rate
of a gold piece for each line! Later this Zoticus, with the
approval of Ammianus was even instrumental in obtaining for
Lydus a wife who brought with her a dowry of one hundred
pounds of gold and who according to Lydus himself 'excelled all
women who at any time have won a reputation for sobriety'. We
are not surprised after all this that early promotion had given
Lydus an exceptional appointment when he was accepted as the
first *chartularius* on the staff of *ab actis,* who was head of the
important branch in the Prefect's office which dealt with appeals
in non-criminal cases. The *chartularius* assisted an *adjutores,* an
official of a special type who was appointed to help senile heads
of departments no longer capable of carrying their full load. The
court of *ab actis* was much concerned with matters of property
and finance and constituted a regular record office, requiring
elaborate minutes and records of all its proceedings. This gave
great scope to the particular bent of Lydus, who waxed almost
lyrical in his description of the work.

But times changed. Justinian came to the throne and his
reforming zeal was soon sweeping through the offices, cutting
out at least some of the inevitable dead wood. Lydus appears to
have lost his highly-placed connections and was no longer
persona grata with his chiefs. He disliked all interference with
the ancient forms and was particularly upset when Greek
replaced the formalized Latin in which the proceedings of the
Prefecture had hitherto been obscured. Consequently he found
his services being attracted to more academic and literary activities. He was commissioned by the Emperor as a sort of Historian
Royal, to write a history of the war against the Persians
(probably that of A.D. 527-32) and was made a professor in the
University.

It appears that the reforms adversely affected the importance
of the Praetorian Prefecture, which had lost control of the postal
system and arms factories to the *Magister Officiorum* and had to
receive one of the latter's staff as *princeps.* Lydus was critical,
too, of the division of the staff between the judicial and the
financial officials, regarding the latter as upstarts and inveighing
passionately against the raising, in preference to men of letters
or barristers, of such finance clerks as Marinus the Syrian and
John of Cappadocia to the Praetorian Prefecture. He was particularly critical of the exactions of the latter, which he alleged
impoverished the provincials, although it is in fact known that
John of Cappadocia, besides feathering his own nest, was success-

ful in filling the public coffers. The personal effect of the changes was that with nearly forty years in the service, the highest post in the office open to him, now that the position of *princeps* had been assigned to an outsider, was that of *cornicularius,* to which indeed he had been promoted, but the perquisites of this office were also much reduced in consequence of the changes.

Lydus retired after completing forty years of service, with the title of *clarissimus,* the rank of count of the second class and a testimonial from his chief which refers to him as 'John the great writer', a label that is said to have pleased him more than any official title.

There is much in the story of Lydus that illuminates not only the early public service of Byzantium, but also the attitudes of the typical official throughout the ages: the addiction to procedures, the inherent conservatism of outlook, the natural resentment of changes that modify original expectations and diminish opportunities for advancement, the existence of 'passengers' who in the absence of an effective retirement system have to be tolerated although no longer of much use to the administration. Perhaps, as a parallel with our own times, we can appreciate more clearly the reactions of an official with a literary and academic background against the employment in his own sphere of experts from other fields. But before we rail against bureaucracy — a human habit that seems to go back to the very beginnings of government — it is as well to remember the other side: the assiduous devotion of the official to the service of the State; his loyalty to his chief and his pride in his career; above all, and one can discern this in the mind of Lydus, his desire to devote his energies to the general welfare. If at times he is prone to take more than his due from the common pool, or contrariwise to regret the conditions that prevent his doing so, one has to remember that his faults stem not from the fact that the official belongs to a species that is something less than human but that the very nature of his work leaves plenty of scope for ordinary human failings.

From the career of John Lydus the two authorities to whom we are indebted for these facts draw quite opposite conclusions. Thus Ure ends his admirable chapter in 'The Bureaucracy': 'But if we accept the high authority who told us that corruption can come only from within, then amongst those to whom we might with reason ascribe the gradual decline and ultimate end of the imperial system Johannes Lydus and his like must be given a high place.'[22] A. H. M. Jones, on the other hand, in his stimulating essay on 'The Roman Civil Service' states:

'It is easy to poke fun at the Byzantine bureaucracy, but cumbersome and corrupt though it was, it served some useful purposes. The emperors relied on the clerical grades, perhaps not altogether in vain, as a check against the far more arbitrary extortions and illegalities of the administrative officers, the provincial governors in particular. The permanent clerks of the *officia* not only knew the regulations better than the governors, who served only for a year or two; they also had a less pressing need to get rich quickly and could content themselves with more or less regular perquisites, hallowed by custom; and being permanent residents they could not but have some fellow feeling for the ordinary provincials.'[23]

Perhaps it is fairer to end upon a note of interrogation: if Byzantine officialdom was as bad as some surviving records appear to indicate, how was it possible, in the light of its long chequered history, for the great Empire to continue for an entire millennium, and at a time when a divided West was struggling out of chaos and strange forces were sweeping in from the East? Does the result not rather suggest the existence of a more effective public administration than it is usual to credit to the Roman Empire of the East?

REFERENCES

1 George Finlay, *History of the Byzantine Empire* (1877, Dent's Everyman Edition, 1906) and N. H. Baynes & H.St.L.B. Moss (Editors), *Byzantium*, (Oxford, 1948).
2 P. N. Ure, *Justinian and His Age*, (Penguin, 1951), pp. 102-20 and Wilhelm Ensslin on 'The Emperor and Imperial Administration' in *Byzantium, op. cit.*, pp. 268-307.
3 J. M. Hussey, *The Byzantine World* (Hutchinsons, 1957), p. 139.
4 A. M. Andréadès on 'Public Finances' in *Byzantium, op cit*, pp. 76-7.
5 Ensslin on 'The Emperor and Imperial Administration' in *Byzantium, op. cit.*, p. 289.
6 Georgina Buckler on 'Byzantine Education' in *Byzantium, op. cit.*, pp. 150-63.
7 Psellus, *Chronographia*, translated by E. R. A. Sewter as *Fourteen Byzantine Rulers*, (Penguin, 1966).
8 Buckler, *op. cit.*, p. 218.
9 Andréadès, *op. cit.*, p. 74.
10 A. H. M. Jones, *Studies in Roman Government*, (Blackwell, 1960), pp. 171-2.
11 Finlay, *op. cit.*, pp. 184-5.
12 Ensslin, *op. cit.*, p. 279 and 285.
13 Ensslin, *op. cit.*, p. 288.
14 Hussey, *op. cit.*, pp. 136 and 140.

15 Ensslin, *op. cit.*, p. 293.
16 Finlay, *op. cit.*, pp. 86 *et seq.*
17 Finlay, *op. cit.*, pp. 149 *et seq.*
18 Finlay, *op. cit.*, p. 159.
19 Finlay, *op. cit.*, pp. 373-95.
20 Finlay, *op. cit.*, p. 377.
21 Ure, *op. cit.*, pp. 113 *et seq.* and A. H. M. Jones, *op. cit.*, pp. 172 *et seq.*
22 Ure, *op. cit.*, p. 120.
23 A. H. M. Jones, *op. cit.*, p. 175.

CHAPTER 7

BIRTH OF THE WEST : A.D. 500 to 1066

Although, towards the end of the third century, Diocletian had consolidated the power and integrated the administration of the Roman Empire under his personal control, it was also he who superseded the Augustan Principate by a sort of dual-imperialism that was nicely patterned to fall into two distinct parts as soon as the situation became ripe. Not that this seemed likely when Constantine, early in the fourth century, superseded for the time being Diocletian's separate *augusti* and combined the entire Roman realm for the first time under the mantle of one religion — Christianity. But, in transferring his capital to the favourably situated site of Constantinople on the Bosphorus, he inevitably shifted the Roman centre of gravity eastwards and a weakened and morally reduced Rome was to prove no match to the probing vigour of the barbarians already storming the long-drawn northern frontiers. The continuance of Roman rule in the East for another thousand years, the first part of which has been considered in Chapter 6, and the rapid decline of Rome in the West present scholars with a problem that has called forth a store of solutions from among which final certainty is never likely to emerge.

No doubt administrative weaknesses came somewhere into the picture, but this could hardly have been the whole story or even the key defect. Of the two essentials for the continuance of empire — namely the effective concentration of power and the existence of an efficient administration — it is difficult to believe that fourth century Roman administration suffered from some fatal defect that rendered the Western Empire's survival impossible when it is evident that the application of similar principles in the East at least contributed something to Byzantium's continuance. It seems that the root cause must be sought in the realm of power, which in the East was able to withstand attacks from without and tendencies towards disintegration from within and to make the most of an efficient administrative machine, while in the West the process of weakening through continual barbarian assault and absorption created problems that efficient administration could not alone have solved.

Under successive attacks of Angles, Saxons, Visigoths, Vandals, Huns, Ostrogoths and many others the Western marches of the Empire crumbled and if Roman institutions continued to function, as there is evidence that they often did, no doubt they were so changed by the new economic and social situation that they soon tended to lose their original *raison d'etre* and even became a burden upon communities calling for simpler administrative solutions and means.

A partial restitution of the Empire in the West under Justinian after A.D. 535 when the Roman standards were carried westwards against the Ostrogoths in Southern Italy, the Vandals in Northern Africa and the Visigoths in Southern Spain, was to be short-lived, for the spirit of Rome itself had decayed, and even in the heart of Italy the power could not be wrested from the Lombards whose kingdom stretched northwards to the Alps. On the western and northern frontiers of the momentarily reinflated Imperium were the extensive Kingdoms of the Visigoths, occupying most of Iberia and a section of Southern Gaul, and the Kingdom of the Franks extending across Gaul and Germany to the Elbe. Justinian's herculean offensive efforts in the West and defensive efforts in the East succeeded only momentarily, at an exorbitant cost to all the citizens of the vast Empire. In any case unimagined hazards lay ahead. Already, the birth in A.D. 570 of Mohammed, son of Abd-allah of Mecca, was the portent of a massive challenge not only to Rome but to all contemporary civilization.

It would be hopeless to attempt here even a brief summary of the complicated history of those fateful centuries following the withdrawal of the Roman legions from the frontiers of the north, somewhere towards the end of the fourth century. All we can do is consider some of the administrative situations that were developing during that Age of Chaos, situations that were to make their considerable impress eventually upon the administrative picture of the Modern Age. We shall look at the public administration of the new Kingships of the West, the Church of Rome, Islam, and the Anglo-Saxon Kingdoms.

RISE OF THE WESTERN KINGSHIPS

The withdrawal of the Roman legions from Britain, Germany and Gaul did not mean the immediate or universal replacement of the Roman administration. The consequent breakdown of communications and loss of records has led to exaggeration of the 'Dark Ages' that were to follow. For centuries the local inhabitants had absorbed and accepted the Roman way of life and had come to prefer its refinements to the rude tribal habits. Sometimes the invading or infiltrating tribes destroyed; sometimes, after driving out the inhabitants, they just abandoned the Roman settlements as something incomprehensible to them and left them to neglect and decay; often they settled down alongside the present inhabitants and began straightaway to learn their methods and absorb their customs. Tribal traditions and methods of government were quickly modified by the new situation and an amalgamation of the two schemes of administration gradually took shape. The precepts and examples of Rome continued to live in men's minds after the actual institutions had ceased to be effective in the very different and inevitably more primitive social and economic situation that had emerged from the ruins of the older society.

Despite the existence of democratic insttutions among the Germanic tribes, the new leaders were essentially charismatic and the royal authority, especially among the Franks,[1] was impressive. Any man who refused to appear before the King's tribunal could be outlawed, which meant dispossession and death, for not even the delinquent's wife could give him sustenance without herself falling under the ban; while those who were employed about the King's person had special privileges and protection.

The Royal Household — a highly mobile centre of power — was the only central administration, and for many years there were no specialist administrators as such. As soon as the royal sway became too wide for personal control to be effective, a system of territorial administration was devised, of districts under viceroys, or representatives of the King, with the main tasks of preserving law and order and collecting the royal dues or fines. This is the pattern of tribal government wherever it may arise, but the special conditions of the already civilized Roman West were bound to prescribe modifications in this simple design. Yet despite the considerable impact of these special conditions tribal ideas were to persist for a long time and to contribute to the feudal system that was later to emerge.

The Merovingian Franks[2] (*circa* 500-750) had to grapple with problems in Gaul which were quite beyond the capacity of the tribal institutions. Here the numerous settled Gallo-Roman population had been accustomed to being governed as a *diocese* from Rome. Thus a new central administration had to be introduced and additional officials appointed, while the local administration had to be modified to exercise effective control of the highly sophisticated inhabitants. In the outcome Roman and

German institutions were to combine in varying proportions according to local need. In addition, as a further dimension, the influence of the institutions and ideas of the Christian Church were to contribute to this remoulding of political structures.

Under the Merovingian Kings the Roman idea of the State was in eclipse. The new rulers were personal leaders demanding personal obedience and offering personal protection. The King's relationship with the people was personal; they were his subjects in fact and the link came to be sanctified by oath. Under this system governmental decision continued to be valid only during the ruler's lifetime. The realm was the property of the King and all revenues were his due. The King could do what he liked with his own. Upon his death a new allegiance called for legislative and administrative renewal. His realm would be divided among his sons as any other private property. It is possible that the idea of a distinct public administration still lay at the back of men's minds from the Roman experience, but administrative institutions suitable to the emergent society had to be worked out by rule of thumb, aften expensively and sometimes with much suffering.

The Merovingian King exercised paternal rights over his subjects and could issue orders and interdicts as any Germanic leader, but he also exercised certain powers rooted in Roman practice, such as the right to create currency and to levy taxes. The shadow of the Empire manifested itself in the adoption of the doctrine of *lèse-majesté* as a protection of the royal person but the ruler's despotic sway was greatly diminished by the restricted nature of the governmental means at his disposal. The *Palatium,* or Royal Household, was a mere shadow of its imperial prototype: it consisted of councillors, officers and bodyguards, but there were no offices, or bureaux, to form a central administration. It was just the ruler's mobile household. For counsel on any matter whatsoever the King called in anyone he chose, layman or ecclesiastic. His domestics acted as ministers, chief among whom was the *Major Domus,* or Mayor of the Palace, who was estate manager with control of all household personnel. The Mayor of the Palace came to wield great influence and growing power. During a king's minority he might exercise the royal power, which included command of the bodyguard, presiding over popular assemblies, and control of administration. His closest assistants were the *Comes Palatii,* or Counts of the Palace, who looked after matters of royal justice and could act as ambassadors or undertake military assignments, and the Referendary, who was the sole survivor of the Roman system, with the duty of preparing edicts and orders, looking after and affixing the royal seal, and handling correspondence. Among the more menial officers was the *Comes Stabuli,* or Count of the Stables, who looked after the horses and as a matter of course came to exercise military powers, and the Seneschal, who was responsible for supplies and organizing the domestic services. These domestics, beginning as freedmen, came to acquire high rank. Under the protection of the ruler they enjoyed immunities which placed them on a par with the leading citizens and great proprietors. The members of the *Palatium* acquired an *esprit de corps* of their own, and gradually became a corporate power to which the King himself often had to bow. The Mayor of the Palace in particular acquired autonomy and was able to challenge the King. Towards the end of the seventh century he had grown sufficiently powerful to dominate the nobility and reduce the King to a puppet, a situation that has frequently arisen in history, where an influential administrator by acquiring governmental powers has been able to usurp the ruler's authority and become supreme governor, without actually occupying the throne.

The writ of the Merovingians was exercised in the localities by *Comes,* or Counts, usually appointed from the palace staff and invariably exercising all the royal powers and enjoying royal immunities. From the sixth century the *Comes* came to be assisted by a *Vicarius.* The King also, when circumstances demanded, appointed Dukes who had military powers and as such ranked above the Counts. The public services were concerned mainly with justice and finance. The former was dispensed through the King's tribunal and the common courts. The latter was reduced to its simplest terms, for the royal expenses were those of an ordinary household. Officials and troops were maintained on a subsistence basis. Public works were executed through the *corvée* or forced labour. The cost of the court and royal family had to be met but in travelling from place to place the burden of upkeep was circulated among the King's hosts whose duty it was to see that the royal entourage was properly cared for while under their jurisdiction. The King also derived income from his own considerable estates or *villae,* as grand proprietor. Each villa was managed by a *decanus* who had direct control of the domestic staffs but was under the general supervision of a palace official known as *Domesticus super villae.* Each royal villa was an autonomous realm separated from the *pagus,* or county, with its own court and system of taxation.

Other income came from fines and confiscations under

Germanic law and voluntary loans from freemen (which were usually voluntary only in name). For a time certain Roman imposts continued to be levied, through the Counts, on the Gallo-Romans, but with attempts to extend these imposts to the Franks and the growing confusion in the system itself serious difficulties began to arise until, in A.D. 614, Clotaire II (A.D. 584-629) promised not to extend the system further. Duties on goods upon entry into towns and ports — excise and customs — and the direct requisition of stores by officials were easy means of supplementing the royal income. There was no separate State treasury: all these imposts accrued to the royal chest and would have been excessive had not the ruler usually reduced his patrimony by rash spending and the transfer of lands and property to make sure of the loyalty of influential subjects.

During the seventh century the several Merovingian kingdoms had generally fallen under the control of their Mayors of the Palace and a precarious unity was achieved only under Charles Martel, victor over the Arabs at Tours in A.D. 732, and his son Pepin the Short. When the latter died in A.D. 768 his realm was split into two kingdoms under his sons, one of whom died three years later, opening the way to the other son, Charles, to reunite the two and then by conquest to extend his sway southwards beyond the Pyrenees to the Ebro and in Italy beyond Rome, and northwards to the Elbe and the Danube. Such was his power that the Church enjoined his protection and in Rome on Christmas Day, A.D. 800, Charlemagne (A.D. 742-814), as he had come to be called, was crowned Emperor by the Pope. Thus the lay and ecclesiastical governments of the West were brought into close liaison and the Holy Roman Empire was born, more as an idea than a continuing reality but an idea that continued to inspire the loyalty of European men until its final abandonment in 1806.[3]

With the enthronement of Charlemagne the idea of the State came back into men's minds, at any rate so far as the reinstatement of the power of Rome was involved. Charlemagne regarded himself as the legitimate successor of the Roman Emperor, his conquests as a reoccupation of parts of the lost Imperium, and he accepted as one of his supreme duties the protection of the universal Church of Rome. Already under the Merovingians the idea of the interpenetration of church and civil government had been taken over from the East and, Byzantium being no longer able to protect the Church in the west against the Lombards, the Pope had conferred this protective duty successively upon Charles Martel and Pepin. It was then that the concept of the Frankish King as successor to the Imperium had become something more than a pious wish. But the idea of personal rule and dominance continued to overshadow the wider concept and Charlemagne, despite his enlightenment, regarded himself as supreme master of life and death of his subjects. The existing assemblies were purely consultative. Except in Lombardy and the Papal territories, all the peoples of the new Empire were considered as subjects of the ruler, local domination being exercised through the existing institutions. Charlemagne continued to exercise all the powers of his predecessors — of executive order, military command, and total jurisdiction — but to these were now added power to legislate in the same manner as a Roman Emperor.

These legislative acts, known as *capitularia,* were of four types, namely (1) *per se scribenda,* emanating from the ruler himself and having to do with matters of administration, both lay and ecclesiastical, as well as certain juridical matters; (2) *pro lege tenenda,* having general legislative force throughout the Empire; (3) *legibus addenda,* filling in or amending national laws and covering private and penal matters; and (4) *missorum,* instructions to the *missi dominici* (see below), dealing with more limited administrative matters.[4]

Charlemagne's realm differed from the Merovingian in having a Germanic majority, in being orientated northwards towards the Elbe rather than southwards towards the Mediterranean, and in being completely separated from Byzantium. On the other hand, despite the renaissance of the idea of the State, the Carlovingian power rested upon the personal link between ruler and subject. Its close association with the Church made the new realm a theocracy. The actual nature of this government has been placed on record by Rincmar, Bishop of Rheims, in his *De ordine palatii* (A.D. 882).

While the *Palatium,* or royal household, continued to be mobile, as under the Merovingians, there was now a royal residence at Pavia in the pricipality of Pavia and a capital at Aix-la-Chapelle, which Charlemagne intended should replace Rome. This *Palatium* continued to be constituted very much as formerly, except that the Mayor of the Palace, the Referendaries and the *Domestici* had disappeared, with the Minister of Finance. Charlemagne himself undertook a regrouping of functions under three grand officers who formed a sort of privy council.

First among these officials was the Archchaplain who directed the ecclesiastical personnel of the palace, represented the Pope to the Emperor, took account of all ecclesiastical affairs in the realm, decided disputes among the clergy and reported on all important ecclesiastical matters to the Emperor. He was also in charge of the palace school. Second, the *Cancellarius,* or Chancellor, replaced the *Referendarius.* He was invariably an ecclesiastic and in this respect subordinate to the Archchaplain. Thus the Chancellery was part of the Royal Chapel. After A.D. 860 the Archchaplain took the title of Archchancellor, but the executive power remained with the Chancellor, who was responsible for promulgation of acts and regulations, for the royal correspondence, for the custody and use of the seals, for the custody of the archives, and for the publication of the royal edicts. With the growth of legislation and increase in administrative complexity the power of the Chancellor expanded. He was assisted by notaries, who verified and dated the acts, and scribes, who copied them. All these officials were clerics. Thirdly, there was the Count of the Palace, who was judge of all secular cases except those involving his peers. He was superior to the Counts, whom he supervised, and was in effect Head of the Imperial Administration. Often the sheer magnitude of the task necessitated the appointment of more than one Count of the Palace. There were other less important officials, among whom the distinction between officials of the royal household and officials of the kingdom began to appear. The former, such as the Constable who had charge of the cavalry, assumed a more general role. To assist him inside the palace the Count of the Palace had a Seneschal. All these lesser officials were laymen.

Charlemagne was advised by two political assemblies; one, consisting of the principal councillors and senior officials, met to consider political, administrative and military matters which needed to be dealt with during the forthcoming year. Plans were thrashed out but the decisions were secret, for this was a closed council. The other assembly, known as the *placitum generale,* in addition to the seniors included also the less important officials and the *vassalli regis.* The Emperor did not participate but this did not mean that he relinquished control of the programme, which he submitted. This assembly, which was purely consultative, gave its views on the matters decided by the senior assembly and their decisions were submitted to Charlemagne who had the final word. This was really an institution designed to broaden as widely as possible the field of consent, although in practice the Emperor seems to have followed the assembly's advice. After Charlemagne the nobles gained power and the advice of the assembly became obligatory.[5]

In order to combine central direction with maximum administrative decentralization — a system essential in the existing circumstances to achieve cohesive rule over such a wide realm — Charlemagne perfected the standing custom of sending out *missi*, or representatives or commissioners of the king, to ascertain that the local authorities were properly carrying out the royal commands. Under a *capitularia* of A.D. 802 this system was comprehensively reorganized. The *missi dominici* were customarily chosen from among the palace staff and usually from among the rich so that there should be less likelihood of venality. They travelled in pairs, covering a certain geographical circuit, or *missiaticum*, which was changed annually. Each team consisted of a *missus ecclesiasticus* (archbishop, bishop or abbé) and a *missus laicus* (duke or count) in order that both branches should be supervised. Each team was a legal entity reaching common decisions and was expected to cover its *missiaticum* four times in the year.

The *missi dominici* exercised the full powers of the Emperor, as modified by the *capitula missorum*. In each locality they summoned the freemen to take oath of fidelity to the Emperor, to publish legislative acts, to collect complaints against officials, to deal with serious legal cases, to consider accusations of immorality and irreligion, and to receive petitions from widows, orphans and the destitute. They also reviewed the troops. Matters of administration were examined in more detail, including *inter alia* the collection of taxes, the certification of the coinage, the proper upkeep of the roads, the conservation of the royal domains, etc. and the proper ordering of the churches and monasteries. The *missi dominici* had full powers to issue executive instructions and to decide legal plaints as well as to discipline officials for negligence or injustice. Inferiors could be dismissed forthwith but in the case of counts or dukes advice in similar terms would go to the Emperor for decision. They were also responsible for ensuring that the servants of the Church carried out their duties properly and exercised true Christian charity. Thus State and Church were indivisible under the Empire; law and morality were one. Here we have a system of government and administration by plenipotentiaries, a super-inspectorate with executive powers. In fact the time was to come when the *missi* were to exercise their powers with less and less reference to the Emperor and it became necessary to send out extraordinary *missi* to supervise the ordinary *missi*. With the weakening of the Empire the *missi* became permanent and were in a position to decide upon their own circuits. The new aristocracy shared in their selection and the *missi*, ceasing to be the true agents of centralization, were now able to usurp the Emperor's authority.

Local administration remained as formerly in the hands of the Counts, who were chosen by the Emperor, although his choice was gradually restricted. Usually they came from among the young scholars of the palace school and were generally members of the old aristocratic families. On nomination the Count took oath of fidelity to the Emperor and became his vassal. The Emperor could revoke such appointments but this was rarely done. By the time of Charlemagne the duchies had disappeared, except in frontier marches where counties were grouped under a Duke, who, in addition to the ordinary powers of the count, had special military responsibilities for local defence. In general the *Vicarius*, as the Count's deputy, became more closely assimilated with the *Centenarius* who had charge of the hundred and in fact the basic unit became known as the *vicaria*, which in the ninth century consisted of groups of hundreds. As the agent of the Count, the *Vicarius* exercised executive, administrative and military powers and, unlike the Merovingian *Centenarius*, also had judicial powers. Later a new deputy, or Viscount, appeared to assist the Count, and where a Count assumed charge of several counties a Viscount was placed in charge of each. Since neither in theory nor in practice was there any real division in the Empire of Charlemagne between state and church the ecclesiastical institutions were part of the local administration, providing services connected with the health and morals of the people, which were considered as amatter of course religious rather than lay responsibilities. In view of the importance of church government it is proposed to consider its form and development separately in the following section.

Relations between Emperor and Pope were close, the one representing the temporal the other the spiritual aspects of a single dominion over the people of the Empire. Such was Charlemagne's force of character and dynamism that his was the predominant power, the Pope usually endorsing his policies. Under his successor, Louis the Pious, this situation was to be reversed, for independence and sovereignty were restored to the Pope, who was shortly to assume the power to designate the Emperor.

Although the idea of the Holy Roman Empire was long to continue to inspire the minds of Western men and there were to be numerous attempts to make the idea a political reality, the concept had already achieved its most concrete development under Charlemagne and, despite the sincere attempts of his able but less dynamic and dominating successor, the Carlovingian realm went into rapid decline. Its weaknesses were exemplified in the division of property and power among the sons of the Emperor under the laws of succession and were further probed by the devastating attacks of the Normans. The resources no longer existed to concentrate the power and maintain the administration of so large a realm as a single political entity. Resources in men and material were too thinly spread and communications too primitive and precariously maintained for the sustenance of adequate administrative co-ordination from the centre. It was natural in the circumstances for administration to operate from a series of autonomous power centres around the strong points and demesnes of powerful nobles and prelates. The system of land tenure and personal allegiances that already operated gave rise to a hierarchy of contractual relationships which became known as the feudal system, in which the rule of the kings within the several kingdoms of the West was largely concentrated upon their immediate vassals, who as personal overlords could be as powerful in their own spheres as the ruler in his.

THE CHURCH OF ROME

The emergence of the Christian Church from its simple beginnings in the Apostolate of the Twelve to a world-wide organization with extensive temporal as well as spiritual powers is a development that no student of public administration can ignore. In the period under review, when religion and government were inextricably interwoven both in men's minds and in practical affairs, the Church was destined to become an institution of outstanding importance. Hitherto church and state had been one: it remained for the Christian Church to inaugurate a development that would result in their separation and substantiate to the full Jesus Christ's diplomatic answer: 'Render therefore unto Caesar the things which are Caesar's; and unto God the things that are God's.'[6]

In the beginning the Church already had an ordered hierarchy of apostles, prophets and teachers[7] and soon the first simple communities began to form amidst the heathen peoples of the West. 'In effect the church of the first age may almost be said to have consisted of a laity grouped in local communities, and a ministry which moved from place to place to do the work of missionaries to the heathen and of preachers and teachers to the converts.'[8] As a definite organization began to appear the Bishop came to be accepted as leader and head of his compact Christian community whose spiritual needs he was competent to look after personally and intimately without the aid of assistants. He was originally elected by his flock and it was not until the fourth century that the clergy began to participate and eventually to take a predominant part in his selection. It was the growing success of the new religion that was eventually to render a more complex organization necessary. In the first churches presbyters and deacons had been selected locally from among the first converts to provide for the simple needs of religion, and incidentally to act as embryo administrators in keeping the group together. These offices and others became generally accepted, especially during the third century, and subsequently a regular hierarchy of posts began to emerge. Apart from the increase in size of the congregations, the building of large church edifices created new needs for their servicing and maintenance, while the natural assumption by the Church of the functions of a gigantic friendly society called for more deacons to act as relieving officers. These deacons, under the direction of an overseer, visited the sick and needy in their homes to dispense the alms contributed by the more fortunate members of the community. In the course of these charitable peregrinations the priests had excellent opportunities to become acquainted with the characters and spiritual strengths and failings of their flock and it was part of their duty to report to the Bishop on cases calling for the penitential discipline of the Church.

In consequence of these new duties the original orders of bishop, presbyter and deacon had to be supplemented by new grades, so that during the third century a large community such as Carthage or Rome had seven types of officers. Subdeacons and acolytes had been added to take over the personal and secretarial duties originally performed by the deacon, exorcists and readers had been added as subordinate members of the liturgical ranks. All these grades had been enumerated by Pope Cornelius to Fabius of Antioch in A.D. 251, but it was during the following century that they came finally to constitute a well-defined hierarchy.

Inevitably, as the organization of the churches became more rationalized, the new administrative structure became less flexible than the earlier simple scheme and the principle of promotion of the clergy from grade to grade, no doubt with the pattern of the *cursus honorum* of the magistrates of Rome clearly in mind, became part of the traditional procedure. The friendly personal link between the bishop and his flock had thus been imperceptibly removed by the interposition of an organization that success and expansion had rendered necessary, and tensions inevitably developed between bishop and presbyter which often brought the

latter independence rather than subordination. While the individual churches maintained close contacts, and indeed their members regarded each other as belonging to the same brotherhood,
the bishops continued for long to operate as independent units,
no doubt meeting their close opposite numbers informally when
the occasion arose, which was probably not frequently in those
times of indifferent mobility. The structure so far described
applied to the separate units, but a spontaneous movement to
co-operate through councils developed under the spur of necessity and gradually more formally organized meetings came to be
planned until, at Arles in A.D. 314, a *concilium plenarum* or
General Council, was summoned by Constantine to settle a
quarrel that had been raging in Africa between the partisans of
Caecilian and the partisans of Donatus.[9]

In accordance with the basic doctrines of the Church these
bishops were originally all equal, irrespective of the size and
importance of their churches, but with the gradual emergence
of the system of conciliar co-ordination that is being visualized
it came to be recognized that some of the bishops were more
important than others. Inevitably, the spiritual equality which
was the essence of the Christian doctrine came to be modified in
practice by the injection of power into the general organization.
Now we have a picture of the structure of the Church embodying
two hierarchic levels, one within each local church community
under the individual bishops and the other among the bishops,
culminating with the Bishop of Rome.

At first the supremacy of the Bishop of Rome was purely
moral, for he had no judicial, administrative, disciplinary, or
even doctrinal authority over his brother bishops.[10] Constantine
conferred a special mark of favour on the Bishop of Rome when
he gave him the Lateran Palace and raised a basilica over the
tomb of Saint Peter, thus distinguishing the Bishop as Peter's successor. When Constantine left for his new eastern capital it was
natural that he should leave the Bishop of Rome with a particular
authority. Thus, if Rome was losing its position as the political
capital it was destined to acquire the distinction of becoming the
moral capital of the West. The position was legalized in A.D. 325
at the Council of Nicaea, when primacy among all the bishops
was conferred upon Rome, Alexandria and Antioch. The Bishop
of Rome thus emerged as Pope at the head of the bishops of the
West and, while he continued to be elected by the clergy and
people of Rome in the presence of the bishops of the neighbouring sees who gave their assent and consecrated the election, the
elements of kingship were already present. For example, most

influential among the electors were the senior city officials and the more important church dignitaries who wielded the greater influence. By A.D. 385 the Pope's right to legislate, by the issue of Decretals, was recognized and a decade later the first appeals appeared before the Papal Court. It remained only for Pope Leon I, in A.D. 440, to set up a Papal Chancellery and to organize an ecclesiastical hierarchy with administrative functions mainly in mind.[11]

Everywhere, with the breakdown of the Imperial Administration, the Church began to acquire estates and with them to extend its temporal commitments. Throughout the West the Church stepped in to provide administrative services which had hitherto been the sole concern of the civil authorities. In this way the theocratic links between Church and Empire, Pope and King, which were a characteristic of the Carlovingian age and were to continue for many hundreds of years, were made acceptable to the people who came to recognize the arrangement as part of the natural order of affairs and were inevitably confused when quarrels arose between the ecclesiastical and royal agents.

It was in the City of Rome that the most significant development occurred in the assumption of secular responsibilities and powers by the Church and reinforced the need of the Pope, as a powerful ruler, to exercise temporal powers in order to protect the Church's growing properties against robbery and rapine. With barbarian attacks ever imminent it would have been suicidal to rest content with the spiritual power of a religion not yet in the least acceptable to most of the invaders.

In Rome itself the old urban government had continued in form, but it had begun to give way to the ecclesiastical authorities when the *Curiales,* representing the rich citizens, had been content to hand over certain civic burdens to the Bishop, who thus acquired responsibility for a number of estates. Although, by the *Pragmatica sanctio*[12] the maintenance by the State of the public buildings in Rome had been guaranteed, during the seventh century the care of the aqueducts and the preservation of the city walls passed over to the Papal administration. This process was unspectacular but persistent. For example, when next we hear of the *Praefectus urbis* nearly two hundred years have gone by and this once strong arm of the administration of the Imperial Capital had unobtrusively become a pontifical official.[13] The hospitals and charity organizations that had graced Rome in her heyday now became the care of the Pope's functionaries and corn, collected from far and wide as church dues, continued to flow into the granaries of Rome, even from the traditional corn-

fields of Sicily, for distribution to the populace under the benevolence of the Pope. Thus the Pope's image came to replace that
of the Emperor, and all this had begun while the Emperors were
still in office. In Rome the growth of the new power, before the
old power had abdicated, ensured a continuity to the Imperial
institutions which other centres were not usually so fortunate as
to enjoy. The same continuity also ensured that the Papal administration should to some extent bear the stamp of its Byzantine
predecessor.

With the increasing Latinization of the West, following Diocletian's reorganization of the Imperial Government into two
distinct realms, East and West had continued to drift apart, but
there was no formal break in the Church. Equality between the
Bishops of Rome and Constantinople had been affirmed by the
Council of Chalcedon (A.D. 451) although the Pope was then
conceded honorary precedence. Reunion with Rome continued to
be the aim of some of the Eastern Emperors and this idea persisted in men's minds, providing one of the reasons for the
Crusades until the Fourth Crusade, by its ruthless sack of Constantinople in A.D. 1204, raised a final barrier between the two
wings of Christendom. The coronation of Charlemagne in A.D.
800 had no doubt been the event that finally decided the issue,
for the Pope then recognized the importance of having a power
in the West strong enough to provide the protection against the
barbarians that Byzantium could no longer guarantee. He was
also concerned to frustrate Charlemagne's serious project of
reconstituting old Rome at Aix la Chapelle which he had chosen
for his capital, a plan whose success would have permanently
shifted the centre of power within both Empire and Church away
from the Mediterranean to the German borders and thus stolen
a march upon the future.

The Pope himself was already a temporal power in Rome,
where for many hundred years the Papal State had been emerging
out of the accumulated landed estates of the Bishopric of Rome
and, with the weakening of the Imperial power, he had come
to exercise political leadership in Rome and Italy. As we have
already mentioned, the Papal administration had gradually
absorbed the administrative and judicial offices of the city and
the finances of the two administrations had become inextricably
intermingled. By the time of Adrian I (A.D. 772-795) the dominions
of the Pope had practically reached the limits which were to
continue until 1860. A new state had appeared on the map of
Europe although, on account partly of its peculiar origins, partly
of the counter-claims of the Emperor, its status remained vague.

IP

It was not a *regnum,* rather a *terrae seu patrimonium ecclesiae,*[14] but despite its many vicissitudes it was to provide an element of administrative continuity between Imperial Rome and the Modern World.

THE IMPACT OF ISLAM

The Holy Roman Empire was not the only theocratic system that inscribed its imprint on the governmental and administrative map of the West during the first millennium. The emergence of Islam in an obscure Arabian town in A.D. 570 was to lead to the creation of an extensive realm and a worldwide culture which was to challenge in its all-conquering drives the might of both East and West Rome, only to be rolled back from the very heart of Europe at Tours by Charles Martel in A.D. 732. The administrative characteristics of this impressive spiritual and political success story are still imperfectly understood and it may well be that the records no longer exist that could provide final conclusions. But there can be little doubt that our ignorance in the West is to a large degree due to a lack of interest in a major human effort that failed at the final stage, despite many brilliant successes whose impact, however, was felt largely on the periphery of Western power. In fact the attacking waves were to flow in, long beyond the period covered by the present volume.

There is no proof that at the outset Mohammed intended his message to penetrate beyond his own land of Arabia whose inhabitants had been brought under the new faith before his death in A.D. 632, with the exception of Jews and a few Christians and Magians who were permitted to retain their own faith on condition they recognized his overlordship and paid a special *jizya* or poll-tax.[15] It was later, under the Caliphs, or Successors, of the Prophet and Commanders of the Faithful, that expansion really began. By A.D. 750 the power of Islam extended in Asia to Transoxiana and the Indus Valley; in Africa across Egypt and the full extent of the northern coast to Morocco; and in Europe to the Douro and Ebro in the Iberian Peninsular, including the Balearic Islands, Sardinia and Sicily. This phase reached its apoges under the Ommiad Caliphs, particularly during the Caliphate of al-Walid (A.D. 705-715). The Islamic Empire was held together by the proselytizing faith of the converted and the drive of military conquest. The Arabs were not great organizers like the Romans or inventive in administration. They retained the customs and institutions of the conquered, merely placing their own leaders and officials in key positions. The Umayyads were replaced by the Abbasids — descending from Abbas, uncle of the Prophet — who, during their period of rule from A.D. 750 to 1258, added a cultural quality which marked the high tide of Islamic civilization and made a powerful impression upon the West. By this time the simple leadership of Mohammed had been replaced by a highly despotic, and luxuriously aristocratic and oriental, court which bore little resemblance to the original inspiration of the Prophet. It was at the beginning of this phase that Harun al-Rashid (A.D. 786-809) ruled in a Baghdad whose glory had been transmitted to us in the *Arabian Nights*. Drawing upon the world for its material riches and encouraging scholars of all races and creeds to its schools the Abbasid realm in the East presented a startling contrast to the semi-barbaric court of Charlemagne, with whom Harun al-Rashid maintained amiable diplomatic relations. A contracted but still powerful Byzantium stood as a third force, while internal strife and the impacts of the Seljuk Turks and the Mongols under Genghis Khan were by the thirteenth century to make way for the Turks as successors and representatives of Islam.

It was upon a tribal society that the Prophet constructed the theocracy inspired by the new faith, a four-grade society made up of (1) the chief and his family, (2) the group of free families that acknowledged the chief, (3) the *mawali* or freedmen and the various descendents of freedmen, and (4) the slaves. According to the Prophet's original charter the membership formed one *umma* over against the rest of mankind, believers who shared the burden of each other's debts and collectively guaranteed the security of the community.[16] Political power was wielded by Allah and his apostle, Mohammed, and there could be no distinction between church and state (neither of which in fact existed as such). Add these basic ideas to the fluid nomadic habits of the Arabs and it is not easy to discern a definite system of public administration. The existing institutions of the Byzantines, the Greeks, the Persians and the Romans in the conquered and contiguous territories were freely adopted, and adapted to provide a workable administrative organization for the new empire.

We are fortunate in possessing in Ibn Khaldun's remarkable *Muqaddimah* (An Introduction to History, *circa* A.D. 1332-1406) an authoritative account of early Islamic institutions. His description of the government offices begins with the fourfold functional division of the ruler's duties in which he will require help. Such help would thus be afforded (1) with the sword, (2) with the pen, (3) with advice and knowledge, and (4) by keeping people from crowding upon the ruler and diverting him from the supervision of their affairs. The existence, no doubt at a later stage, of specialist offices as subdivisions of each of these spheres is visualized: thus we encounter 'the pen of letters and correspondence', 'the pen of diplomas (or warrants conferring privileges, notes entitling to payments) and fiefs', and 'the pen of book-keeping'. The sword included 'military operation', 'police', 'postal service', and 'administration of border regions'. All such governmental functions adhered to the Caliphate and were subject to the religious law which was the only law. Jurists were therefore intimately concerned in all governmental and administrative activities. There was no separation of powers.

It was some time before individual posts emerged. In the early days the Prophet was in the habit of calling in the men around him for advice, especially Abu Bakr who came to be known as Mohammed's *Wazir* (the Vizir of oriental courts). Otherwise the Arabs in general were too illiterate to undertake writing and book-keeping tasks which, as far as they were needed in a society habituated to oral communication, were left to Jews and Christians and others, and specific ranks did not yet exist. Religious law forbade the Caliph from keeping petitioners away from the gates, but with the assumption of royal authority one of the first actions of the ruler was to bar access to the masses. For this purpose an official was appointed to protect the person of the ruler with the title of *Hajib,* or doorkeeper, always an important Islamic functionary. Abd-al-Malik (A.D. 685-705) is said to have directed a doorkeeper whom he was appointing with the admonition, 'I have given you the office of keeper of my door (and you are entitled to turn away anyone) save these three persons: the *muezzin,* because he is missionary of God; the person in charge of the mails, for it (always) is something (important) that he brings; and the person in charge of the food, lest it spoil.'[17]

With the extension of royal authority the position of Vizir, as general councillor, assistant and supervisor of the other servants, became formalized and recognized as the most important official about the court. The control of military and police matters came into his hands. Secretarial work was left to clients, usually Jews or Christians, but to preserve secrecy a special Secretary was appointed who was, however, less important than the Vizir, since his intervention was only required for written matters at a time when the most important business was still conducted orally.

Under the Abbasids the official ranks proliferated and became more important. The Vizir in particular tended to receive the

delegated executive authority of the Caliph, with supervision of
the pen as well as the sword. A seal to authenticate the royal
documents was introduced and placed in the hands of the Vizir,
who in the days of al-Rashid even received the title of 'Sultan'.
The only office he did not absorb was that of Doorkeeper, largely
because, despite its importance, its menial duties were disdained.
It was not a big step then to the time when the Vizir acquired
full control of the executive powers — although to comply with
religious law formal appointment as the Caliph's delegate was
still necessary — and the identity of the Caliphate was lost.

Under the Umayyads in Spain at first the older type of Vizirship flourished but later an interesting specialization came about.[18]
Separate Vizirs were appointed for the several functions, namely:
(1) government accounting, (2) official correspondence, (3) care
of those who had suffered wrongs, and (4) supervision of border
regions. All these Vizirs had a special office at the Court where
they sat on carpets spread out for them and there executed the
orders of the ruler, one of them being appointed as liaison between the group and the Caliph. His constant contact with the
ruler gave him greater authority than the others. He sat on a
raised seat among them and was distinguished by the function
and rank of *Hajib,* or doorkeeper, a post which retained its
leadership until the end of the dynasty.

As the functions of central government became more complicated, especially under the Abbasids, the Vizir and other top-
rank officials came to need more and more assistants in order to
get through the day's work. Definite specialist offices, or *Diwans,*
appeared which may be considered the modest forerunners of the
modern government department or ministry.

Prominent among these departments was the *Diwan* of Financial Operations and Taxation which was responsible for management of the royal income and expenditures and acted as pay-
master of the soldiery. It was necessary to collate and write down
the rules set by the chiefs of tax operations and stewards of the
dynasty. Such essential information was entered in a book known
as the *diwan* and it was from this that the place in which the
officials worked derived its name. But there were other interpretations. Ibn Khaldun is not decided about its actual origins,
for he suggests two amusing explanations. The first was that a
king who saw all his secretaries at their calculations thought they
were talking to themselves and uttered the word *dewaneh* which
was Persian for 'crazy', and the word was adopted and became
shortened in use. The second story also attributes the title to
the Persian meaning of *diwan* as 'devils', an allusion to the

officials' quick comprehension and capacity for drawing sense out of random facts. Accounting offices of this type, although of outstanding importance, did not appear until a dynasty had become powerful and interested in efficient administration. It is first met with under the Muslims in the reign of Omar (A.D. 634-44), although there already existed the Persian and Byzantine finance offices as examples. Ibn Khaldun remarks: 'This office constitutes a large part of all royal authority',[19] on the grounds that it is one of the three basic pillars of such authority, which were soldiers, money, and 'means to communicate with those who are absent'.

Next there was the *Diwan* of Official Correspondence and Writing, a type of institution needed only by the dynasties of sedentary societies. As the more complex society developed Arabic tended to become corrupt and its practice a craft. Official office could then be entrusted only to those who know the language well and the growth of secretarial practices would follow as a matter of course. The secretary became important among officials. His work is clearly described: he 'issued documents freely, and signed his own name at the end of them. He sealed them with the seal of the ruler, which was a signet upon which the name of the ruler or his emblem was engraved. It was impressed on a red clay mixed with water and called sealing clay. The document was folded and glued, and then both sides were sealed with the seal. Later on, the documents were issued in the name of the ruler but the secretary affixed his *alamah* (signature) either at the beginning or the end. He could choose where he wanted to put it as well as its wording.'[20] Another important function of the secretary was the *tawqi*, the arrangement whereby he sat in front of the ruler during public audiences briefly taking down decisions concerning the petitions which were being considered. Such decisions had subsequently to be set down in writing for issue to the petitioner, and this was a task, we are told, that required a great deal of stylistic skill. Consequently posts as *tawqi* were sought after by writers who wished to acquire similar skills. Indeed this was a high position which had normally to be filled from among those members of the upper classes who had high scholastic abilities. Where the ruler chose to select a secretary from the rank and file he had many conditions to consider. That this was sometimes necessary is evidenced by the survival of a delightful epistle addressed by the secretary Abd-al-Hamid (died A.D. 750) to his fellow secretaries. From the paragraphs of this document now quoted it is abundantly clear that much of Abd-al-Hamid's advice could have been adopted by any professional body throughout the ages:

'And now: May God guard you who practice the craft of secretary-
ship, and may He keep you and give you success and guidance.
There are prophets and messengers and highly honoured kings.
After them come different kinds of men, all of them made by God.
They are of different kinds, even if they are all alike in fact. God
occupied them with different kinds of crafts and various sorts of
businesses, so that they might be able to make a living and earn
their sustenance. He gave you, assembled secretaries, the great
opportunity to be men of education and gentlemen, to have knowledge and (good) judgment. You bring out whatever is good in the
caliphate and straighten out its affairs. Through your advice, God
improves the government for the benefit of human beings and
makes their countries civilized. The ruler cannot dispense with you.
You alone make him a competent ruler. Your position with regard
to rulers is that (you are) the ears through which they hear, the
eyes through which they see, the tongues through which they speak,
and the hands through which they touch. May God give you, therefore, enjoyment of the excellent craft with which He has distinguished you, and may He not deprive you of the great favours that
He has shown unto you.

No craftsman needs more than you to combine all praiseworthy
good traits and all memorable and highly regarded excellent qualities, O secretaries, if you aspire to fit the description given of you
in this letter. The secretary needs on his own account, and his
master, who trusts him with his important affairs, expects him, to
be mild where mildness is needed, to be understanding where
judgment is needed, to be enterprising where enterprise is needed,
to be hesitant where hesitation is needed. He must prefer modesty,
justice, and fairness. He must keep secrets. He must be faithful in
difficult circumstances. He must know (beforehand) about the
calamities that may come. He must be able to put things in their
proper places and misfortunes into their proper categories. He must
have studied every branch of learning and know it well, and if he
does not know it well, he must at least have acquired an adequate
amount of it. By virtue of his natural intelligence, good education,
and outstanding experience, he must know what is going to happen
to him before it happens, and he must know the result of his actions
before action starts. He must make the proper preparations for
everything, and he must set up everything in its proper, customary
form.

Therefore assembled secretaries, vie with each other to acquire
the different kinds of education and to gain an understanding of
religious matters. · · ·

*   *   *   *

None of you should have too sumptuous an office or go beyond
the proper limits in his dress, his mount, his food, his drink, his
house, his servants, or in the other things pertaining to his station,
for, despite the nobility of the craft by which God has distinguished
you, you are servants who are not permitted to fall short in their

service. You are caretakers whom one does not permit to be wasteful or spendthrift. Try to preserve your modesty by planned moderation in all the things I have mentioned and told you. Beware of the wastefulness of prodigality and the bad results of luxury. They engender poverty and bring about humiliation. People who (are prodigal and live in luxury) are put to shame, especially if they be secretaries and men of education.

Things repeat themselves. One thing contains the clue to another. Let yourselves be guided in your future understandings by your previous experience. Then, choose the method of doing things that is most definite, most accurate, and that promises the best result. You should know that there is something that defeats accomplishment, namely, talking about things. The person who does it is prevented from using his knowledge and his ability to think. Therefore, everyone of you, while he is in his office, should endeavour to talk no more than is sufficient; he should be concise in the matters he brings up and in the answers he gives; and he should give thought to all the arguments he advances. His work will profit from that. It will prevent too much preoccupation with other things . . .'[21]

Could any better evidence be quoted to support the universality of the substance of good administration?

Among the important services under the Caliphate was the *Barid,* or postal system, which was maintained for the carrying of official messages throughout the Empire. It acted both as an intelligence service and an essential communications network upon which the entire administrative system was patterned. This was not of course an invention of the Caliphate, or, as we have already seen, the existence of an efficient postal service was an essential of the earliest empires of Western Asia. The connection is evident in the employment of Persian and Byzantine titles and methods. The system achieved its highest efficiency under the Abbasids, when relays were organized at suitable stages along all the main routes, while new routes were laid out for the purpose. Messages were carried either by runners or by horsemen or camelmen. Even carrier pigeons were sometimes employed. The maintenance of the *Barid* was a vital local responsibility.

In the capital there was a special *diwan* under the *Sahib al-Barid* chief master of the posts, who became one of the Caliph's most important and influential officials. His was a highly specialized post, for he was responsible for the organization of the posts throughout the realm and the appointment of officials. The Caliph depended upon his information on routes and staging for his own travels and for the organizing of military expeditions. The route books compiled by officers of the *Barid* were the earliest Muslim geography books.[22]

As an outcome of his specialist knowledge and contact with local organizations the *Sahib al-Barid* became the general supervisor of provincial officials.

The *Ifriqiyah,* or chief of police, was the head of another important office, which was first created by the Abbasids to investigate crimes and execute legal punishments, activities not appropriate to the religious authorities who exercised the office of magistrate, although there were instances where the Chief of Police also exercised magisterial powers in the case of capital crimes and punishments. Among the Umayyads in Spain this function operated at two levels—of the great police and of the small police. The great police had jurisdiction over both the upper and lower classes and particularly over government dignitaries and their families, as well as anyone connected with them as clients. The chief was chosen from among the great personalities and had his seat at the gate of the palace. He was attended by *raje,* or footmen, who occupied places nearby which they did not leave except to go about his business. This office could be a stepping stone to the heights of the vizirship or to the office of doorkeeper. The chief of the small police was concerned only with the common people.

Another important department was the Mint, where the *dinars* and *dirhams* used in commercial transaction were stamped with an iron die upon which designs or words were engraved in reverse, a process about which Ibn Khaldun gives us valuable information. This was an office necessary to the royal authority, he says 'for it enables people to distinguish between good and bad coins in their transactions'. There was also the *Diwan* of the Seal which was composed of the secretaries whose task was to expedite the letters of the ruler involving the use of the seal in the way already described.

The pattern of the central administration varied considerably as the power of the rulers waxed and waned, and the relative importance of the individual offices changed accordingly, fluctuating particularly with the relative prestige of the Vizir and the Doorkeeper. There was no concept of a tightly organized administration under a co-ordinating council of ministers. Powers were assigned to individuals by the ruler and the *diwans* developed spontaneously to cope with the increasing volume of administrative work involved in the government of the Empire. As the processes became more complex and the extension of operations called for more assistants, more specialization and detailed supervision became necessary and further officials were called in to supply the required skills. But, by the very nature of the Islamic community, much of the administrative work had to be carried out on the spot, so that there were limits to which centralization could be carried in this particular political system. It is always a virtue in public administration to deconcentrate as much as possible away from the centre. But with communications so primitive the real problem was the opposite one of maintaining a co-ordinated control over those to whom responsibility was confided over the vast expanses of the Empire. The provincial administration should now be briefly reviewed.

From the beginning an agent was sent out to the localities to collect taxes. This official, known as the *Amil,* accompanied the *Amir* who commanded the troops sent to enforce payment and suppress rebellion. The system of dual agents was to continue and to be developed further. At first the *Amir* was invariably superior to the *Amil,* but with the consolidation of Islam and natural increase in the relative importance of finance, the *Amil's* relative power increased, so that on occasions where the Treasury's interest had become paramount his decision could be decisive. It is recorded that in Iraq in Omar's time—he died in A.D. 644—a more complicated tripartite division was adopted, for Omar sent out three officers, one to lead in prayer and war, one to take charge of justice and finance, and a third to measure the newly acquired lands for revenue purposes.

It was not easy to maintain this sort of control. Under weak rulers local leaders tended to take over control of the situation and to appoint the governors. However, there was a tightening up under the Umayyads, when control from the centre was restored and a simple form of local government was maintained. In the main the pattern of local administration varied with the already existing system. The Arabs themselves at the outset had neither the skill nor the inclination to become administrators and more often than not local control was left in the hands of tribal chieftains or village headmen.

The Abbasids, despite their power, were unable to maintain the unity of the Islamic world. For a time the Empire was divided between the Eastern Caliphate of the Abbasids with its capital at Baghdad and the Amirate of Andalusia under the Umayyads of Cordova, but later disintegration was to go further. It is interesting to speculate how far lack of effective administrative means was a fundamental determining factor in this power-split. Of course the white heat of the original inspiration could not last and the external weaknesses which had facilitated the original successes were almost bound to become less helpful, nor could the efficiency of charismatic leadership be expected to continue at a sufficiently high level to prevent disruption, but there can be little doubt that the inherent administrative weaknesses of such a widespreading and loosely integrated political structure must have had something more than marginal effect upon the outcome.

Certainly, administrative co-ordination will have become less difficult in the realms that had broken away, but this may not have amounted to much. In the Eastern Caliphate the simpler administrative methods of the nomadic Arabs were finally eclipsed and a much more sophisticated system of public administration evolved. The Abbasids retained the system of sending *amir* and *amil* together from Baghdad except that Iraq, owing to its proximity to the capital, enjoyed a special relationship to the administrative headquarters. Thus, the fertile region of the Sawad was placed under ministers of state instead of the usual governor. There was in Baghdad a *Diwan* of the Sawad, control of which was most eagerly sought. Similarly the district of Badurayya on the right bank of the Tigris, actually stretching right up to the perimeter of Baghdad, had its own minister and *Diwan al-Karaj,* which constituted a qualification for the vizirship. The remaining districts of Iraq were placed under a single *wali* or *amil* appointed by the Caliph himself, or the Vizir when he was invested with executive patronage. Elsewhere kinship to the sovereign invariably afforded a natural claim to office. Governorships could also be obtained by purchase. In the same way the *amil,* instead of being a salaried official of the central administration, might be a tax-farmer who purchased his appointment for a fixed sum nad made what profit he could, with all the accompanying oppression that has invariably accompanied such administratively irresponsible methods wherever they may have been adopted. Not that these defective administrative arrangements were the inevitable precursors of political decline. On the contrary, with the weakening of central control it was almost inevitable that *amir* and *amil* should come to terms and share the spoils of their province. It is true that this would also involve the connivance of the official of the *Barid,* or posts, but in a situation of weakness and corruption even this important safeguard could cease to matter much.

As we have seen, the Islamic system of government was essentially theocratic, so that all the administrative arrangements that have been touched upon were entirely dependent upon religious law, and the executive and judicial branches were one and the same. Our picture of the administration, however, would not be complete without some reference to the military organization which was an aspect rather than a separate branch of the government of Islam. This has been apparent with reference to the powers of the Caliph and his vizirs and provincial *amirs.*

Warfare was already a way of life in pre-Muslim Arabia, where it constituted a periodic activity of tribal life, ostensibly for plunder and revenge but basically as a relief from the monotony of desert existence.[23] Victory for Islam became an over-riding impulse of the new Islamic polity. Wielding the sword for Allah was an essential governmental duty of the Caliph and the military aspects were no more separable from his overall function than were the religious. Administration, so far as it could be distinguished as a specialist activity, served all aspects— religious, judicial, military and civil — and the latter would have the least significance to contemporaries.

The Caliph had final responsibility for war and peace, though he might delegate execution to his Vizir. Significantly, when the Caliphate was at its height the military part of government possessed a high degree of efficiency. The military administration had its beginnings in the diwan or register of the troops by which the *ata,* or stipend, was granted to each soldier. Originally recompense had rested entirely upon plunder, but inevitably this became insufficient and money had to be brought into the Treasury by the imposition of taxes upon subjugated lands. Grants of land also became a common means of reward. Eventually the recruitment and payment of the troops became the responsibility of the *Diwan al-Jayash,* or Ministry of the Army. In the realms bordering the Mediterranean, which were extensive when Islam was most powerful, there was also an office of Admiralty, under the *Almiland,* a word of Christian origin. He was concerned with the techniques of navigation and servicing the fleets, and was responsible to the official in charge of 'the Sword'.

Like the Prophet before him the Caliph was supreme commander of the troops though, as in Rome, it was not easy to prevent the ultimate power from falling into the hands of the soldiers, who could murder the ruler and appoint his successor. Next to the Caliph were the generals, whom he appointed. They often included his sons, but normally military prowess, as determined by success in battle, was necessary to the continuance of the system and the commanders were therefore chosen from among those with wide and proven experience of warfare. The generals appointed the officers below them. Under Omar a system of gradings became established. In order of precedence after the Amir, or Commander, were the commanders of the *ta'biya* (which was the basic unit whether on parade, on the march or in battle), the commanders of the *irafa,* or tenths, the standard bearers (who ranked highly) and the tribal chiefs. In addition to the fighting officers there were also the physician; the *qadi,* who had control of all booty and saw to its equitable division; the *da'iya,* or advocate, who put forward the claims of the men; the *ra'id* whose duty it was to find camp sites; the interpreter; and the scribe. This was not a particularly complicated organization but fully adequate to the needs of the situation. There was no provision for training, for it was assumed that the tribesmen were already skilled in military operations which had hardly developed beyond large-scale raiding. On the other hand, for essential supporting services, a definite administrative structure had emerged.[24]

Islam was to have its great moments of triumph and enjoy great achievements in learning and culture, as well as those in religion and warfare already mentioned. Governments were to be responsible for great constructional works, especially in the building of mosques, fortifications and irrigation systems, and for these appropriate administrative means had to be contrived. It was eventually to contribute to modern administrative effectiveness the arabic numerals and the use of paper from China as an essential writing medium. This is not an experience to be summarily dismissed, but the picture given here of an administration emerging without design to serve the needs of a civilization that found most of its means ready-made elsewhere seems a fair one, which sufficiently explains why Arab administration did not contribute a continuity factor to existing Islamic society or provide an administrative legacy to its successors as other governmental systems have done.

ANGLO-SAXON KINGSHIPS

In the lands beyond the fringes of the Carolingian Empire — Britain and Scandinavia — institutional developments were similar to those in the wider realm though they were usually less advanced and there were local conditions that were later to give rise to striking historical deviations. With the withdrawal of the Romans the conquest of the southern parts of Britain by Anglo-Saxon invaders from the coasts of Germany and Scandinavia took place between A.D. 450 and 600, a 'Dark Age' that has left only scanty records. By the end of this period, however, the tribal chiefs, who settled in the cultivatable lands of the island, were already assuming the character of settled kingships, and it is known that a heptarchy of kingdoms—Northumbria, Mercia, East Anglia,

Essex, Kent, Sussex and Wessex—had already been established. Christianity had been introduced under the Romans, whose law was to survive as the canon law, but a heathen period had supervened with the invasions and it was only in A.D. 597 that St. Augustine, on the invitation of King Ethelbert of Kent, came to Canterbury and the Church of England was founded. The building of churches and monasteries during the following centuries established settled centres of learning where documents could not only be produced but preserved. In this way the means for effective administration, both human and material, were being shaped.

During the next two hundred and fifty years a process of consolidation went on, and the kingdoms of Northumbria, Mercia and Wessex in turn achieved supremacy. Towards the end of the eighth century raids from the north again gathered momentum and it was under the pressure of aggression by the Danes, who now came to settle in the land, that the unity of England was eventually forged during the tenth century. The stage was set, after a further period of Danish conquest under Canute (A.D. 1016-35) and his sons, followed by a brief Anglo-Saxon interlude under Edward the Confessor and Harold, for the Norman Conquest of A.D. 1066.

Recent discoveries suggest that during the early years of these struggles, advances in civilization in England were in no way inferior to those occurring in other parts of the old Roman realm. Thus, under the Mercian supremacy, King Offa maintained relations on an equal footing with Charlemagne, with whom, in A.D. 796, he concluded the first commercial treaty in English history. In Anglo-Saxon England there existed many of the political and administrative institutions and customs already noted in connection with the Frankish realm: the itinerant court living off the country; administration of the King's domains by his household servants; personal relationships determining duties and rights not only between King and leading subjects but between the latter individually and the lesser nobility and freedmen, responsibility in the localities located in the shires, or counties, and hundreds under royal appointees; the constitution of fortified centres as the first burgs or boroughs with certain privileges; the emergence of specialised administration in the Royal Household; and the tentative rebirth of the idea of 'public' administration which had withered with the Roman withdrawal.

The public administrative pattern had long consisted of a disjointed multiplicity of separate households stemming from a multiplicity of rulers, such as those numerous kings in Sussex

whose existence is indicated in the charters issued by Aethelwalh
(c. A.D. 675) in connection with the Saxon cathedral of Selsey.[25]
On the other hand the mere existence of such charters also suggests the existence of *scriptoria,* or writing offices, and there is
evidence that the ecclesiastical authorities were already perform-
ing public tasks, for in A.D. 749 Aethelbald issued a charter to
all the churches in his kingdom freeing them from all public
business except the essential duties of repairing bridges and maintaining fortresses. In the same way Offa's relations with lesser
kings were authenticated and these documents bear witness to
the existence of something more than mere retainer groups about
the throne. Different styles in the script and titles employed indicate the operation of increasingly complex administrative
routines. Another public sphere in which important advances took
place during Offa's reign was the minting of money. The work-
manship of the King's monayers showed important advances—
advances no doubt influenced by expanded commercial intercourse with Europe—and the continuous history of English
coinage may be said to begin with Offa.[26] It was then that the
penny first appeared, as a silver coin.

With our knowledge of Offa's able statesmanship, pieced together from mere fragments of evidence—his independent part
in continental affairs, equal contact with Charlemagne, and his
recognition of the value of Papal authority over the English
Church as an aid to his own political manipulations—it is a great
pity that more information about his purely administrative
arrangements has not survived. It would be surprising, in view
of Offa's wide outlook, if the germ of a real public service could
not already be discovered in the organization of his household
staffs.

At the best, however, the administrative content of government was still primitive. The main expense of the King's
entourage, which prominently included his fowlers, huntsmen and
grooms, was rooted in their entertainment during the court's
circulation which was possibly subjected to some planned rota
in order to spread the burden. Certain services are mentioned
in charters of the eighth and ninth centuries as due from holders
of unenfranchised land. These included the cartage of goods for
the King's use and constructional work on his estates. The three
burdens specifically mentioned in a charter of Wiglaf of Mercia
(c. A.D. 830)[27] were the building of royal villages, the *feorm* or
food rent of the king and ealdormen, and hospitality to the
King's servants. These were generally accepted duties which
nevertheless are not clearly defined.

The Witenagemot continued from earlier days in the royal government as an advisory council of influential and knowledgeable persons of the type that rulers throughout history have considered it expedient to call upon for advice. It was not a representative or democratic institution in the modern sense. A common law code for England emerged in Alfred's code, although he himself lays claim to no wider title than 'King of the West Saxons' (A.D. 849-901). While this was the first legislation by an English king for a century it had a special significance, for by this time continental kings had ceased to exercise their traditional legislative powers. Stenton concludes: 'In England alone, through Alfred's example, the tradition was maintained to be inherited by each of the two foreign kings who acquired the English throne in the eleventh century.'[28]

Only now was administration in the localities beginning to attain its later structure. In the several kingdoms there existed different local divisions or *regiones,* organized for the maintenance of the economic life of the community, but it seems that Wessex was the first to achieve a system of shires and hundreds as a consciously organized administrative system, the smaller unit being concerned with the adjustment of taxation, the maintenance of peace and order, and the settlement of local pleas.[29] It seems that, by the beginning of the eleventh century, in England south of the Tees except in areas where Danish influence prevailed, this system of local administration had become universal.

By the reigns of Edward the Confessor (A.D. 1042-1066) and Harold II (A.D. 1066) a co-ordinated system of government existed in England but the administration, although fully competent to meet the needs of the simple governmental structure, was inevitably piecemeal and not discernable as an entity. It was severally associated with management of affairs in the localities and the numerous household units. The basic problem of exercising power over the larger areas prescribed by the emergence of the consolidated kingdom was primarily one of co-ordination. In Europe Pope and Emperor were already grappling with the problem of reintegration which the dissolution of the Roman Empire had imposed upon the West. The forging of an appropriate administrative system was to be a vital element in the solution. In England it fell to the latest invaders, the Normans, to take the next step.

The central administration was still the personal administration of the ruler, in the shape of the royal household, an itinerant organization that subsisted upon the compulsory hospitality of the localities. The household officials were such as would be needed in any contemporary household to perform the personal services required by the noble head and his family. These were working officials, for the honorary element that was later to become so influential at royal courts had hardly yet entered upon the English scene, although it is on record that, as early as the reign of King Ethelwulf (A.D. 839-858), Oslac, father of the king's wife, served in courts as a butler. Nor was there a high official of the calibre of Mayor of the Palace, as at the Carlovingian Court.

Early charters with their formalized language have long indicated the existence of trained clerks forming a writing office for the king. One such is even mentioned by name in A.D. 993 by Ethelred II (A.D. 987-1016) in a grant of land to Ælfwine, his faithful writer.[30] It is not unreasonable, therefore, to register Ælfwine as the first known English civil servant. As yet there was no evidence of a formal chancery.

From the will of King Eadred (A.D. 946-955) it appears that his principal servants were the discthegns, who served at the table, the hraeglthegns, who looked after his clothes, and the *birele,* or butlers. These were probably equivalent to the stewards, chamberlains and butlers of the later Anglo-Norman court. There also existed an inferior type of *stigweard,* or steward, in Eadred's household, as well as a horse-thegn, no doubt the forerunner of the marshal, who was later concerned with the stables. Stenton suggests that 'it is unlikely that Duke William, when he visited King Edward's court in 1051, can have noticed much that was unfamiliar in its arrangements'.[31] In the palaces and castles of the nobles and bishops, in the churches and monasteries, in the courts of the sheriffs, and in the strongholds of the burghs, improved managements and new administrative methods were already being sought. In fact, in England and throughout the West the stage was being set for the emergence of a new pattern of public administration.

REFERENCES

1 M. C. Pfister on 'The Franks before Clovis' in *Cambridge Medieval History,* Vol. I, (Cambridge, 1911,) pp. 292-301.
2 Jacques Ellul, *Histoire des Institutions,* Vol. I, (Presses Universitaires de France, 1955), pp. 667-707.
3 James Bryce, *The Holy Roman Empire,* (1864).
4 Ellul, *op. cit.,* p. 715.

5 Ellul, *op. cit.*, p. 721.
6 *St. Matthew*, XXII, Chapter 21.
7 Referred to by St. Paul in *First Epistle to the Corinthians*.
8 C. H. Turner on 'The Organization of the Church' in *Cambridge Medieval History*, Vol. I, p. 144.
9 Turner, *op. cit.*, p. 165.
10 Ellul, *op. cit.*, p. 515.
11 Ellul, *op. cit.*, pp. 535-6.
12 L. M. Hartman on 'Imperial Italy and Africa' in *Cambridge Medieval History*, Vol. II, (Cambridge, 1913), referring to *Pragmatica sanctio pro petitione Vigilii* as source of information about administration, p. 223.
13 Hartman, *op. cit.*, p. 229.
14 P. Partner, *The Papal State under Martin V*, (British School at Rome, 1958), p. 6.
15 R. Levy, *The Social Structure of Islam*, (Cambridge, 1957), p. 3.
16 Levy, *op. cit.*, pp. 272-5.
17 Ibn Khaldun, *The Muqaddimah: An Introduction to History*, (A.D. 1377, edition of the Bollingdon Foundation, New York, in three volumes, 1958), translated by Franz Rosenthal, Vol. II, p. 9.
18 Ibn Khaldun, *op. cit.*, p. 12.
19 Ibn Khaldun, *op. cit.*, p. 23.
20 Ibn Khaldun, *op. cit.*, p. 26.
21 Ibn Khaldun, *op. cit.*, pp. 29-35.
22 Levy, *op. cit.*, p. 301.
23 Levy, *op. cit.*, p. 407.
24 Levy, *op. cit.*, pp. 426-7.
25 F. M. Stenton, 'Anglo-Saxon England' in the *Oxford History of England*, (Oxford, 1943), p. 58.
26 Stenton, *op. cit.*, p. 222.
27 Stenton, *op. cit.*, p. 286.
28 Stenton, *op. cit.*, p. 273.
29 Stenton, *op. cit.*, pp. 289-90.
30 Stenton, *op. cit.*, p. 349.
31 Stenton, *op. cit.*, p. 632.

CHAPTER 8

THE OFFICIAL AND HIS ADMINISTRATION TO THE ELEVENTH CENTURY A.D.

A scholar of the West in the early years of the eleventh century of our era, looking back over the reaches of universal history, would have discerned little to suggest a natural progress in government through the ages and even less to indicate the existence of administration as a distinguishable activity. While he would probably have been able to observe in his immediate Eurasian environment — the West, Byzantium, Islam, India and China — much that unfortunately has not been preserved for us, the comparatively poor communications between the main power centres, even of such a compact landmass, would have rendered impossible the sort of conspectus which is becoming increasingly achievable as a result of modern communications and scholarship. Had our scholar been a student of Confucianism he would certainly have understood the possibility, and indeed desirability, of a division between the political and the administrative in government, but as a scribe in a monastry in Britain he could have been forgiven for concluding that the heyday of government had already occurred in some past Golden Age.

During the few thousand years that settled communities had then been developing beyond the long nomadic stage — a short enough span in human experience — most types of political community had emerged somewhere or other and consequently many different kinds of administration had been devised and adapted to changing governmental situations. In fact it is not unreasonable to regard the whole period as one vast testing time of man's political capacity, upon the quality of which his eventual survival might well depend.

The simple tribal community, with its families and clans; the compact city state, with its distinct democratic aspirations; the larger realm, embodying both settled and rural communities; and the widespreading empire, collecting under one rulership a number of realms and other political formations: all had been tried at different times and places, and all continued in being somewhere in the world at that very moment. Under leadership that had varied in its capacity to interpret and make the most of the existing social and economic conditions, communities had waxed and waned, and governments had changed with the accidents and climate of the times. Chiefs had become kings, and kings emperors, mainly because they had the capacity to provide the effective leadership which the situation happened to demand, and the idea of government as an essentially personal responsibility persisted. Kings and emperors still looked upon the management of the realm or imperium in the same terms as the management of their own household. The activities of government associated with the ruler's court — often still a highly mobile institution — were the personal services of his own servants and retainers. Rule was despotic even when it was also benevolent, depending very much upon personal loyalties and a system of relationships based upon a scale of rewards and punishments.

The smaller units of the tribe and city were naturally governed by charismatic leaders or small aristocratic councils, although the latter, with the need for increasing citizenship participation, tended to become more and more widely based until, notably in the Greek cities, democratic forms came into existence. It was in the larger realms and empires that problems of the transmission and delegation of power became increasingly acute. Sparseness of population and difficulty in communication often rendered the problem of maintaining an empire almost insoluble. Effective power usually depended upon the mobility and prowess of the military arm and force was accepted as the most potent administrative factor, while the main problems of administration were often side-tracked by means of treaties and by placing outlying areas under vassalage. The importance of road systems to effective government from the centre in the Achaemenian and Roman Empires is not easily exaggerated. Such empires continued after their heyday less because of their own internal solidity than of the existence of greater weaknesses beyond their borders. They were very vulnerable to any strong counter-power that happened to emerge at their own moment of weakness. The overwhelming but short-lived successes of Alexander provide an outstanding example of this, which also suggests that, while military prowess could go a long way in rendering imperial government possible, some vital stabilizing element was needed. Was this not the proper function of public administration? Given the right economic and social situation, the existence of leaders of sufficient calibre and foresight, the requisite military force, and the acquiescence of the people, such realms could be moulded by outstanding leaders and held together by good use of such administrative resources as were even then available.

The ruler, usually adopting the ritualistic and repressive methods of oriental despotism, whether he travelled much himself or stayed in his capital, was always concerned to know what was going on in other parts of his realm. Having secured his military control, often as a result of his own prowess, his chief problem was the maintenance and improvement of his system of communications, both to facilitate the transmission of order and instructions and to ensure the flow back of economic resources and information. The postman and the inspector, even if dressed in military style, were prominent among the first public officials.

The phenomenon of the division of labour manifested itself at the very outset of social development and the appearance of government as a conscious activity was concurrently involved both in the devolution, or separation, of powers into different hands and the progress of specialization, but it was a long time before the governor saw any real distinction between his religious, military and more modest administrative functions, except that the latter would first be allocated to others while he would cling on to the sources of power as long as possible. It has been seen how vitally the original governments were involved in religion: for example, not only in the temple states of Sumer and the extensive realm of the Pharaohs, but even in the more sophisticated systems of Greece and Rome where religion continued to be a government responsibility and, in the guise of soothsaying and augury, to influence the activities of administrators. The struggle between Emperor and Pope in the West has only to be mentioned to emphasize that right up to the very end of the period reviewed the spiritual and temporal authorities, where they had become separated, still figured equally as governing institutions and as active providers of public administration. Under the Islamic Caliphate and in China the two aspects continued to be even more intimately connected.

The military power was certainly an essential factor in government and the early leaders needed to be militarily competent. It was only in the city states that this power could be effectively diffused, through the organization of the citizen body for military purposes — although even there military predominance often occurred — and more attention could be given to the civil activities of the state. In the Greek states and Republican Rome this was apparent but, as the latter grew in extent, the tendency towards military usurpation became endemic. Aided by the weakening grip of incompetent emperors after the Augustan era, the army became increasingly the power behind the throne and even the throne itself, when its incompetence in non-military matters led eventually to the breakdown of the system.

During all the struggles for power, spiritual and military, that went on both within the states and externally, activities that we should today define as administrative had to be performed and the effectiveness of the particular government would certainly depend to a considerable extent, upon the quality of its administration. The growing complexities of civil administration would become burdensome to the leader interested in the exercise of power and he would be compelled for his own comfort not only to call in his officials for advice but to delegate responsibilities to them. He would soon learn that the collection of grain and the organization of labour gangs would be more effectively achieved by the employment of those who had the requisite knowledge and, preferably, understood the outlook and capacities of the local inhabitants.

There was as yet no designed administrative specialization but in choosing his deputy the ruler discovered that for the running of his household and the civil affairs of his realm it was as well to appoint a person with certain managerial capacities. The office of Vizir emerged widely as the right hand of the ruler and, while he was not usually without religious and military functions, the control of these as the fount of power remained with the ruler, leaving the Vizir usually to concentrate more on civil matters. He was primarily an administrator with a large amount of delegated executive power. Of course under a weak ruler the balance could easily tip in favour of the Vizir who might reduce his chief to a figurehead or even become an usurper whose inside knowledge would assist him in carrying on the succession. This happened in all the systems examined, nowhere more frequently than in the Byzantine Empire. Under these circumstances, the line between the ruler, as power wielder, and the administrator, as manager, cannot easily be drawn.

In those systems where the harem formed an important part of the ruler's household there was another factor that tended to modify the shape of the administration. As a matter of course power tended to settle into the hands of eunuchs specially vested with responsibility for court management and a conjunction of factors, such as their inside knowledge and access to family secrets, nominal inferiority and legal incapacity, both impelled and enabled these eunuchs to become a separate and dangerous power under the throne and to interfere in the wider administrative sectors of the government. Such eunuchs were able to exercise independent administrative authority in the Chinese,

Byzantine and Islamic systems and even to occupy leading positions.

DEVELOPMENT OF BASIC TECHNIQUES

Administration is so essentially a social activity in which a high degree of co-operation and co-ordination is needed to create a sort of communal memory that the importance of records as a fundamental administrative instrument does not need to be emphasized. Without the continuity factor of the written record public administration would have continued to suffer serious restriction. But administration is necessary to and indeed does exist in a pre-literate society and early chiefs and kings were compelled to devise administrative ways and means and to recruit persons to their households who had a natural flair for such activities. The obvious importance of effective power-manipulation as a main ingredient of primitive government — indeed of all government — should not be allowed to mask the fact that the leader who also had administrative talent at his disposal was better equipped to make his rulership effective, as well as acceptable, to the subjects whose continuing support he needed if his period of rule was to be satisfactorily prolonged. If leadership skills are still a matter for discussion in our seventh millennium of governmental experience when they are coming increasingly under examination, how much more was this so in the eleventh century when so much would have been attributed to the will of God, or the good offices of several gods! It is surely not far-fetched to suggest that the skills of the leaders then depended upon those same management processes and experiences that are still but obscurely understood. If this be conceded, then surely the first developments in administrative technique must be sought in the earliest days of governmental development and it is not illogical to suggest that a first major step was made by those rulers and their assistants who evolved a system of records to replace the less reliable and less durable individual memory, even though the fixing and conveying of information by rote had often been developed into such a fine art that information handed down through a number of generations can often be proved on investigation to have a high degree of truth. The need to add an element of permanency and transferability to the spoken word presented a vital challenge to human ingenuity which was variously solved at different times and places.

There can be little doubt that while the invention of writing can be attributed in some degree to administrative impulse, other factors were important, such as religion, which in the case of

Sumer impelled the temple corporations to introduce records in order to facilitate and rationalize their day-to-day transactions. The first writing was representational, facts and even ideas being depicted by drawings, which later could be simplified into signs. The impulse to convey meanings by scratching marks on caves and rocks, or marking trees, or leaving indications alongside forest tracks, goes back to the very beginnings of humanity and it is very probable that the rationalization of this process was begun at least as early as the cave painters who, some fifteen to twenty centuries B.C., were already developing suitable means for their main purposes. Out of the early pictographs emerged the hieroglyphic writings found in Sumer, Egypt, China, Crete and elsewhere. In Egypt their use was to continue into the Christian era, while in China this form has continued to the present day, and here it should be added that, despite the universally recognized disadvantages of the hieroglyphic, in its Chinese development it has had an undoubted administrative virtue of establishing and maintaining for a very long time over a large geographical area the means for ensuring effective communications despite inevitable variations in speech.

In practice the grave disadvantages of the inflexibility of the hieroglyphic and the need on the part of the writer to learn and memorize many hundreds, possibly thousands, of different pictographs were gradually overcome by the development of syllabic systems of writing, which made the building up of words and phrases much easier, and which eventually led to the alphabet of a limited number of letters representing the basic sounds from which an infinite vocabulary could be constructed. It was the Phoenicians, spurred on no doubt by the urgent economic necessities of a world-wide trading community, who invented the first alphabet, somewhere about the turn of the eleventh century B.C.

A study of the development of writing is also a study of the development of the beginnings of conscious administration, and particularly of public administration which was the handmaid of religion and government. Apart from the actual form of writing there is the equally important problem of media. Writing requires a suitable base for its very existence and appropriate tools for its production. The first permanent signs were probably chiselled or incised on the stone surfaces of caves, and the cave paintings of the prehistoric era mark a considerable advance, with the invention of colouring matter and tools for its application. No doubt similar signs had been habitually made on more portable but extremely perishable materials, such as leaves and bark, and most of the technical problems of writing had already been solved. What was still lacking was a suitable base for writing on which would be both portable and reasonably permanent and therefore suitable for the transmission of messages and the keeping of records. For a considerable time such materials as bark and wood may well have been employed but all traces of these early experiments have been lost. The survival in China of inscribed bamboo and bones more than hints at the potentialities of that vanished age.

Three widely used media mentioned in the text have survived to pass on information that would otherwise have disappeared without trace, namely the mud brick of the Euphrates-Tigris Valley, the papyrus of the Nile Delta, and the more universal paper of the later period. The mud brick had the advantages of moderate portability and considerable permanence. It was easily obtainable and usable and had its special influence in moulding the writing techniques and conditioning the administrative procedures required for dealing with this particular medium's limitations. It was, however, the discovery of how to convert the papyrus plant, which flourished in the marshy lands of the Nile Delta, into sheets and rolls upon which writing could be imprinted, that paved the way to important developments. Here was a medium that was both abundant and portable, if somewhat fragile. The basic processes of administration could now be multiplied and extended to meet the needs of an expanding government. Records could be kept in abundance, and messages and commands conveyed with a maximum of facility. But the restriction of cultivation of the plant to certain climatic conditions limited its geographical use and the search for a more generally serviceable material went on. Certainly the skins of animals, so widely used in primitive societies for a multitude of purposes, were sometimes employed as a base for writing, but this was an uneconomical use and even parchment, which had been developed by the second century B.C. and was used by the Greeks in place of papyrus, was a comparatively expensive medium.

It remained for China, early in the second century A.D., to discover how to make paper out of much more widely available vegetable matter, including old linen and rags, but this was kept a secret until A.D. 751 when the Arabs extracted the information from captured Chinese paper-makers. Yet it was still some time before paper was widely used in the West where, after the incorporation of Egypt in the Islamic dominions, supplies of papyrus were cut off and the more expensive but, fortunately for posterity, more durable parchment had to be used. In the meantime, more rapid writing had been evolved by the introduction of continuous script and the substitution of pen for brush. Thus, by the eleventh century A.D. all the basic means for effective office work and record-keeping had become available.

The emergence of the seal was also important. As a means of identification at a time when governors were still often illiterate and also as a security aid, the seal can almost be said to have appeared as a matter of course. It was natural that the owner of goods should seal their containers with clay or wax on which his mark would not only indicate his ownership but also act as a safeguard against the petty pilfering that is endemic in all societies. It was but a step to use similar means to authenticate a document or mark containers or 'files' of records stored in an office. Such seals, often finely artistic in form, were already in daily use in pre-literate Sumer as early as 3500 B.C.

With the gradual emergence of administration as a specialized governmental activity, of an organization specifically to deal with the transmission of instructions and regulations, the handling of information from agents, and of ordinary correspondence as well as the keeping of records and inventories of all kinds, public administration had already assumed its basic form. In regular offices numbers of scribes would be working together under the guidance of the political leader, who might himself be immersed in the details of administration, as were the viziers of the early courts, in the East, and the Mayors of the Palace, in the West. We should not therefore be surprised to find Hammurabi, in Babylonia at the end of the third century B.C., dictating his daily instructions to a secretary, very much in the same way as any modern administrator, certainly up to the time of the introduction of the dictating machine. Similarly the discovery, amidst the ruins of early palaces, of remains of archive rooms fitted with shelves for storing in an easily accessible manner inscribed tablets or papyrus rolls, foreshadows the modern office with its filing bays.

Similar parallels are to be found with other office procedures: e.g. for copying, by the use of inscribed rollers capable of making a series of duplicate impressions when run across a series of soft clay tablets; or dictation to a number of scribes for simultaneous transcription; or provision for security means of inscribed tablets with an outer clay envelope on which the inner message could be duplicated to provide corroboration later; or the use of short-hand by the scribe to save his master's time; or, finally, the use of bilingual writings to meet the requirement of governments with alien subjects using different languages and where the administrators themselves were chosen from among such subjects, who were often culturally more competent for this sort of work.

One certainly gains the impression that the senior public administrator of the eleventh century A.D. was facing daily tasks that differed little from those of his successor in succeeding ages and that a scribe of that period transferred to, say, an eighteenth century public department would have had very little to learn.

THE EMERGENCE OF SPECIFIC SERVICES

Public administration, it is evident, had many different types of government to serve, its functions and structure being strictly determined by the form of government, subject to place and time and the important influences of history. Its primary obligation was service to the government and, in addition to the normal executive activities, this included functions of a religious, military, legislative and judicial nature. It was a long time before specific administrative services could be distinguished and the services of specialist officials be requisitioned. The early officials were generalists, but nevertheless one cannot avoid being impressed by the broad functional scope of their activities. Somewhere or other most of the government services known to the modern world appear to have been attempted and our eleventh century spectator would certainly have been surprised, and perhaps professionally envious, had he known even the little we know about certain public services that already belonged to the distant past. In the present section it is proposed briefly to survey these multifarious services under ten spheres of governmental activity, bearing in mind that some regimes in some periods were much more advanced and administratively prolific than others.

(i) *General Management.* While from the outset rulers exercised the executive power and operated without any thought of a separation of functions, the ruler's personal assistants were involved in administering, and their first responsibility was the management and servicing of the estate or household. Their primary function was the maintenance of the ruler's family and dependents, a logical extension of the basic activity of the preceding tribal phase. As civilization expanded estate management was to broaden gradually into state management, but during the whole period under review, from the earliest communities of Sumer, Egypt and China to the more extensive governmental systems of imperial Babylon, Persia, Rome and Byzantium, the concept of the royal household continued to flourish. The Islamic realm never even looked like discarding it. Perhaps only in the compact city states of the Mediterranean, where economic and strategic conditions allowed a high degree of citizen participation in state management, was the personal idea of household management superseded by a wider concept. Even then charismatic leadership was ever round the corner to restore the older viewpoint.

Out of this embryonic form of public administration certain definite activities were gradually to develop. Thus the increasing importance of ceremonial at the court was not only to affect the status and conduct of officials but also to give them special duties to perform. Indeed this continued to be a characteristic of oriental systems and its exigencies often became a serious brake upon the administrators, deflecting their energies to sterile purposes. Even in Imperial Rome, once the republican experience had receded, oriental influences were gradually to overwhelm the admirable example set by Augustus during the Principate.

In systems where a multiplicity of wives or female slaves was permitted, household management was radically affected by the institution of the harem, and the introduction of eunuchs as servants of the inner feminine realm led to the development of a counter-power and a sort of administration-within-the-administration. Struggles between the state officials and the eunuchs considerably deflected the development of public administration in, for example, China and Byzantium.

At quite an early stage the more menial servants of the household were to lose influence to the scribe, whose talents were essential to the developing records system. At first this was a particularly arduous discipline, especially when a large number of hieroglyphs, or even syllables, had to be memorized, and where scribal practitioners could not be obtained in any other way, the court itself was compelled to undertake their instruction. In a sense this is where public education services began. There were training schools attached to the public offices of early Egypt, while China, at least from the Confucian era, considered government and education as almost synonymous.

With the accumulation of archives a special branch of public administration emerged, concerned with the organization and preservation of public records. The advances already made in this field in Sumer and Babylon are evidenced by the inscribed clay tablets dealing with official transactions that have survived in quantity and are still in course of translation and interpretation. Closely associated with these state archives were the records of dynastic events which were preserved by early rulers. A notable instance is the so-called Palermo Stone, a fragment of diorite marked with hieroglyphics which list some of the early dynasties of Egypt. In China this tendency gave birth to history as a purposive activity of public administration, in contrast to other regimes where the historical aspects of public records have usually been considered merely incidental to their main purposes, a fact that subsequent generations have had good reason to regret. An allied service was the library, which had existed long before the destruction of the famous establishment in Alexandria by fanatics during the seventh century A.D. Thus, we know of the Assyrian, Ashurbanipal's great interest in this field, and the development of the art of library management had already begun.

With the expansion of the basis of government the ruler's need to keep himself informed about what was happening elsewhere led to the appointment of inspectors who went out, often with executive powers, to see that the ruler's commands were being properly executed and to report back. Such inspectors, as the eyes and ears of the ruler, figured in most of these early power systems and theirs was to remain an important technique of public administration even when other systems of communication became available. Governments needed all the information they could get and every possible means was employed, every traveller being a potential agent for the king. Thus intelligence in the broadest sense had already become an important official activity.

So far we have noted household management, ceremonial, scribal work, education, archives and libraries, history, inspection and intelligence as basic functions of public administration about the throne, but this provides but a restricted view of the scope of government administration even for those times. Administration is but the servant of the wider powers, and activities under the nine following headings indicate the broad ramifications of public administration during the period. They all link up in some way with the administrative activities already mentioned, for in this sphere no clear cut classification is possible: all the several aspects interweave.

(ii) *Religion.* It could well be argued that this was the inspiration and therefore the originator of government and that public administration could have begun here, as in fact it did. Both in Sumer and Egypt it was the gods who ruled, the priests and kings being merely their agents, and even in more sophisticated times religion and government were for long inseparable. The attention given by officials to signs and augeries in the supremely rational systems of the Greek cities and Republican Rome can only be understood in the light of the drum-head ceremonies that continue to be an integral part of services before battle of the even more rational European nations today. It was in the nature of Christianity that religion and government should become differentiated within the wider community, but even in the eleventh century the issue was only partially resolved: in Byzantium the church remained an integral part of the state system, while the division between state and church in the West left the latter with many of the traditional responsibilities of public administration, especially where the welfare of the poor was concerned. It was part of the Islamic philosophy that state and church should be indistinguishable, while in China the Confucian philosophy had superseded the earlier cults and, as the accepted inspiration of officialdom, defined the terms on which public administration was to operate. At the time of our review therefore religious activities still figured prominently among the functions of officials, and there was close administrative interlinking between the two spheres and frequent interchange of personnel.

(iii) *Defence.* The first duty of government was the preservation of the lives and property of the community, and originally this depended almost entirely on the power of the ruler who could call upon the support of every able-bodied male. Defence against aggression from without and the maintenance of law and order within continued to be a primary task of all governments. At first the military organization was simple and there was little call for permanent administrative arrangements. Soon, however, such matters as the sharing of spoils and the distribution of rations called for records, and a scribe might be needed to specialize in this work. The Vizir or Magistrate would be responsible for both military and civil matters and the administration would deal with both types of action indiscriminately. But with the increase both in size and complexity of the military establishment, scribal and other administrative posts would appear within the military organization, although such officials would continue to be interchangeable with the more purely civil side. Even in Imperial Rome it was to be some time before separate military and civil careers emerged. Under Islam there was a significant arrangement whereby the *amir,* who was both military and civil leader, was supplemented by an *amil,* a financial official with direct responsibility to the central government.

In early communities the preservation of internal law and order was usually a military responsibility, although watchmen would be chosen from among the citizens to patrol the streets and walls of towns. Occasionally the idea of a civil police force would be realized, as in Rome under Augustus when three urban squads were organized for this purpose under the *Praefectus Urbi,* an officer of senatorial rank; but the close relationship with the military arm was demonstrated by allocating nine military cohorts to reinforce the civilian force in case of necessity. Fire hazards were also serious in cities such as Rome, with narrow ways lined with matchboarded tenements, and a fire brigade became necessary. The first step in this direction is attributed to an enterprising *aedile,* M. Egnatius Rufus, who first set up his own private organization, which was destined to become a state service in 22 B.C. and later to be professionalized. As with police and fire guards, so with prisons which were always needed in the administration of justice, whether in the guise of military guard house or fearful dungeon of palace and strongpoint. There is the interesting example of the use of the quarries at Syracuse in the time of Cicero for the detention of criminals from all parts of Sicily. But in the main such prisons as existed were used for the detention of persons awaiting punishment, or the incarceration of unfortunates to satisy the whims and hatreds of the powerful, and not as a publicly organized system of punishment and rehabilitation in the modern sense. Yet more advanced ideas had already developed in China, where Po Chu-i made prison reform one of his particular interests while serving as Omissioner in A.D. 808. It is significant that his involvement was due initially to the discovery that a number of prisoners had been sent to local gaols and subsequently forgotten.

(iv) *Local Operation.* In a tribal society executive power would be shared by the chief with the headmen of settlements and villages, who were probably members of his family. With the growth of towns and larger communities the need for a more regularized system of delegation soon arose and the realm would be divided into districts over which the King or Council would appoint governors to carry out the local administration. Often such administrative powers would go with the leadership of the military forces, particularly where such were stationed on or near the borders. In this way Egypt was divided into *nomes,* which were based upon the irrigation needs of the area. Over each *nome,* the Nomarch as royal representative acted as military commander, judge and clerk of works, and also had responsibility for the general welfare of the people of the area. In Athens the basis of local administration was tribal on an ingenious pattern and there was the interesting case of the forty-eight *naucrariae* which had special responsibility for the supply and manning of ships for defence. It was not unusual in larger realms for this local government pattern to include three distinct tiers, as in China under the Han, which was divided into provinces, each with a number of prefectures, further divided into districts. In the smaller realms of the West the division for administrative purposes was into counties and hundreds, or their equivalent. The Counts in charge of the larger areas were appointees of the King, responsible for maintaining his authority in the area.

(v) *Production*. Whether this or the following function — supply — should receive priority of consideration is open to argument. Goverment is primarily concerned with regulation and ensuring its own share of the product rather than in setting up as producer on its own account, and it is not until the advent of socialism as a philosophy of life that production becomes an accepted responsibility of public administration. Nevertheless, at the tribal and household stages there is no separation between production and government, the latter growing out of the former with the extension of specialization. Royal household administration, concerned as it was primarily with the maintenance of the king's family and entourage, was closely involved in agriculture and stockraising. The priests in the temple corporations of Sumer were intimately involved in the irrigation and farming of the dependent estates, while in Egypt the whole realm was looked upon as the personal estate of Pharaoh. There, irrigation was concentrated under his control within what may well have been history's first great administrative department.

The importance of extensive water-works of various kinds in these river-valley civilizations produced a form of society whose very existence depended upon the successful rule and administration of a strong centralized government which had sufficient resources and authority to organize the necessary services and defend the works from outside aggression. Because of the special basis of such societies Prof. K. A. Wittfogel, in his *Oriental Despotism* (1957) has christened them 'hydraulic societies'. In such societies officials were, as a matter of course, closely involved with production. Apart from this all governments must have been actively concerned in the production of weapons, clothing and pottery.

(vi) *Supply*. Originally comprised under the heading of estate management, it was the function of government to broaden the basis of supplies available to the community, both from within the country and from abroad, and the nature of the official's participation changed radically. He became involved in regulatory activities and in the encouragement and even the provision of facilities to improve the supply situation. When trading began markets emerged spontaneously but officials were soon responsible for their regulation. For the effective sustenance of the community storage facilities had to be provided — an early development in socialism. The widespread survival of the ruins of water cisterns and grain stores from most of the early civilizations thus provides important archaeological evidence of the concern of public administrators with supply problems. To these may be added the well-known often quite massive *amphorae,* or wine jars, of the Mediterranean cities which so frequently astonish the modern traveller.

Concern with crops and the flow of the waters also caused the official to be interested in heavenly phenomena and their possible effects upon the weather. Astronomy was an early science to develop and calendar-making was already an important public activity by the epochs of Sumer, early Egypt and China.

With the expansion of the realm the ruler's need for information about the outlying areas called into being the first important statistical activity of public officials: namely, the census, which is so frequently referred to in surviving records of the early societies. It applied to manpower and was initially important in estimating the potential military resources of the community. It would also provide basic information whenever large labour forces had to be deployed, as for the irrigation works already mentioned, the vast prehistoric earthworks and the construction of such edifices as Stonehenge. For the levying of tithes and other charges the size of crops and herds would also be essential and the census could be made to disclose such information, though one cannot imagine that the public's response would have been enthusiastic.

Out of the levying of tithes, as a proportion of output, for the support of temple or court, taxation began to emerge as an established practice of governments and the basis of later systems of public finance was laid. For this purpose ways of counting and accounting had to be evolved, and this was to be a slow process. Yet even as early as Babylon written instruments to facilitate trading had been introduced. The financial arrangements adopted by public administrators remained at a somewhat primitive stage, although the public finance of the communities examined was no doubt adequate to the burdens placed upon it by the governments. Thus, the Roman numerals, which were widely used at the time, and continued in use long after our period, were extremely inflexible and acted as a brake upon the development of more effective financial methods. Yet the Arabs had already shown the way, through the perfection of ideas obtained from the Hindus, by producing a system of numerals which has since been universally adopted for our day-to-day affairs.

It may be that the widespread practice in Greece and Rome of placing responsibility for the provision and financing of important services on the shoulders of the rich helped to simplify the system of public finance, or to extend its scope without actually improving its techniques.

Money is the spontaneous invention of trading communities and the regulation of the means of payment would soon become the concern of public administrators. The invention of coinage by the Greeks was a great boon to trade. With the need to ensure standards of quality and weight in such coins, their manufacture became an established responsibility of public administration and both in Greece and Rome the mints were organized by the government with a consequent extension of its capacity to regulate commerce and to improve its own financial methods.

(vii) *Communications.* Communications exist long before government has been formalized, in the bush trail mapped by habitual use of runners and carriers between settlements or the invention of craft for transport on rivers and along sea-coasts. The natural advantage of navigable rivers in this connection can hardly be exaggerated, while the geographical advantages of the Mediterranean Sea in the development of Western civilizations is too well understood to need emphasis here. Although the hazards of open sea navigation were not easily faced until much later it is to be remembered that the Phoenicians were at an early stage enticed out of the Mediterranean by the prize of tin, to venture northwards in the Atlantic to the British Isles, while the invaders of the latter came mainly across the Baltic and Germanic seas from the north.

It was, however, with the growing problems of governing empires that public administrators found themselves faced with real difficulties in maintaining communications and organizing transport services over long distances. Sumer, Babylon and Egypt had their river systems for easy transport within their domestic fields, but as the empires spread across the hinterlands of Persia and India road construction became an important public responsibility. The Achaemenians in particular planned a road network with the administrative needs of the central government prominently in mind. They devised a communications web across their realm which facilitated the mobility of the armed forces, as well as instructions, information, supplies and, indeed, the officials themselves to the most distant frontiers, and beyond. Regular postal services were organized, solely for government purposes, with defence posts set up at suitable intervals along the routes. The Indian civilizations supplemented their river highways with similar roadways, as did China, by the construction of canals on which heavy loads could be economically transported. That these were no light tasks for the officials is amply supported by written evidence that goes back at least to the Sui Dynasty. It was perhaps in Imperial Rome that road development reached its climax with routes so well surveyed and constructed that many of them continue in use to this day. This efficient road network must not be underestimated when reasons for the long survival of Byzantium are being sought. The land communications of the Islamic Empire were much less efficient, for the Arabs tended to keep to those routes already constructed by the Persians and Romans across the conquered territories or to the age old caravan routes, although it is to be remembered that they for long maintained by their efficient seamanship close control of the shores of the Mediterranean. Effective communications and mobility are so much the *sine qua non* of administration that a history of the development of public administration could be solely based upon a just appreciation of the transport systems of the several civilizations.

(viii) *Construction.* The primitive defence work of earth or palisade clearly begins in the pre-governmental phase as a natural communal activity, but it becomes more and more important with every extension of government. Defence works of earth, stone or brick; the construction of fortresses and palaces, the building of tombs and other ceremonial places; the various productive and communications activities already discussed, all served to place the public works organization in a prominent position from the outset. We have seen, for example, how Pharaoh's viziers had need to be competent architects and builders, often themselves officiating as clerk of works. The impressive performance of these early builders has left its imprint upon the magnificent ruins that have survived in so many lands. The majority of them were most certainly the work of governments under the guidance of officials. It is only necessary to mention the Pyramids of Egypt, the Great Wall of China, the Palace at Knossos, and numerous Greek theatres and Roman amphitheatres whose ruins are scattered throughout the Western world. The drainage systems of Knossos and the Indus Valley cities, and the aqueducts of Rome also suggest constructional advances that had reached out towards the modern world and were receding into a Golden Age status by the eleventh century. In the contemporary West the resources were no longer adequate to the emulation of such achievements. It is still something of a mystery how the technological and administrative problems of some of these achievements were solved. Clearly the men of those early ages were as intelligent as their modern counterparts, and it is in the light of such a conclusion that the public administration of the time must be assessed.

(ix) *Social Services.* Royal household management in its very essence included social service to its members as part of its function, but as government extended into wider fields the administration of such services tended to be left with family or temple. For long they remained outside the governmental sphere, although it is clear that wherever the ruler and his officials had to deploy large bodies of troops, workers or slaves some attention to their social welfare had to be given, for economical if not for humanitarian reasons. It seems probable, therefore, that the cruelty of slave-driving has been exaggerated by historians, since overseers would soon learn that they obtained better results from the labourer when discipline was imposed with some discretion. Contemporary reports may tend to suggest otherwise, for sensationalism is not necessarily a modern invention and kind treatment rarely makes news.

One of the first services to develop outside the sphere of public administration was education, much of which has always had to be undertaken in the home. Literacy was so important to the conduct of public business that the earliest states had to make provision for the training of officials, as we have already seen, but the education of the people for long remained a matter for private enterprise, except in special cases like Sparta where the regimentation of the citizenry was essential to the achievement of state policy. In Egypt and indeed elsewhere, the scribes became a profession which exercised an influence even wider than the state, much education being provided through informal establishments. On the other hand wherever the training of top officials was in question the government was inevitably involved in the provision of higher education. This was certainly the situation both in China and Byzantium. The priesthood, often the sole literate class, was always closely associated with teaching, so that when church and state became separate the former tended to maintain its close interest in the provision of schools. Under Islam of course there were no such distinctions.

Social welfare services were also a natural household responsibility and early governments would have had little reason to become involved. It is here, however, that the city states were able to make an individual contribution for they were organized on a personal basis and were often able to provide more effectively communal services normally left to the family. The Greek cities, particularly during the Hellenistic period, provided health and recreational services, the financing of which was frequently borne by the richer citizens. There were state-run hospitals in Rome and Byzantium, as well as such communal amenities as public baths, while spectacular entertainments were often provided on a lavish scale, calling for concerted efforts on the part of the responsible officials. Public assistance must have been important wherever large urban communities grew up and, again in Rome, the organization of grain supply and distribution became an important official responsibility. From time to time, both in India and China, services for the sick and indigent were publicly provided, as well as grain distribution. From Persia in the Achaemenian period, when an extensive commercial system had been built up, the existence of labour exchanges has been authenticated. When state and church drew apart in the West the latter continued to administer the public social services in the localities.

Despite totalitarian and occasional socialistic interludes, public administration during the early millennia, in so far as it transcended the personal service of the ruler and his court, was mainly concentrated upon the primary functions of defence, regulation and supply, leaving other communal activities to non-governmental institutions. Nevertheless, sufficient evidence survives of the widespread existence of public social and welfare services that we are justified in concluding that, were all the facts known to us, our picture of the concern paid to such services by public administration under certain regimes would be an eminently favourable one.

(x) *External Relations.* Despite poor communications and natural barriers of mountain and desert, contacts between early peoples were widely maintained through war and trade, although governments were not in the habit of organizing regular foreign services. Nevertheless the practice of diplomacy was well understood by governors and rulers long before specific diplomatic services were formed. Specially appointed missions were frequently despatched to foreign courts. These usually consisted of nobles or leading citizens who were able to do credit to their king or government and possibly to contribute out of their own pockets towards the expenses of their mission. Soon a strict protocol for the conduct of such embassies had been devised. Sometimes traders resident in foreign centres would act as agents for their governments, sending back information with travellers proceeding homewards and receiving information and instructions from those travelling outwards. Diplomatic correspondence on baked tablets discovered a Tell-el-Amana bear witness of the extent to which such arrangements were developed.

With nomadic movements on their frontiers a periodic occurrence, the Egyptians had gone to the trouble of organizing a tight system of immigration control, whereby information about travellers was placed on record and entrance permits issued. Byzantium had a carefully devised procedure for the reception of foreign envoys, through whom treaties might be arranged and concessions granted. The Greeks and Romans are known to have sent commissions of inquiry abroad: for example, by Aristotle when he gathered information about the many city state constitutions, and by Rome when drawing up the Twelve Tables.

TOWARDS PROFESSIONALISM AND BUREAUCRACY?

Throughout history the rulers, when filling the highest governmental posts of vizir or minister, have usually if not invariably thought in terms of status and power rather than of a specifically visualized administrative competence. For most of the period and even in the most extensive and highly organized systems the relationship between leader and administrator has remained substantially a personal one. Only in the highly responsible city states, where all citizens were expected to participate in the management of affairs, was this relationship seriously modified by the peculiar status of the magistrates, and even here such impersonal institutions as selection by lot were not to continue for long. Moreover, selection by the favour or whim of the leader was to persist even where, as in China, examination tests were also applied.

This does not mean that the chief officials were necessarily without specific administrative competence, for kings and emperors had to have the arduous tasks of government performed and the best of them developed their own skills in choosing the right man. One of the first principles of the administrative art to be learned was how to hold the balance between competence and mediocrity among the top officials, to decide how many 'passengers' the system could support. Aristocratic classes grew up with the idea of statesmanship as a class vocation and certainly the priestly orders were well-equipped for administrative office. As early as the days of the Sumerians, talent in management and co-ordination were being manifested. Because of the importance of family traditions and the constant influence of a father's precept and example in inculcating proper administrative attitudes, recruitment of the sons of officials often found a special place in the system.

The early rulers were likely to select good all-rounders, generalists as we sometimes call them, for the highest positions, although it must not be overlooked that the holders of special skills, in military, engineering and such matters, might be given preference. In all the systems mentioned the nobles and the wealthy were the preeminent aspirants to high administrative office, although wherever scribal ability became important, with the growing use of writing procedures in government, apprenticeship to the scribal profession could provide an avenue for others into the ranks of officialdom.

But the scribes always had to struggle, in China as well as in the West, against the effects of patronage and frequently against the powerful influences of well-placed groups like the eunuchs, while at more modest levels there were the lower servants of the household and even the household slaves to be provided for. The shape of officialdom at the more menial levels could be diverse, for the slaves could be either public or private, the freedmen as servants owed allegiance either to the king or to individual nobles and high officials.

Thus it is more realistic to regard the public service of most of the early governments as a plurality of officialdoms of varying status rather than a broadly conceived hierarchy under the leader. Even the highly organized public service of Imperial Rome remained a series of careers, each with its own class basis. Certainly the early emergence of the office as a letter-writing, authenticating, and recording unit and the gradual growth of financial procedures, tended to establish the middle and lower levels of officialdom as a specialist occupation of a recognizable type and numerous facts in the text substantiate the image of the office and its routines as having both perennial and universal validity.

There is much evidence that the administrative machinery of the larger state systems — Egyptian, Achaemenian, Imperial Roman, Byzantine and Chinese — had been developed to a high degree of complexity and had achieved a high level of competence. In Imperial Rome a system of departmentalization according to administrative process had been organized, while under several Chinese dynasties and the Mauryan Dynasty in India a complicated scheme of functional departments had been devised. Such bodies were in a position to undertake executive as well as administrative responsibilities.

The council as an advisory body in government goes back to

the earliest stages, for the tribal chief, however autocratic he might be, found plenty of reasons for having a group of intimates with whom to discuss current problems and future plans, and this led later to the use of the plural or collegial executive for administrative purposes. Admirable as such a body could be for consultation, as an executive it entailed dispersion of responsibility over a number of heads and led to a lack of decisiveness, which is so frequently a consequence of board leadership. Yet the collegial organization was of the very essence of the Greek city state, where it had the obvious advantage of bringing as many citizens as possible into current administration. It was also widely employed in Rome, especially under the Republic, when the magistracy was organized on collegial lines, and boards were widely entrusted with administrative responsibilities in China.

It cannot be said that there was at any time a clear line drawn between government (or public) and non-government administration, particularly in city states where the management of affairs was everybody's business, and the organization and financing of particular services were confided to wealthy citizens who might even compete for the privilege. There is the notorious case of the Roman *publicani* to whom, for a price, the state farmed out certain taxes. Indeed the farming of government responsibilities in this way as an alternative to extending the state's administrative machinery and personnel, was always prevalent and was to continue for some time to come, not usually with very happy results.

Whenever large administrative services developed complicated systems of personnel management were called into being, and despite the attendant burdens thus thrown upon the shoulders of the governors, failure to evolve an adequate administrative machine at such a juncture would lead inevitably to declining governmental efficiency, with the possibility of much more serious consequences. The change over from Republic to Imperium in Rome could be interpreted in terms of administrative development, and the first imperial leaders were confronted with no more urgent task than the replacement, by up-to-date machinery, of the creaking administrative organization that had been so suitable to the more compact realm. In Imperial Rome, while the Princeps or Emperor remained personally responsible for the appointment and regulation of his administrative staffs, a complex system of personnel administration was evolved, dealing with such matters as recruitment, remuneration, education and training, promotion, discipline and retirement. A graded system of salaries was worked out, varying in accordance with the importance of the several careers, and there was a carefully staged *cursus honorarum* for the awarding of honours. But all these arrangements had already been introduced in China, where management of the public services was entrusted to a series of administrative boards. From Byzantium a number of, what may be called, staff manuals have survived. In most public administrative systems the services of officials were paid for by fees which the officials themselves collected, a practice which led to obvious misuses, and appreciably added to the widespread, and in some ways natural, unpopularity of officialdom.

Usually the officials were strictly under the personal control of the ruler who, as in Imperial Rome, had the final power of life and death over his servants. His position *vis-à-vis* his officials was very similar to that of the Roman *paterfamilias* to his own household. But there were built-in safeguards, such as in the Greek cities, where there was a regular inquest in open court on the credentials of the aspirant to office and subsequently upon his performance. Roman magistrates were subject to similar checks, which despite their good intentions had the grave disadvantage of inducing unenterprising administration, and here there were also administrative courts before which certain defaults and misdemeanours on the part of officials could be examined. In China, officials, who were equally servants of the imperial master, could direct memorials to the Emperor, and the custom was for a good deal of latitude to be given to complaints thus reported. This custom was wisely contrived as a much needed safety valve in such a vast personnel body. Most of these systems embodied a censorate as part of the machinery of government, notably the Ephorate of Sparta and the Collegium of Ten at Carthage. Such institutions, when allowed to operate properly, introduced a salutary and constructive element of self-criticism into power systems that were inevitably despotic. Not that it would be sensible and in accordance with human experience to conclude that the critics themselves were ever popular with their masters, whose normal acceptance was more likely to be pained than enthusiastic. No bill of rights existed to stop the oriental despot from having his servant decapitated, if such was his immediate inclination.

Given the existence of large public services in a position to exercise or usurp considerable governmental powers — particularly when their chief was weak or not very much interested in administration — it is proper to ask what evidence there is of the prevalence of bureaucracy during these early millennia. By 'bureaucracy' we mean an administration service that exercises undue and irresponsible power or usurps the executive functions of government. Obviously in large-scale administrations, such as those of Egypt, Persia, China, Rome and Byzantium over which complete control must have been difficult to exercise under the most favourable conditions, there must have been periods when the administrators were on top, but this appears to have occurred invariably when the governing power was weak or preoccupied, and there is little evidence that governing bureaucracies ever existed for long or as a constituted form of government. Modern theories of bureaucracy, despite the eminence of some of their proponents appear to be based upon inadequate data, for quite apart from the destruction of so much original material it is certain that much basic administrative experience, that would be essential to the formulation of a really valid theory, was never placed on record. There can be no doubt whatever that any system of government that required the services of a powerful administrative corps would be likely from time to time to come to depend upon its efficiency rather more than was healthy for the working of the system. On the other hand such an administrative body is by nature a stabilizing element in the machinery of government and there must have been plenty of occasions when a government's failure to develop adequate administrative means had a decisive effect in bringing about its own failure and decline. The Islamic Empire, despite its outstanding successes, was probably one such case. To base a theory of historical change on the growth and decline of bureaucracies is like arguing that the tail wags the dog, although it has to be admitted that theorists rarely confine the use of the term 'bureaucracy' to mean a power grasping administration, but also import the idea of large-scale complexity and round-about procedures for which the term is also so frequently used. The widespread employment of a term that has autocratic, structural and inefficiency connotations is unfortunate and to be deprecated. It would certainly have been better to use one of several existing terms that are generally understood, such as 'officialdom', 'public service' or 'administrative service', or perhaps to have propounded a new technical label, such as 'admincorps', without any of the widely accepted derogations of 'bureaucracy'. It is in its more critical and narrower sense that the term is used in this present work.

THE HUMAN OFFICIAL

Generally, the records are too meagre for the public official in history to emerge, except occasionally, as a person in the round. Inherently a subordinate, if an essential one, it was the official's vocation to be seen and not heard, and usually he had to rise to political status to leave behind a permanent portrait of himself, as with the vizirs of the Pharaohs who inscribed their autobiographies upon their carefully prepared tombs. On the other hand, despite the general defectiveness of the records, we are left with no narrow concept of the official's role. From statesman-manager under the throne down to mere stylus-pusher at the feet of his master the official was a man of parts. Whether as menial worker in the temples of Sumer or script-magician inscribing dragon bones in Shang China, his indispensable, if modest, role can be fully appreciated. Yet his life cannot be completely understood if we ignore the peculiar hazards of his office, which were often not far round the corner. In the massive tombs of Ur and by the Nile his mummified body has survived in the entourage of the dead king, strategically placed amidst the corpses to serve his master in the other world, which included as a matter of course the ruler's secretarial scribe ready to indite his commands in paradise.

The ever-present possibility that by mere whim his master might decree some punishment he had perhaps not deserved, even to the cutting off of his head —a favourite pastime of oriental despots, including some of the Caliphs of Islam — would tend to make the official circumspect and conservative in outlook, while the less frightening built-in checks and balances, such as those adopted in Greek city state administration, would have a similar effect. Even with the Chaldeans, who had the earlier inventions of the Sumerians at their disposal and who themselves made valuable advances in astronomy and town planning, the attitudes of officialdom were centred upon the past rather than the future; while the influences of ancestor worship as well as of the all-pervasive conservatism of Confucianism were sufficient to ensure that the Chinese official, competent as he usually was, should also find his inspiration in the past. Similarly, in Egypt under the professional inspiration of the scribes the hieroglyph continued in use long after more flexible methods of writing had been invented.

Often inspired by the wise admonitions of their leaders, or by the gradually evolved professional code of their particular service, there is much evidence that public officials usually strove efficiently and loyally in the service of their masters, even if the concept of public service was missing and tendencies towards bureaucracy were often present. But they would need to have been less than human to resist the temptations frequently thrown in their way. Their position often enabled them to make greater profits than the rules visualized, for example when levying fees for services rendered, or *sportulae* as in Imperial Rome, which were unreasonably burdensome. Occasions might even arise when Egyptian officials consorted with outside enterprise, to rob the royal graves, to whose secrets they had access and whose sequestered hoards they might even be forgiven for considering misapplied.

Yet when they had done their best and functioned according to rule with high competency and a sense of justice, their position as public administrators could render them very unpopular with the people. Nor is this surprising when they came as tax collectors, or snoopers, into the private affairs of all and sundry. No favour is shown to the tax gatherer in the Bible, and evidently this is not entirely due to the fact that he was the agent of an alien power. Such incidents as the reprisals taken for the murder of a tax collector at Antioch in eleventh century Byzantium were not calculated to improve the official's reputation. However benevolent the ruler's intention the public official was his minion and therefore an inevitable scapegoat for his mistakes. The tradition of unpopularity was to continue long into the future and still survives in the folklore of the West.

Although their presence can usually be sensed behind the leaders, in the wings of history, the officials for most of the time remain shadowy beings. When they do find themselves in a position to blow their own trumpets, to grasp the opportunity offered by the tomb inscriptions of Egypt, the persons concerned have usually drawn so close to the seats of power as to have relinquished the status of official for that of politician and statesman. But at least in some of these tomb pictures we discern lesser officials working in the household of the vizir, or individually exercising immigration control on the frontiers, or perhaps taking down details of war booty, and so on. As scribes they are just ordinary workers wearing no distinctive uniform.

Usually when they do survive by name they are notabilities in their own right, although in China the lists of officials of even middling rank go·back a long time. Occasionally we hear about an Axotas at Pylos in Greece, a modest inspector of crops, probably attached to the palace staff, or a Gnaeus Flavius, scribe to the *aediles* in Rome, who was himself to rise to the magistracy in 304 B.C., or an Ælfwine, writer to the Anglo-Saxon King Ethelred, who may be honoured as the first known English 'civil servant'.

However, the great often began modestly and from their

biographies much can be learned of the vicissitudes of an official's life in early times. Such a one was Weni, of Dynasty VI in Egypt, who had begun as steward and must have been very able to have risen to such important positions as judge, general, and master of works and hydraulics. Nor could such versatility at the top have existed without the support of considerable professional capacity from the lower ranks of the several official branches below him. Another interesting Egyptian example was Methen, servant of Snefru of Dynasty VI who had risen from small beginnings in the preceding reign to so many high political and administrative posts that he has a claim to be considered arch-pluralist of all time. We are justified in concluding that he had outstanding capacity for delegating, that essential but by no means widespread virtue of the administrator.

Also amongst the famous Egyptian vizirs is the much-quoted Ptahshepses, whose career is reputed to have stretched through both Dynasties IV and V and thus to have endured so long as to give him the right to the title of most permanent of permanent officials! Certainly such a performance indicated a good deal of competence, not a little good fortune, and an outstanding capacity for yesmanship. The latter characteristic of officialdom is more than endorsed by Ptahshepses's own tomb inscription, which displays so much braggadocio as to make him rather untypical of a class, who normally prefer to hide their personal lights from public inspection. But then the Egyptian philosophy of death was bound to have a special influence upon its addicts!

Turning to Rome, where statesmanship and administration alternated with military and judicial responsibilities in the tasks of magistrates, we certainly find in such careers as those of Cato the Younger, at the end of the Republic, and Frontinus, during the Principate, much evidence of high administrative competence, while their reactions to their subordinates suggest that the personnel problems of their times were not so different from those encountered by their modern successors. Cato took steps to overcome the inevitable amateurism of the magistracy — an amateurism which the old hands of the scribal fraternity were not slow in taking advantage of — by paying special attention to the detail of his work and closely examining the official activities of his subordinates in order to know if and when they went wrong. Nor was he slow in admonishing them for their deficiencies and in bringing them before the appropriate administrative tribunal whenever they had seriously broken the rules of the office. Cato also set a good example in his own attendances at office. Characteristically he took a particular interest in financial expense and saw that his subordinates recorded their financial activities accurately, such matters as were too often permitted by other magistrates to take their course. Frontinus also had the habit of studying the technical detail of the work under his control. This habit had significant results when he became responsible for Rome's waterworks at a time of serious scandal. He was able to search out the frauds, which were being connived at by members of the staff, and by tightening up management control, especially of the labour gangs, to root them out and prevent their recurrence.

Of all the officials that have thrown their shadows across our pages none has come more prominently to life or typified the immemorial official more illuminatingly than John the Lydian, who served under Justinian. It is true that during his retirement, he wrote a book about the public service in the age of Justinian that would have been sufficient to hand down his name to posterity, but he began as a modest scribe and does not seem to have risen above what we should call executive or middle rank.

John the Lydian began, as so many officials have begun throughout the ages, with the patronage of an influential friend and the protective cloak of a senior official who was also a relative, and by pleasing his patron, he continued to do well in various scribal capacities. His perquisites at one time comprised the extraordinary fortune of an amiable wife with a good dowry! In this wise he rose effortlessly to a substantial executive position in an important legal branch of the Prefect's office. But the tide was destined to turn with the advent to supreme power of Justinian, whose reforming broom swept through the offices and not only removed those with whom John was *persona grata,* but inaugurated structural and procedural changes which were not to his taste. John was passed over by, as he thought, less worthy men with unorthodox ideas and even the promotional *cursus* was altered to his disadvantage, a hazard that many civil servants have to face at one time or another. However, he served his time out, making some valuable literary contributions in the meantime, and retired after forty years service with an honour of the second class. Clearly John the Lydian was a highly competent scribe, with considerable literary abilities, but he hated change and failed to keep up with the times: he hated too, as all officials hate, the invasion of experts with new fangled ideas into his particular sphere. It is easy, however, in seeing him as the typical official, to overemphasize his role as stick-in-the-mud favourer of forms and routines, and to fall into the common error of overlooking his inherent loyalty, his persistent service to his chiefs, and his urge to devote his life to the general welfare which, if it still centred in a state personified by the Emperor, was an essential step towards that broader commonwealth raised not for the glory of an individual or a class but for the benefit of the whole people.

It is apparent from our broad survey that the devoted government official had emerged at an early stage in the development of society and that men of right intention and adequate capacity for this office already existed when mankind was still young. For the complex administration that was to be needed to service the more complicated human societies that were eventually to emerge, it was not the man but the inspiration and the necessary technological instruments that had to be devised. Up to the eleventh century A.D. the required evolution had been steady if slow, and for a time it was to appear that further advances would be just as measured. Today we know that there were startling changes ahead, and it may well be asked whether the immemorial official, whose virtues continued to be sufficient right into the twentieth century, is at last doomed to extinction? Yet human capacity has too often responded with surprising resilience and success to past challenges for any but the cynic and misanthrope to answer 'yes'.

PRE-COLUMBIAN CIVILIZATIONS

Omission from the present volume of any reference to America calls for explanation. As is well known today — though it was beyond the ken of our eleventh-century forbears — there already existed in the central and southern parts of America societies which were as advanced as any in the West. These were the numerous communities of the Aztecs, the Mayas and the Incas, who inhabited an area stretching from modern Mexico in the north to modern Peru in the south. Since the existence of these 'empires' was not to be realized before the discovery — some would say 'rediscovery' — of America by Columbus towards the end of the fifteenth century, and since their history was only to be gleaned retrospectively through the actions of the Spanish Conquistadors, it is considered appropriate to leave their discussion to Volume II.

INDEX